The Transpersonal in Psychology, Psychotherapy and Counselling

# The Transpersonal in Psychology, Psychotherapy and Counselling

Andrew Shorrock

palgrave
macmillan

First published 2008 by
PALGRAVE MACMILLAN
Houndmills, Basingstoke, Hampshire RG21 6XS and
175 Fifth Avenue, New York, N.Y. 10010
Companies and representatives throughout the world

PALGRAVE MACMILLAN is the global academic imprint of the Palgrave Macmillan division of St. Martin's Press, LLC and of Palgrave Macmillan Ltd. Macmillan® is a registered trademark in the United States, United Kingdom and other countries. Palgrave is a registered trademark in the European Union and other countries.

ISBN-13: 978–0–230–51776–9 hardback
ISBN-10: 0–230–51776–5 hardback

This book is printed on paper suitable for recycling and made from fully managed and sustained forest sources. Logging, pulping and manufacturing processes are expected to conform to the environmental regulations of the country of origin.

A catalogue record for this book is available from the British Library.

A catalog record for this book is available from the Library of Congress.

10  9  8  7  6  5  4  3  2  1
17  16  15  14  13  12  11  10  09  08

Printed and bound in Great Britain by
Antony Rowe Ltd, Chippenham and Eastbourne

*With appreciation for all my friends, colleagues, and clients without whom this book would not have been possible.*

*With deep love and gratitude to Antonella, whose tireless encouragement and expertise supported the project moving beyond the realm of ideas, and to Topaze and Virginia, constant reminders of the wonder of life.*

# Contents

# 1
# Introduction

In my professional life I have been asked many times the simple question: What is transpersonal psychology, counselling or psychotherapy?

The answer is straightforward: it is a broad transcultural theory of human nature that posits that human beings are more than physical and psychological beings, with some form of spirituality being a reasonable bet. Oh, and by the way, it is also a discrete field of study that could be conceived as having had about 40 years of academic recognition. Not surprisingly, this off-the-cuff response never seems to be enough, and commonly leads onto many more questions, ones that whilst seeking a deeper elaboration, reveal the questioners' theoretical assumptions and their beliefs, not just about the helping professions, but also their understanding of the world. These further questions may cover a wide range of topics and could include diverse areas such as spirituality, paranormal experience, religion in its many variants, cults, psychopathology and philosophy. These then lead onto even more questions, and for the polite or genuinely interested, they can take three different directions:

a. The questioner wants to posit even more complex questions and possible answers from yet more diverse fields
b. The questioner's eyes glaze over with therapist's hmm hmms
c. The questioner suggests to go for a coffee or (hopefully) a beer as they want to tell me about an experience that they had when...

All of this may hint at the complex nature of the beast, as well as, I suspect, that spirituality is for many an area that brings strong feelings and associations. Moreover, to add further complexity for the clinician, as well as the interested layperson, the literature that explores the field

1

can be so overly simplistic so as to seem naïve; or, alternatively, it can be so complex that a prior knowledge is needed just to understand the terminology used, let alone understand what is being discussed. If this were not enough, just like in other areas of psychological thinking, some theoretical schools espouse limited viewpoints, as their postulates need to fit within set theoretical confines.

Yet, it appears to me that a great many of those who present, or are referred for psychotherapy, counselling or any of the myriad definitions of self-growth, bring material that touches upon areas of functioning that best-fit descriptions loosely associated with the subject that matches the umbrella-term 'spirituality'. Here, I am not just talking about those individuals who could be considered or diagnosed as suffering the effects of abnormal psychopathology. In fact, I have met many sane and well-functioning individuals from all corners of the world who claim to have had experiences or beliefs that cannot be explained by any orthodox worldview that does not accept that mankind is, or has access to, a realm of experience that is somehow greater or more than everyday consciousness.

Although psychologically 'healthy', individuals may have a sense of life that is more than that meets the eye, I have also worked with many who could certainly be best-described as being 'disturbed'. Whilst for countless individuals their experience of suffering has no link to anything that could be described as spiritual, for many this is, however, clearly not the case. And like with many areas of disturbance there is a wide-ranging spectrum that is possible to place individuals upon.

Perhaps, at one end there would be the benign 'space cadets' who create worldviews that include the transpersonal as a means to make sense of their world, with the other end of the spectrum inhabited by individuals who may be a danger to themselves or others with coping mechanisms/behaviours that fit generally accepted definitions of psychoses. Even here, though, diagnostic challenges can be met, as shaving your head begging for alms and wearing red robes is considered the norm in some neighbourhoods, and more than eccentric in others. And making promises and begging for favour from an unseen super-being and regularly attending meetings in medieval buildings is also the norm in some parts of town.

With such a broad canvas this then gives me, as a clinician, great scope; yet, as a self-proclaimed transpersonal therapist I would no more steer clients/patients towards or away from exploring, for instance, their sexuality, their relationships with significant others or their understanding of world, than I would from their understanding, or experience, of life having some form of spiritual element.

Moreover, as recognized by many psychological schools, all areas of human functioning can and do relate to each other, as well as having an effect upon all areas of the lifespan. With all the foregoing in mind, I would ask you to suspend any belief you bring to this book and the field, as I try to answer the question in the first paragraph in a little more depth.

## What to expect from this book

This book could end up as one of those works with a vaguely interesting title that seem to sit upon your bookcase waiting to be read one day; if this is so thank you for purchasing it, though this would not go towards meeting the original aim that provided the impulse to write it. This work is designed first and foremost to be a means to aide finding some answers to the question 'what is transpersonal psychology, counselling or psychotherapy?' I also hope it provides a means to offer food for thought and to galvanize further exploration as you look inside yourself, at those who populate your life as well as the universe in general for *your* answers to the question. I would imagine that this would be an ongoing work in progress, for I presume that you, like me, and indeed the field of transpersonal psychology are also a work in progress.

However, I think it is important to recognize that, as Alfred Korzybski (1879–1950) reminds us, 'the map is not the territory' and, although all the information I have gathered can be considered to help build a picture of transpersonal psychology, I could only give, in one single book, brief descriptions of the many maps. If this were not enough, many of the cartographers I introduce, although viewing the same terrain as their fellows, have done so from a different angle, and thus have at times described what can appear to be a different landscape.

With this in mind, this work is not intended to make any claims that are in any way definitive or somehow representative of a fixed immutable truth. Throughout this book, whilst considering the transpersonal, I also explore what may not be the transpersonal. Unfortunately, often the 'what-is' and the 'what-is-not' are one and the same, though viewed from differing angles. This state of affairs can appear at times confusing as well as engender ambivalence; therefore, to aid the understanding of the field I found it necessary to look behind the theories to find those bodies of knowledge that underpin or inform their claims. Having done so this then makes it possible to gain a deeper understanding of the work of the thinkers who claim to be transpersonal theorists, which in turn allows a discussion of the place of the transpersonal in the clinical setting and the universe at large.

Simply put, with a broad field of exploration and a plethora of possible angles from which to view the field from, this work attempts to offer many perspectives that can be used to discuss 'The Question'. Although some of the postulates I describe would be more in line with my own views and some I have needed to research in more depth, I have tried to give all an equal say and have made explicit where I stand, as I felt it important not to discount some of the ideas I put forward. Moreover, with such a rich landscape that has already been explored by many others, I was spoilt for choice and could not possibly follow all areas that may potentially speak of transpersonal psychology. Finally transpersonal psychology, for many, is not a valid area of research, simply because its theories suggest functioning beyond ego boundaries, with its praxis as well as its theories seen to exhibit phenomena that do not meet the test re test criteria of the prevailing scientific hegemony. Thus, the prevailing transpersonal maps do not often meet consensually agreed constructs for validity and therefore may be unacceptable, purely because they do not fit within the confines of what is considered the norm.

I spent quite a lot of time deciding upon the most useful way of presenting my findings, as, with such wide-ranging interests that encompass many bodies of knowledge any work that seeks to present, transpersonal psychology and its application could approach the task in any number of ways. Therefore, in order to try bringing some coherence and clarity to the proceedings, this book is divided into four chapters.

The first chapter has a fairly narrow focus, and after introducing the book offers a general overview of the field, with a definition and brief history of transpersonal psychology. It also begins to identify theoretical confusions, with a brief foray into what is not transpersonal psychology and some of the ways that researchers approach the field.

The second chapter takes a much wider view than the first; it picks up on some of the themes already identified and dips into the bodies of knowledge that underpin transpersonal psychology. It also looks towards the four forces of psychology, with a look at how the best-known schools of psychology recognize and support or disagree with their theories of human nature that accept transpersonal functioning.

The third chapter builds upon the second and reveals the work of some of the past and present transpersonal theorists. A brief overview of the main theoretical positions is offered; however, no thinker is seen to provide a model that is better or more valid than any other. Thus this chapter is not intended to be a comparative portrayal of the various theories, although it may stimulate debate, as models that explore similar phenomena are presented.

The final chapter naturally moves from the 'what-is' to the 'how you apply the diverse theoretical models'; it moves from questions exploring what transpersonal psychology is and the field's theoretical underpinnings to a portrayal of how the diverse theoretical models are applied in the clinical setting. And once again, as in all things related to transpersonal psychology, no approach is presented as 'the' pre-eminent or most efficient application of transpersonal theory. A case for when as well as how to adopt a transpersonal perspective is also given consideration, with recognition that a transpersonal element can be included by clinicians that practice within models that may not traditionally look beyond ego functioning and interpersonal dynamics. Although no method is highlighted, a discussion of differential diagnosis is given, as this is a clinical consideration that is deemed to be important by the majority of transpersonal theorists and clinicians.

Overall, the work is intended to give an overview of the field and its application, as well as revealing how the transpersonal is viewed from the major schools of psychology. Besides, some readers may find it useful to dip into the areas that interest them most, whilst others may find it useful to explore the work in a more systematic way. I hope that there is much that you find to agree or disagree with, and that, at the least, the more self-aware reader has the opportunity to recognize their own biases regarding the transpersonal and be afforded the opportunity to find how their worldviews arose. Before moving on to explore the field itself, I want to make clear that throughout this work I use the terms transpersonal psychotherapy and transpersonal psychology and transpersonal counselling interchangeably. I also in the same manner use clinician, therapist, practitioner and counsellor to denote a professional who applies psychological thought, if this was not enough I also do not limit myself to one term for individuals, persons, people and human beings.

# 2
# Definitions and a Potted History of Transpersonal Psychology

When exploring the transpersonal, a good beginning is to take some time examining the definition of the term transpersonal itself, whilst briefly placing it in historical context. This is important, for, unlike theoretical schools such as behavioural psychology, which can be seen as having and relying upon a narrowly focused epistemology, transpersonal psychology has its roots in and springs from a multidisciplinary movement that comes from a wide spectrum of diverse fields. These include bodies of knowledge that often would be seen as strange bedfellows, such as religion, psychology, neurobiology and philosophy.

In order to examine any body of knowledge clear definitions are important; in the case of transpersonal psychology the need to ascertain that my reader and I are talking the same language is important because transpersonal phenomena can be regarded as factors in the assessment of an individual's level of psychological health.

I am privileged in that I do speak several variants of psychobabble and the need for clear definitions is often highlighted in my work with other professionals whom I work with. For instance, as a psychotherapist I have often found that when discussing tentative diagnosis and prognosis with doctors (trained and situated within the allopathic medical model) we often use similar language though with differing meanings. A good example of this would be my use and understanding of the psychodynamic concept of schizoid-type defence mechanisms. This concept, without care and clear elucidation, can be translated by doctors as a suggestion that the patient is suffering from some form of schizophrenia.

Therefore, I begin with a brief exploration of the history of the term transpersonal as well as its use in psychology.

The recognition and the consequent legitimization of transpersonal psychotherapy as a valid stance from which to view the human condition can be traced to the early 1960s, when it began to be considered by many to be the 'fourth force' in individual therapy. The term 'fourth force' is attributed to A. Maslow (1993), one of many thinkers of this time who, like his contemporaries such as V. Frankel (1975) and R. Assagioli (1993), pursued an active interest in the transpersonal and its relationship to psychotherapy. His work has had a great impact and influence upon the whole field of psychological thought. And when exploring the genesis of transpersonal psychology Maslow is often credited with being the father of transpersonal psychology. He was not a practising therapist, unlike the greater number of influential theorists whose work can also be seen as affecting many of their contemporary and successive theorists, such as Frankel (1975), Freud (1961b) and Winnicott (1975) to name but a few.

Although he was to address similar issues to those that existential philosophers examine, it would be unwise to count him as a true existentialist, for the main concern of his work was with mankind's essence rather than existence. Maslow is arguably best known for his hierarchy of needs model, which has found its way into mainstream thinking. However, the larger part of his life's work was the examination of values, ultimate meanings, spiritual concerns and theories regarding the concept of self-actualization. He began formulating tentative theories concerning self-actualization as early as 1942 and carried on till his death in 1970.

Yet, we need to look further back in time to see the roots of what was to become this fourth force or transpersonal approach to psychology. Assagioli and Jung are two figures who spring immediately to mind. Both were formulating their ideas of the transpersonal as central tenets of their theories in the second decade of the twentieth century. Singer (1983) gives Jung the credit of introducing the term 'transpersonal' in the field of psychology (ueberpersonliche) as early as 1917. Though upon examining Jung's work (1973), it is apparent that he in fact is referring to the collective unconscious and not using the term with its present meaning.

Going further back I could argue that William James had already recognized the importance of the transpersonal with the publication of *The Varieties of Religious Experience* (1958), in which he examined spiritual experiences from a psychological stance, though using terms such as metaphysical, spiritual and soul. It was not just in this piece of work that he gave importance to the transpersonal. In his seminal work *The Principles of Psychology* (1981), originally published in 1890 (which he had started 10 years earlier), he made clear within the chapter

*Consciousness of Self* (pp. 279–380) his hypothesis that we all have an aspect of ourselves that he termed the 'spiritual self'.

James was not the only early theorist to claim that the transpersonal needs to be included in psychological discourse. A lesser known figure the Canadian Richard Maurice Bucke (1837–1902) (known as Maurice Bucke), who spent a great deal of his life researching and writing a book entitled *Cosmic Consciousness* (1901, 1992), which was published the year before his death, in 1901, and is still in print today. In addition to describing his own mystical experience, he posited a theory that recognizes three main stages of consciousness that can be seen as belonging to a developmental spectrum, the last of which, 'Cosmic Consciousness', would certainly fit the greater majority of definitions describing the transpersonal.

Within this same era it was not just those from the burgeoning new science of medico-psychology who spoke of the transpersonal. Philosophers such as Underhill (2001), who is recognized as still providing the seminal inquiry into mysticism, wrote of the importance of the transpersonal. She proposed that mystics seek to gain a direct comprehension and communion with the transpersonal. She phrases it as 'a direct communion with (...) transcendental Reality' (p. 68), going on to claim that it '(...) usually lies below the threshold of our consciousness; but in certain natures of abnormal richness and vitality, and under certain favourable conditions, it may be liberated' (p. 68). Although in embryonic form the field can be traced back to the beginnings of the twentieth century, it was not until the flowering of the human potential movement in 1960s that transpersonal psychology could be said to have received wider recognition.

This brief exploration of the history and origins of transpersonal psychology does not reveal what is meant by the term 'transpersonal psychology'; therefore I now turn to the literature for a clear definition.

For me the obvious starting point was my *Dictionary of Psychology* (1995). However, I was unable to find a mention of the term 'transpersonal'. I did not find this so surprising, as transpersonal psychology anecdotally seems to be considered an innovative approach even though the term transpersonal has been firmly established in the lexicography of the psychotherapeutic community for over 40 years.

With no luck consulting my dictionary I turned to other works, and I could find many theorists and commentators who offered elucidation. I found that the one given by Wellings succinctly encapsulated my own understanding. ' "Transpersonal" has become an umbrella term for naming those experiences where consciousness extends beyond (trans) the individual or personal. These experiences are filtered through the individual person, hence the word trans—personal' (Wellings & Wilde McCormick, 2000, p. 2).

Although this is succinct and clear, it could be applied to a great many fields. So, keeping this as a starting point, I was keen to include the psychotherapeutic aspect, which Wilber, I felt, did eloquently, 'It [transpersonal psychology] fully acknowledges and incorporates the findings of modern psychiatry, behaviourism, and developmental psychology, and then adds, where necessary, the further insights and experiences of the existential and spiritual dimensions of the human being. We might say it starts with psychiatry and ends with mysticism' (Wilber, 1994, p. x).

Although considered one of the best-known thinkers in the field, Wilber is not the only theorist to give a definition that encompasses the enormity of the field of transpersonal psychology. In the past 40 years a wide range of clinicians and theorists have increasingly used this term, and many have given what I see as a clear definition, such as Fadiman and Speeth as quoted by Boorstein (1996),

Transpersonal psychotherapy includes the full range of behavioural, emotional and intellectual disorders as in traditional psychotherapies, as well as uncovering and supporting strivings for full self-actualization. The End State of psychotherapy is not seen as successful adjustment to the prevailing culture but rather the daily experience of that state called liberation, enlightenment, individuation, certainty or gnosis according to various traditions.

(Boorstein, 1996, p. 3)

In the same work Groff gives the following definition,

Transpersonal psychology is a branch of psychology that recognizes and accepts spirituality as an important dimension of the human psyche and of the universal scheme of things. It also studies and honors the entire spectrum of human experience, including various levels and realms of the psyche that become manifest in non-ordinary states of consciousness (NOSC). Here belong, for example, experiences and observations from meditation and other forms of systematic spiritual practice, spontaneous mystical raptures, psychospiritual crises ('spiritual emergencies'), psychedelic therapy, hypnosis, experiential psychotherapy, and near-death situations (NDE).

(Boorstein, 1996, p. 44)

Continuing and speaking of the legitimacy of transpersonal orientation he points out that

> ... many professionals refuse to accept that the transpersonal orientation represents a legitimate scientific endeavour. They dismiss it as an irrational and undisciplined product of a group of eccentric, mystically oriented professionals and paraprofessionals that are not familiar with the most basic principles of traditional science. The main reason for this criticism is the fact that the findings and conclusions of the transpersonal disciplines are incompatible with the most basic metaphysical assumptions of the Newtonian-Cartesian paradigm and with the materialistic philosophy that has dominated Western science for the last three hundred years.
>
> However, this attitude completely ignores the fact that many of the pioneers and chief representatives of the transpersonal movement are people with solid academic backgrounds and often impressive professional credentials. They have departed from the traditional conceptual frameworks, not because of their ignorance of the most basic principles of Western science, but because the mainstream conceptual frameworks failed to account for and explain too many of their important observations and experiences.
>
> (Boorstein, 1996, p. 45)

This last quote highlights that it is important to look at the issue of credibility and validity. Something that I too feel is important because just being able to name something may not mean that it has any importance or relevance to any other thing, though before exploring concerns regarding validity I wished to include a last definition of transpersonal. I chose Tart's preface to *Transpersonal Psychotherapies*, from the first issue of the *Journal of Transpersonal Psychology*, in 1969, because it places transpersonal psychology in relation to other schools and is an early definition from within the field.

> TRANSPERSONAL PSYCHOLOGY is the title given to an emerging force in the psychology field by a group of psychologists and professional men and women from other fields who are interested in those *ultimate* human capacities and potentialities that have no systematic place in positivistic or behavioristic theory ('first force'), classical psychoanalytic theory ('second force'), or humanistic psychology ('third force'). The emerging Transpersonal Psychology ('fourth force') is concerned

specifically with the *empirical,* scientific study of, and responsible implementation of the findings relevant to, becoming, individual and species-wide meta-needs, ultimate values, unitive consciousness, peak experiences, B-values, ecstasy, mystical experience, awe, being, self-actualization, essence, bliss, wonder, ultimate meaning, transcendence of the self, spirit, oneness, cosmic awareness, individual and species-wide synergy, maximal interpersonal encounter, sacralization of everyday life, transcendental phenomena, cosmic self-humor and playfulness, maximal sensory awareness, responsiveness and expression, and related concepts, experiences, and activities. As a definition, this formulation is to be understood as subject to *optional* individual or group interpretations, either wholly or in part, with regard to the acceptance of its content as essentially naturalistic, theistic, supernaturalistic, or any other designated classification.

(Tart, 1975, p. 2)

I would hope that the chosen quotes have given a good indication of what transpersonal psychology is all about, though they also highlighted that it is a vast field. Besides, I am not the only one to have looked for definitions; a review of the literature Lajoie and Shapiro (1992), Walsh and Vaughan (1993), Shapiro et al. (2002), Caplan et al. (2003) as well as Waldman (2006) have also done the same.

Lajoie and Shapiro (1992) offer a paper that, like my search, revealed the field to be one that encompassed a very broad scope of interest. They took 40 definitions that had appeared within the literature between 1969 and 1991. And what I find useful in their work is that they identified five key themes that were common within these definitions: states of consciousness, ultimate potential, functioning beyond the ego boundaries, transcendence and spirituality. No one of these five, whilst encompassing the interests of transpersonal psychology, is regarded to be more important than another. Although not every thinker or clinician within the field may agree totally with the above categories, and semantic debate could ensue regarding their exact meaning, I think that they fairly represent the interest and scope of transpersonal psychology.

Lajoie and Shapiro's commonly found themes are not the only work that tries distilling the transpersonal down to fundamental areas of interest. Cortright (1997) uses another device and defines eight basic assumptions,

Our essential nature is spiritual – Consciousness is multidimensional – Human beings have valid urges toward spiritual seeking, expressed as a search for wholeness through deepening individual social, and transcendent awareness – Contacting a deeper source of wisdom and guidance within is both possible and helpful to growth – Uniting a person's conscious will and aspiration with the spiritual impulse is a superordinate health value – Altered states of consciousness are one way of accessing transpersonal experiences and can be an aid to healing and growth – Our life and actions are meaningful – The transpersonal context shapes how the person/client is viewed.

(pp. 16–21)

Sutich (1996, p. 10) gives a much looser set of three basic assumptions, ones that had been mooted in the early days of the recognition of transpersonal psychology. In the same work Walsh and Vaughan, discussing transpersonal therapy, look towards its goals instead of identifying basic assumptions. They are clear that

The goals of transpersonal therapy include both traditional ones, such as symptom relief and behaviour change, and, for appropriate clients, the introduction of a variety of methods aimed at the transpersonal level. The latter include the provision of an adequate conceptual framework for handling transpersonal experiences; information on psychological potential; realization of the importance of assuming responsibility, not only for one's behaviour but for one's experience; discovery of the possibility of using all life experience as a part of learning; experiencing the existence and potentials of altered states; and understanding the usefulness, limits, and dangers of attachment to fixed models and expectations. In addition to working through psychodynamic processes, the therapist may also assist the client in beginning to disidentify from them.

(Walsh & Vaughan, 1996, pp. 21–22)

Here the importance of including the aims of traditional or orthodox therapeutic schools and the inclusion of transpersonal functioning is recognized with both being seen as having equal weight. It is also established that working with the transpersonal is not appropriate for all.

Daniels (2005) brings his focus purely upon theoretical issues and does not look towards the application of transpersonal psychology. He takes another stance to those I have so far portrayed, as he bypasses debates regarding basic tenets and definitions. Having said that, he recognizes that, 'All theories in transpersonal psychology have the common aims of clarifying our understanding of the nature of transpersonal, and accounting intelligibly for the process of transformation' (p. 26).

Here the onus is upon 'transformation', with the recognition that, as the field matures, there is a bias towards developmental models, and it is the thrust that development takes that he explores. Looking towards transpersonal theory, he splits the various models into two groups: those that can be considered as being situated within and looking towards experiences that are immanent and those that are better described by being transcendent. He regards this distinction as being useful when trying to understand the differences between the various transpersonal theories on offer, 'The immanent-horizontal-descending position argues that transformation is to be sought through greater connection to the world of nature, to other people, the body, the feminine, or the dynamic ground of the unconscious' (Daniels, 2005, p. 26), whereas the transcendent or ascending position can be thought of as a means whereby transformation can be sought through the realization of mystical or divine states that are regarded as being metaphorically above or beyond the physical universe.

He positions the work of well-known transpersonal thinkers along an axis that at one end has the ascending and at the other the descending. Within this schema he recognizes that Ken Wilber's work moved from early theories that fit the descending category to the ascending in his later thinking. However, whilst I find his continuum a useful device to roughly place differing transpersonal theorists upon, I think it is overly simplistic, as many theorists recognize that transformation can be seen as being achievable through both positions; Assagioli (1990) is a good example.

Although in Chapter 4 where I review the major transpersonal thinkers this device is not adopted, it emerges when looking at Wilber's linear and hierarchical model of human development and Michael Washburn's more pluralistic or non-linear developmental model.

It may also be useful to bear in mind that the terms 'immanence' and 'transcendence' are familiar in philosophy and are commonly used to highlight a dichotomy between Asian and Western philosophy, with immanence said to typify Asian, especially Chinese, philosophy and religion, whilst transcendence is seen to be prevalent in Western thought and religion.

Finally, before moving beyond an exploration of definitions for the field, I think it is worth noting that Hutton (1994) uses a differing approach to understand what transpersonal psychotherapy is. Instead of concentrating upon transpersonal as phenomena, he seeks instead to reveal how transpersonal psychotherapists differ from other practitioners.

His findings reveal that transpersonally orientated therapists utilize all four forces of psychology to define themselves and tend to be more eclective in their use of techniques, with the suggestion, '...that transpersonal psychology may be better suited to the study of psychoreligious and psychospiritual concerns than other psychological and psychiatric disciplines' (p. 167). He then concludes that the main factors that distinguish transpersonal clinicians from others is that, 'The practitioners of transpersonal psychology tend to report having had spiritual experiences, follow some spiritual practice, and believe that such experiences are important. They have had training in transpersonal psychology and believe that spiritual issues are relevant to psychotherapy' (p. 167).

Having briefly related some of the many definitions of the field and identified key areas of interest cannot fully answer the question posed at the start of this book, as for many the 'proof of the pudding is in the eating'. It highlights however that, although transpersonal psychotherapy may not have its own entry in my dictionary, it is nonetheless recognized as a valid and legitimate part of psychological thinking and practice, as many clinicians, and theorists alike, 'bother' with the transpersonal perspective because they appreciate and recognize that it should justifiably be a part of psychological practice.

## The recognition of transpersonal psychology by the medical model

The idea that a transpersonal view of anything is able to offer a valid viewpoint is a contentious issue in the present academic climate, and is explored through a discussion of the philosophy of science in the next chapter.

However, the fact that many professional governing bodies, especially those that are situated within the mainstream medical model, recognize the need to include a transpersonal orientation within their ranks may for some transpersonalists offer some hope of legitimization.

In 1996, for instance, the British Psychological Society (BPS) created the Transpersonal Psychology Section (Fontana & Slack, 1996). My own professional body 'the United Kingdom Counsel for Psychotherapy' recognizes and accepts upon their register of accredited psychotherapists many clinicians who describe themselves as transpersonal psychotherapists as well as those whose orientation includes the recognition of the transpersonal.

The professional recognition of the transpersonal is not just the case in the United Kingdom, as there are worldwide transpersonal psychotherapy organizations that have acceptance and recognition for their professionalism and validity from within the established psychological professions. However, this is not always apparent at first glance, for, when speaking of the transpersonal, we need to be mindful of the use of terminology, as not all thinkers or clinicians in the fields of psychotherapy or psychiatry use the classification transpersonal. A good example is the *Diagnostic and Statistical Manual of Mental Disorders Fourth Edition (DSM IV) American Psychiatric Association* (1994). It includes the diagnostic category 'Religious or Spiritual Problem' (Code V62.89). It states that,

> This category can be used when the focus of clinical attention is a religious or spiritual problem. Examples include distressing experiences that involve loss or questioning of faith, problems associated with conversion to a new faith, or questioning of other spiritual values which may not necessarily be related to an organised church or religious institution.
>
> (p. 685)

Because of its terminology the DSM IV category may appear a long way from the picture I have been painting. However, upon closer examination of the rationale for the inclusion of this category, we can see that it is in fact nearer to the definitions I have already discussed. Lukoff et al. (1998) examining the need for a distinct category covering religious and spiritual problems, relate,

> In a survey of APA member psychologists, 60% reported that clients often expressed their personal experiences in religious language, and that at least 1 in 6 of their patients presented issues which directly involve religion or spirituality (Shafranske & Maloney, 1990). Another study of psychologists found 72% indicating that they had at some time addressed religious or spiritual issues in treatment (Lannert, 1991). In a sample that included psychologists, psychiatrists, social workers, and marriage and family therapists, 29% agreed that religious issues are important in the treatment of all or many of their clients (Bergin & Jensen, 1990). Anderson and Young (1988)

claim that: 'All clinicians inevitably face the challenge of treating patients with religious troubles and preoccupations' (p. 532). While little is known about the prevalence of specific types of religious and spiritual problems in treatment, these surveys demonstrate that religious and spiritual issues are often addressed in psychotherapy.

(Lukoff et al., 1998, p. 22)

Having discussed the prevalence of religious and spiritual problems, he goes on to define the nature of these problems, placing them in two categories, psychoreligious and psychospiritual. It is the following definition of these two categories that was formally submitted in December 1991 to the Task Force on DSM-IV for inclusion as a V Code, a condition not attributable to a mental disorder.

Psychoreligious problems are experiences that a person finds troubling or distressing and that involve the beliefs and practices of an organised church or religious institution. Examples include loss or questioning of a firmly held faith, change in denominational membership, conversion to a new faith, and intensification of adherence to religious practices and orthodoxy. Psychospiritual problems are experiences that a person finds troubling or distressing and that involve that person's relationship with a transcendent being or force. These problems are not necessarily related to the beliefs and practices of an organised church or religious institution. Examples include near-death experience and mystical experience. This category can be used when the focus of treatment or diagnosis is a psychoreligious or psychospiritual problem that is not attributable to a mental disorder.

(Lukoff et al., 1998)

The proposal was accepted in January 1993, though the title was changed from psychoreligious and psychospiritual problems to 'Religious or Spiritual Problem' and the definition was shortened and modified.

Lukoff and his fellow researchers identify themselves as being the transpersonal clinicians and requested feedback when they presented their ideas at the 1991 and 1992 Association for Transpersonal Psychology Conferences. I am aware that there are many who would see this inclusion in DSM as validation and recognition for the field from the psychiatric profession and other clinicians who identify themselves as practising within the traditional medical model. This view, however, is not shared by all. Miller et al. (1997), for instance, see the 300% increase in the number of categories in a 40-year period as symptomatic of a therapeutic culture lead by clinicians who need to pathologize their clientele in order to create a view of themselves as experts, thereby lessening the importance of the part that clients bring to their own healing and consequently emphasizing the therapists' contribution.

The need for clinicians to pathologies, if true, may not be a factor in the inclusion of the transpersonal in DSM-IV. What it may be is that, as Lukoff et al. pointed out, many individuals report some form of what this book calls transpersonal phenomena and it is important to not attribute their experience, if not experienced as ego syntonic, to a mental disorder. And just because those who work within, say, the psychiatric perspective may not use the term 'transpersonal', this does not mean that they will not find themselves working with patients who are seeking to integrate transpersonal experience.

Although I have informed my reader that I will use terms such as transpersonal psychotherapy and transpersonal psychology interchangeably, it is interesting to note that the term 'Transpersonal Psychiatry', though not so common, can be found in the literature, for example in Kasprow and Scotton (1999), Wilber (1998) and Walsh and Vaughan (1993), and it is described in much the same way as transpersonal psychotherapy. Furthermore, Scotton et al. (1986) views classical/traditional psychiatry as a subset of the much larger system, transpersonal psychiatry.

As within all areas where the transpersonal is recognized, initiatives are not bound to one part of the world. Within the United Kingdom 'The Royal College of Psychiatrists', the regulatory body for psychiatrists, recognize, like their American cousins, the importance of the transpersonal in relationship to health and well-being.

Since 1991 the need for the recognition of spirituality has been mooted by influential figures within the college, and in 1999 a Special Interest Group was formed, which, at the time of writing, has a membership that stands at over 1300 members. The Spirituality and Psychiatry Special Interest Group, www.rcpsych.ac.uk/college/specialinterestgroups/spirituality, recognizes that psychiatrists and the psychiatric profession are increasingly interested in spirituality because of potential benefits to mental health. They organize conferences, training events and the publication of papers and research projects for psychiatrists and mental health professionals, and they publish leaflets and provide information for patients and carers. Although they do equate spirituality with the definitions that I have claimed for the transpersonal, examining their literature the influence of major religions, without taking centre stage, has a greater focus.

Regardless of semantic debate, within the medical profession it is not only bodies such as the American Psychiatric Association and the Royal College of Psychiatrists who identify the need to understand and recognize the relationship between an individual's experience and practice of religious belief and psychological health. Also Loewenthal (1995) gives numerous examples of the difficulty psychiatrists can experience distinguishing between behaviour that has become psychopathological and behaviour that has been sanctioned or prescribed by an organized church or religious institution. She includes mainstream religions, such as Catholicism and Hinduism, some of the less well-known, such as the Baha'i faith, and new religious movements and cults, such as the Divine Light Mission.

I do not feel that embarking upon a full-scale exploration of the relationship of religious experiences, religion with transpersonal experiences and transpersonal disciplines is called for in the confines of this study. However, I thought a brief comparison is merited because, without detailed examination, it can be easy to confuse transpersonal and religious experience. Though distinguishable, one would not have to look far to find reason for confusion, for they both could be seen as sharing many similarities, such as an interest in experiences that are commonly described as sacred or spiritual. The distinction Lukoff gives between psychoreligious and psychospiritual problems as diagnostic criterion is one approach that can be employed when finding ways to differentiate between the two.

However, not all those in the field always make differences explicit. Lyons (1999), for instance, addresses one aspect of the transpersonal states, 'The transpersonal movement has the intention of making sense of experiences, which traditionally would have been called "religious". But in using a more "scientific" rather than "mythic" framework it refrains from using religious language, while treating many of the same concerns' (p. 41).

Seeing this as a good example of possible misinterpretation, I turned to Walsh's and Vaughan's (1993) comparison, for it clearly points out areas of overlap as well as differences between the two fields.

> Since some, but not all, transpersonal experiences are experiences of the sacred, and since some, but not all, religious experiences are transpersonal, there is clearly some overlap between transpersonal experiences and religious experiences. Transpersonal disciplines,

however, are also interested in transpersonal experiences that are not religious, and in research, interpretations, psychologies, and philosophies devoid of religious overtones. Transpersonal disciplines espouse no creed or dogma, demand no particular religious convictions, espouse an open-minded scientific, philosophical, and experiential testing of all claims, and usually assume that transpersonal experiences can be interpreted either religiously or nonreligiously according to individual preference. Transpersonal disciplines and religion should therefore be regarded as distinct fields with partially overlapping areas of interest and also significant differences. Likewise, although they share some areas of interest, transpersonal psychology and transpersonal anthropology are clearly distinct from the psychology and anthropology of religion.

(pp. 5–6)

However, it is worth noting that, in addition to lesser-known figures such as Lyons, who finds equivalence between transpersonal psychology and the psychology of religion, more influential figures in the field can also be construed as doing likewise. David Fontana is a good example. Professor of Transpersonal Psychology at Liverpool John Moores University, fellow of the British Psychological society the professional association for academic, clinical, and chartered psychologists in the United Kingdom, and Chair of the editorial team of the journal *Transpersonal Psychology Review* he has been undoubtedly one of the champions of transpersonal psychology in the United Kingdom (Fontana & Slack, 1996).

However, his book *Psychology, Religion, and Spirituality* (Fontana, 2003), that to my mind, offers a well-researched exploration of much that is of primary interest to transpersonal psychology and only explicitly acknowledges transpersonal psychology's existence in passing (p. 29). With possible confusion in discriminating between the two fields, in the next section I examine the psychology of religion, a discrete school of psychology that examines areas such as meaning and faith, though in the context of religion.

I was aware that my own bias as a practicing psychotherapist would lead me to view the transpersonal primarily from within a psychological framework. So I felt it necessary for this study not to look at the relationship between experience and practice of religious belief and psychological health just from a psychological standpoint. It could also be important to metaphorically turn the lens over and recognize that religions themselves may have something to say about psychotherapy and the transpersonal. For this reason I am going to discuss how the transpersonal as an aspect of psychology can be viewed from the vantage point offered by various religious traditions. To conclude this exploration I also address the differences between transpersonal psychology and the many forms of 'Spiritual counselling'.

## Transpersonal psychology: religion with a psychological spin?

To begin the exploration of how differing religious/spiritual traditions interface with Western psychological views and the transpersonal approach, I feel that it is important to recognize that many theorists, who identify themselves as transpersonal psychologists, can be seen as drawing upon religious traditions: whilst sometimes this may be one discrete path within a recognized major faith such as Zen Buddhism, it is also common to draw from a range of religious paths.

## An integrative/eclectic religious influence

It is not surprising to find that some thinkers look towards many differing religious worldviews and traditions to inform their thinking. This could be likened to how integrative/eclective psychotherapists combine different theoretical approaches and theories of human nature in their work.

A good example of a transpersonal theorist who draws from a diverse religious/philosophical background is Vaughan (1985). Examining her work reveals a theorist who has turned towards what could be conceived as maps of consciousness that come from traditional religious thought. She posits that the psychological healing of the whole person is possible by following what she terms an inward arc exploring the superconscious. This, however, is not at the expense of working within the more common approach, familiar to mainstream psychology that explores the unconscious, which she terms 'the outward arc'. She suggests that an analogous metaphorical representation of the inward arc would include the ox herding pictures from the Zen school, the Chakra system of Hinduism as well as the heroic journey and Dante's Divine Comedy from the Western path.

Though Vaughan is not alone in her eclective stance, many concentrate upon one religious orientation, and an obvious candidate to begin an exploration of religious belief and psychological theory would be Buddhism in its many differing traditions.

## Buddhism

Though often regarded as a religion, I have met many who instead see Buddhism as a philosophy that has similar aims to those of Western psychotherapy. Walley in Claxton (1996) clearly suggests this, stating that

> ...the task of Buddhism is first to understand the nature of suffering in its various forms and then to apply methods which step by step alleviate and eventually completely eliminate all suffering and states of dissatisfaction. (...) Buddhism does touch modern approaches towards the care of others directly and it is to these issues that we shall now turn. A position central to Buddhist psychology is the view that the root causes of human unhappiness and dissatisfaction lie within individuals' firmly held attitudes and beliefs about themselves. For convenience these self-cognitions may be referred to as the self-image and in Buddhist terms a person's well-being is directly bound to the fluctuating fortunes of this sense of 'self' or 'I'. Buddhist theory would propose that individuals will become psychologically vulnerable to the extent to which they identify with their self-image and to the extent to which the self-image serves to overshadow the full range of personal experience.
>
> (Claxton, 1996, pp. 195–196)

Mark Epstein (1995), who could be considered one of the best-known Western commentators upon Buddhist psychology, goes further when addressing depth psychology and Buddhist teaching. He recognizes the latter as having a

> comprehensive view of the human psyche. For Buddhism, like the Western traditions that followed many centuries later, is, in its psychological form a *depth* psychology. It is able to describe, in terms that would make any psychoanalyst proud, the full range of the human emotional experience. (...) The Buddha may well have been the original psychoanalyst, or, at least the first to use the mode of analytic inquiry that Freud was later to codify and develop.
>
> (p. 9)

However, through my own understanding of both depth psychology and Buddhist teaching I recognize that Epstein's views could be misconstrued by thinkers who observe human nature from a predominantly psychodynamic or orthodox analytical stance, for from the stance of

Buddhist psychology the building of ego strength plays a minor role. This is contrary to how depth psychology sees ego development as being an important cornerstone in the maturation of a healthy adult individual.

Furthermore, Epstein's entreaty to cultivate emptiness (sunyata) (1999) could be seen, with psychologically orthodox eyes, as indicative of many of the symptoms described by patients displaying symptoms congruent with an unhealthy/disturbed psychopathology. This could include those who are unable to find or maintain a coherent sense of their own self-identity, or defence mechanisms against being overwhelmed by their own feelings of aggression, or alternatives to experiencing a profound sense of inadequacy. In short all experiences that could be seen as having an infantile derivative.

Though the above could be considered a common pathologizing of what is often described by patients as emptiness, orthodox thinking does not completely overlook the potential of possible clinical benefits that exploration may bring. Winnicott (1971, 1974) an influential thinker and theorist within orthodox psychotherapeutic/psychiatric thinking, certainly recognized its importance, seeing it as a valid aspect of the human psyche.

I also feel that it would be wise to recognize at this point that it is not orthodox thinking only that could benefit from an entreaty not to be too quick to pathologize reports of experiences of emptiness. Those who practice from a transpersonal orientation would also be advised to address with care reports resembling emptiness. A good example that springs to mind is the discernment that is needed when one's worldview is influenced by Firman's and Gila's overtly transpersonal model, 'the Primal Wound' (1997), which is discussed in the fourth chapter. Among those who view their clients from this theoretical perspective the less-discerning clinician could confuse, without careful consideration, the Buddhist concept of 'sunyata' with their description of 'non-being'.

Welwood (2002) is yet another thinker who explores the interface between Eastern spiritual practice and Western psychology. He draws primarily upon Tibetan Buddhist thought, and from this perspective he speculates that mankind needs to 'wake up' to our ultimate spiritual nature. 'Enlightenment is not some ideal goal, perfect state of mind, or spiritual realm on high, but a journey that takes place on this earth. It is the process of waking up to all of what we are and making a complete relationship with that' (p. 33). To achieve this awakening he posits that psychological work is needed just as much as addressing the transpersonal, a balance between personal growth, psychological maturity and authenticity on one hand and spiritual development on the other. With his stress upon the importance of psychological functioning as integral to transpersonal development, he suggests that some individuals may choose to not address their psychological material by turning instead to spiritual practices: what he terms 'spiritual bypassing' (pp. 5, 11–12, 207–213) and sees as a defence mechanism. I address this concept in the fourth section.

Walley, Welwood and Epstein are not the only theorists to conceive a psychology that includes Buddhist thought and attitudes. Although many practising Gestalt psychotherapists would claim not to know much about Buddhism, Fritz Pearls, who is commonly seen as one of the founding fathers of Gestalt therapy, studied Zen Buddhism in Japan. The influence of his interest in the Zen worldview is not hard to find underpinning much of his work. His notion that change happens when we cease to change ourselves is accordance with the Zen concept of paradox, and the great importance he placed upon present awareness speaks in Western terms of Zen's directive to the student to practice mindfulness.

It is not just Gestalt, a well-known psychotherapeutic school, that contains the influence of Buddhist thought and teaching. There are other approaches to psychotherapy originated in the West that explicitly claim to draw upon Buddhist practice, such as 'Core Process Psychotherapy' (Donnington, 1989).

Before leaving Buddhism and its interface with Western and transpersonal psychology, I feel that it is important not to give the impression that it is only the humanistic orientated schools, such as Gestalt, that are interested in Buddhist thought. I would recommend Segall (2003) for an exploration of the points of confluence and conflict between diverse contemporary Western psychological orientations and Buddhist teachings. Also Safran (2003) offers a discussion that concentrates upon the relationship between psychoanalysis and Buddhism.

## The Jewish mystical tradition

Another discrete religious school is the Jewish mystical tradition, and an important aspect of which is the Kabala. According to Jewish thinking, within the Kabala a map can be found that charts and gives terminology to inner states and transpersonal realms. It is claimed that it can be used to help individuals towards the balance and integration of spiritual and everyday consciousness in all areas of their life.

The Kabala has a rich heritage and a large body of literature. It can be traced from the classical Hasidism in the eighteenth century to the Cordoverian and Lurianic schools of Safed in the sixteenth century, the Zohar Spanish and French schools of thirteenth and fourteenth century all the way back to a time between the Old and New Testaments. Schacter-Shalomi (1996), a rabbi and lecturer in Jewish mysticism, and Parfit (2006), a psychosynthesis psychotherapist, both offer a discussion of the Kabala. Hoffman's (1981) work also explores how Kabalistic ideas can be seen to have shaped Western psychological thinking.

It is also worth noting that Martin Buber was well versed in Kabalistic thought. His work and thinking has influenced many from the humanistic school of psychology, an influence I discuss in the next chapter.

## Sufism

The esoteric tradition of the Islamic faith Sufism is another religious tradition that places an emphasis upon the transpersonal. As well as addressing purpose and meaning, it places significance upon individuals (and mankind as a race) gaining awareness of our spiritual nature, offering a formula that claims to aid individuals in developing perceptual capacities in addition to those afforded by the intellect and emotion. This of course would also include psychological well-being, the province of Western psychology. Keutzer (1984) quotes Idries Shah, the eminent contemporary Sufi scholar as saying, 'Sufism is itself a far more advanced psychological system than any which is yet developed in the west' (1984).

Examining Keutzer's influences myself, I found that Shah (1996), who offers a comprehensive introduction to Sufic thought, is at pains to point out that Sufism does not offer a one-size-fits-all approach to human development. Sufic instruction may be useful for one person, at a given time, in particular circumstances; though it may be inappropriate or even damaging for another, or at a different time, or in different circumstances. This elasticity and non-pre-determined approach is in accord with many psychotherapeutic schools where clinicians have a clear theoretical stance from which they work, yet carefully choose how and when to use differing interventions.

With statements such as Shah's comments upon Sufism's psychological sophistication, it is clear why this tradition, like Buddhism, is seen by some as being a philosophical/psychological approach to self-realization and not a religion. Moreover, viewed in this light Sufism could be seen as fitting in with Wilber's definition of transpersonal psychology as starting with psychiatry and ending with mysticism, which I quoted earlier.

Shah is not the only thinker from the Sufi perspective whose work is pertinent to this study.

Hameed Ali, who writes under the pen name A. H. Almass (1996), is another. His 'diamond model', according to Cortright (1997), is 'perhaps the fastest growing transpersonal approach on the scene today' (pp. 90–91). Ali, however, maintains that his approach is a spiritual path and practice, not a psychological model. Nevertheless, dissecting the 'diamond model' will reveal a fusion of contemporary object-relations theory, Sufic thought and somatic theory. It aims to aid an individual in shifting the self-identification from that of ego-centred to a greater awareness of their deeper spiritual identity. He terms our spiritual identity 'Essence' and posits that by working through our early wounding we will have an increased capacity to actualize energies such as love and wisdom, with enhanced experience of essence. This is done through addressing both conscious and unconscious psychological conflicts and defence mechanisms. His model has many similarities to the work of some psychosynthesis thinkers such as Firman and Gilas' (1997) 'Primal Wound' theory and Yeoman's (1994) 'Soul Wound' hypothesis. I discuss in greater detail the contribution that psychosynthesis brings to transpersonal psychology as well as a deeper exploration of Ali's work in the fourth chapter.

Although the place of Sufic thought is given little discussion here and has a smaller literature than Buddhist psychology, Deikman (1996) and Keutzer (1984) present a more in-depth discussion of Sufism and transpersonal psychology.

## Spiritual counselling: religion through psychology?

Having briefly discussed the contribution that various spiritual/religious traditions bring to transpersonal psychology, it is important to recognize that transpersonal psychology is clearly distinguishable from the many forms of 'Spiritual counselling' available to followers of specific epistemological religious orthodoxies. Before giving account of 'Spiritual counselling' I feel it valuable to recognize that in the present intellectual climate the academic community with a post-modern tendency is keen to shy away from grand theories, encouraging instead eclecticism and the inclusion of elements from diverse sources. However, I feel that this inclusiveness could further, to the uninformed, the potential for misunderstanding the relationship that transpersonal psychology has to counselling within religious framework. I therefore place in context the essential differences between the two fields.

'Spiritual counselling' has its own rich tradition and can be grouped into three distinct categories:

* Spiritual direction, which is concerned with helping an individual work with the challenges that a pre-formulated relationship with God engenders. Within the Christian tradition it is common for laypersons to take this role after receiving training. Spiritual direction has a long lineage in the West: for example, Ignation Spiritual Direction is based upon the teachings and life experience of St Ignatius of Loyola. A text of *Spiritual Exercises* originally published in 1548 in Latin is to this day used as the core of this approach. For a concise review of differing traditions of Christian spiritual direction see Byrne (1990).
* Pastoral psychotherapy, which aims to aid a formal religious/spiritual practice explicitly directed towards the aims of a particular religious tradition or religious organization. It is therefore not surprising to find that generally pastoral psychotherapy is practiced by a recognized religious authority such as clergymen, Mullahs, rabbis and nuns.
* Psychospiritual psychotherapy, which is an approach that is commonly based in and views psychology from the vantage point of one religious or spiritual tradition such as Buddhism, Christianity and Sufism.

It is this last category that often engenders the most confusion or misunderstanding in its comparison to transpersonal psychology. Clarkson (2002) recognizes this and notes that,

> Where priests or religious people are trained as psychotherapists, they may practice any 'brand-name' of psychotherapy (Jungian, Psychosynthesis, Core energetics, transactional analysis or whatever). However some of these professionals with formal religious roles may also call their practice 'transpersonal psychotherapy' to emphasize the explicit inclusion of the transpersonal dimensions of psychotherapy.
>
> (p. 25)

Clarkson is not alone in recognizing the potential for confusion; West (2000), who claims not to write from the transpersonal perspective, also acknowledges similarities between the two and states that, 'There is a huge overlap between spiritual direction and therapy"' (p. 4).

Having briefly examined the transpersonal from a religious perspective, and highlighted the potential for confusion and misunderstanding that can arise when examining the two fields, I wish to return to the psychological standpoint.

## Psychology critical of the transpersonal

Whilst many of the thinkers who are presented within this work support, or at the least are not antagonistic towards, the inclusion of the transpersonal in psychological thinking, there are some influential thinkers who see it as a waste of time or consider its pursuit dangerous or foolhardy. A good example is Sigmund Freud.

This work would certainly be the poorer if I were not to spend some time exploring the field from the Freudian psychoanalytic perspective. I felt it was imperative to include Freud's thinking because of the importance that his work has imparted upon modern Western culture and in particular psychology. It is essential, however, to bear in mind that Freud, as a man of the turn of the nineteenth century, placed spirituality and what would now be called the transpersonal, solely within a religious framework. He would most certainly not have made any of the distinctions between a religious orientation and the inclusion of spirituality that are discussed in the present milieu. His model of the unconscious mind and the personality structure, as being made up of the id, the ego and the superego, has become an established part of mainstream Western culture. For instance, being accused of a 'Freudian slip' is something that has become part of common experience regardless of the measure of the technical understanding of traditional psychoanalytical thought of either the accused or the accuser. It is not just the layman that has incorporated the thinking of Freud. The influence of his work can be seen as one of the foundation stones of a wide range of theoretical models, such as the psychodynamic approach and object-relations theory. Moreover, many clinicians recognize that Freud can indeed be rightly recognized as the founding father of a great deal of modern day psychological thought.

I see it as ironic that both psychoanalysis and traditional Christianity are two fields that can justifiably be said to claim they are vehicles for the pursuit of truth. Both of their rationales claim this pursuit will bring an individual into a greater sense of harmony with themselves and the world, whilst refining their awareness of their own inner world.

Yet, I thought it fair to say that, though they may indeed share similar purposes and aims, historically both fields seem to have not had much good to say about the other.

My own experience as a clinician working with colleagues in a transpersonal perspective as well as those from a humanistic and psychodynamic orientation is that Freudian theory with its emphasis towards life as deterministic and driven by instinct is openly dismissive of experiences that can be seen as 'spiritual'. Though psychoanalytic thought has a rich and extensive literature that has evolved over almost a century, there is little that openly and directly speaks of religion or the transpersonal. Although the foregoing points towards a paucity of work that combines Freudian thought and the transpersonal, I include in the next chapter a more in-depth exploration of the psychological school that Freud founded.

Freud, a prolific writer whose life work was the examination of the human condition, in *Moses and Monotheism* (1967), *Totem and Taboo* (2001) (Freud claimed this his best written work), *Civilization and its Discontents* (1961b) and *The Future of an Illusion* (1961a) clearly sees man as a herd animal driven by instinct, prone to the psychological tension engendered by the clash and drive of instincts and the influence of the superego. With this he shores up his argument ardently denying the value of religious belief and the possibility of a higher motivating principle. Moreover, Freud declares that the yearning we feel for spiritual experience is in fact a regressive yearning in disguise for the earliest oceanic bliss of symbiosis with mother (1961b), with religion being nothing but an individual's need for a father who would afford a lifelong refuge against existential vulnerability (1961a).

However, it was not just Freud who was addressing the relationship of religion to psychology in the 1930s. Others, such as Waterhouse (1931), took the opposing viewpoint to that of the 'great man'. From the perspective of the present day, it was easy for me to see that thinkers such as Waterhouse, a professor of psychology and philosophy as well as an ordained priest, may have had their own axe to grind. Without being overtly proselytizing, I could view his book *Psychology and Religion*, originally a series of radio broadcasts, as a means of 'defending the faith' from the onslaught of a potential foe, the new science – psychoanalysis.

In more recent times one of the few who explicitly addressed religion from within the psychoanalytic arena is Symington (1998). Although his exploration is primarily within the Judaeo-Christian tradition, he does, however, briefly examine both Hinduism and Buddhism. Symington argues for his proposition that both religion and psychoanalysis need to incorporate each other's values. This marriage would bring about a positive transformation in both. Religion would become more relevant to an individual's emotional life with the inclusion of psychoanalytic thought, and psychoanalysis would be able to contain, and not just pathologize, the spiritual values that help to give an individual's life meaning. He also makes a differentiation between what he describes as primitive and mature religion. Primitive religion he sees as having an ideological stance that encourages magical or mythical thinking in order to provide protection and survival. Mature religion, on the other hand, is rational, thus able to address existential issues, such as forgiveness, good, evil and death. (Elements of both primitive and mature can be combined in all religions.)

As a respected and well-known member of the British psychoanalytic community it comes as no surprise to see his influence in the work of others. Black (1998), for instance, builds upon Symington's work and argues that religion has a psychological function that can be an engine of personal transformation.

Melanie Klein (1975), who is often thought of as the mother of psychoanalysis, arguably the founder of, and the biggest influence upon modern psychodynamic thinking, agreed with Freud's thoughts on spirituality and religion. However, it is ironic that Grof's (1976) exploration of non-ordinary states of consciousness induced by LSD verified some of her postulations concerning early phantasy.

It is not just the classical Freudian psychoanalytic perspective that could be seen to be at odds with the inclusion of the transpersonal as a valid area of exploration towards meeting the aims of psychological well-being. One figure passionate in his criticism of the transpersonal psychology was Albert Ellis, the originator of rational emotive therapy (RET). He can be credited as being one of the founding fathers of cognitive behavioural therapy. Disillusioned by his analytical training he was to formulate many of his ideas in the 1960s and 1970s, the same period during which transpersonal psychology was gaining popularity and credibility. In *Why Some Therapies Don't Work* (1989) – which is subtitled *The Dangers of Transpersonal Psychology* – he vehemently attacks the field of transpersonal psychology or at least his understanding of it. If I had not had prior knowledge of the field and had had to take Ellis as the expert he paints himself to be, I would have certainly been suspicious to say the least of anyone who admitted to being a practitioner of transpersonal psychology. For surely they would have wanted all my money or wished to induct me into some faddish cult or more than likely both! Upon reading *Why Some Therapies Don't Work*, I felt a more appropriate title may have been 'It's dangerous not to follow RET's/Ellis' thinking and methodology'.

Ellis starts by stating that his intention is to 'discuss the potential as well as the current already harmful effects of transpersonal psychology and psychotherapy and will contrast them with the presumably more effective, realistic, and pragmatic approach of rational-emotive therapy' (p. 8). To do this he begins by describing 35 tenets of transpersonal psychology; I did not agree with his list and I could not see it as representing or reflecting others' understanding. Moreover, I had been unable to find a description of the transpersonal that in any way matches his. The 35 tenets include statements such as, 'Because transpersonal views are sacrosanct and include the one and only Absolute Truth, and because enormous harm (such as Armageddon) will befall us if we ignore or oppose these transpersonal truths, we *must* completely believe in and follow them' (p. 14). He attributes this view to the Iranian Islamic fundamentalist Ayatollah Khomeini. I was unable to find any other, from any of the sets of literature I was to examine, who sees Khomeini as a valid authority on the subject of transpersonal psychology. 'The sacred truth is revealed in holy scriptures ( ... ) Transpersonal psychology often advocates that these scriptures be strictly and devoutly endorsed and followed (Franklin, 1973; Luce & Hudak, 1986)' (p. 10) is another of his tenets. Although he proclaims this as a 'fact', I found, upon closer examination, that he attributes it in part to an occult dictionary. I saw this as another good example of his ability to paint a picture that places RET in an exemplary light when compared to his description of the transpersonal. Having given his definition of the transpersonal psychology he goes on to identify 15 commonly accepted goals of psychotherapy, such as the client gaining increased self-acceptance and developing greater degrees of awareness and insight. In the subsequent chapters he explores these 15 commonly accepted goals using a formula which follows a similar pattern for each. A short paragraph briefly outlining the topic followed by an extensive description extolling the virtues of RET justified by a description of the dangers that the transpersonal perspective brings to that particular goal.

When first coming across the title of this book I was hoping to find a work that could give a well thought out and clearly referenced argument from a respected academic who has a critical perspective from which to view transpersonal psychology. This was in stark contrast to what I found: a work that preaches Ellis' own importance, claiming to have the absolute truth on every page, ironically an allegation he makes about those whose practice includes the transpersonal perspective.

Ellis can rightly claim to have an important and influential impact upon many of today's clinicians and thinkers within the cognitive therapy (CT) and the cognitive behavioural therapy (CBT) community. This approach to clinical practice is often the best known and understood by general practitioners in primary care. This is not surprising as it shares many of the ideals and practices familiar to the allopathic medical model, such as solution focus, symptom reduction, technique-orientation and the importance of cognitive over emotional experience.

However, some from this school, such as House (2002), a CT practitioner, strongly feel that the transpersonal is a significant sphere within psychology, and that it needs inclusion. He states this clearly when saying that he believes 'there to be an important role for a type of "spiritualised" cognitive therapy, which:

- transcends CT's narrowly cast empirical-scientific world view
- strongly informed by constructionist theory and postmodern deconstruction
- embraces some limited aspects of Albert Ellis's "rational emotive" therapy (RET) approach' (p. 121).

RET and CT are not unique in having a reductionist and deterministic perspective from which to view the world. Neurobiology as a branch of the Western allopathic medical model also shares this perspective. This, however, does not mean it share Ellis' passionate criticism of transpersonal psychology or his views concerning the validity of exploring the transpersonal. Among the early transpersonal theorists the humanistic/existentialist Rollo May (1969) was particularly concerned about the low level of reflection on the dark side of human nature and on human suffering, and the archetypal psychologist James Hillman (1991, 2004) shares similar concerns. Similar misgivings can also be found being expressed by transpersonal thinkers such as Ferrer (2002) and Daniels (2005). Daniels, who commentates upon theoretical issues in transpersonal psychology, is particularly keen to point out that transpersonal psychology has chosen, by and large, to ignore this area of human nature, a realm first mooted by Jung that is colloquially termed the 'shadow'.

I particularly like Daniels' (2005) description of how personal and transpersonal development can be regarded in a distorted manner as a process

...that involves a wonderful, joyful, entertaining, illuminating, 'happy-clappy', always forward-moving, easy journey of discovery and spiritual advancement. This journey begins when we learn to cast off and leave behind all personal negativity and darkness, adopt an attitude of 'positive thinking', make appropriately positive affirmations, and orientate ourselves and gravitate towards the light, like moths to a flame.

(p. 75)

He clearly recognizes that there is the potential for transpersonal psychology to be misconstrued as being the above, whereas, Ellis for instance, *only* regards it in this light. Although not attributing the potential for the aims and practices of transpersonal psychology to be distorted because of bias in the focus of research, Daniels recognizes that '...research in transpersonal psychology has tended to focus, largely on what we may loosely call the "positive" aspects of transpersonal experience such as ecstatic mystical states, creative inspiration, human kindness and compassion, wholeness and enlightenment' (p. 75). These are areas that I too have seen to be the ones that have most commonly been approached by transpersonal research, though, in my own clinical work, and that of my trainees and supervisees, these areas, with some clients, may never be explored or in the work have little attention placed upon them.

Having highlighted the potential for misconstruing the aims of transpersonal psychology, Daniels then takes one step nearer to sounding like Ellis when he claims that transpersonal development can to the misinformed be encapsulated by naïve myths or, 'dangerous partial truths' (p. 75) that include:

- Transpersonal development may be achieved by seeking out ecstatic and other exciting altered states of consciousness.
- Enlightenment makes you happy.
- Spiritually advanced people are joyful, dynamic and charismatic.
- Spiritual development can be achieved by adopting an enlightening' doctrine, or by discipleship to an enlightened Master.
- Ignore evil – perhaps it will go away.
- The spiritual path can be followed in a self-centred way, by focussing on our own personal and transpersonal development.

(p. 76)

If wild claims such as these were to be a true representation of transpersonal psychology I, for one, would distance myself from the school post-haste. And although the foregoing could be seen as an extreme misconception, I think the field is prone, because of its areas of interest, to being misconstrued as some form of escapist philosophy that preaches through mumbo jumbo. However, although I have not sought out research to substantiate my experience, I have found many times individuals to have all sorts of misunderstandings concerning the whole field of applied psychology, with stereotypical fantasies, such as psychotherapists wanting to encourage their clients to find ways to blame their parents for all life's ills, or professionals being able to somehow sort the clients' lives out in three or four sessions.

I included a brief exploration of the transpersonal from the perspective of neurobiology mainly because clinicians and theorists from all areas of psychology and psychotherapy pursue an active interest in the advances being made in neurological research. Moreover, contemporary neuroscientists themselves, Solms and Turnbull (2002), are increasingly able to direct their neurological research towards subjective mental states such as consciousness. This means that the exploration of subjective experience now need not be restricted only to psychological and philosophical schools. This has been made possible by the increasing sophistication of neurobiological tests, which in turn have been made possible by the advent of sophisticated brain imaging technology and advances in the understanding of molecular neurobiology.

However, our increasing understanding of how the brain and neurological system function, and the lessening emphasis placed upon behaviourism, has not lessened the focus of the majority of research being directed towards finding the determinants of abnormal pathology and mental disorder. Though I have been unable to find material that explains this, I imagine it may be due to the predominantly reductionist stance in the sciences, as well as the majority of research being funded by a pharmaceutical industry driven by a priority that strives to find new medicines, seeing increasing knowledge of inner states as merely a by-product.

Nevertheless, present day research does not exclude the examination of the transpersonal. In fact, it does suggest that transpersonal phenomena may have an effect on the neurological system as well as the neurological system having an effect upon what are perceived as transpersonal phenomena. Zohar and Marshall (2000) talk of 'The "god spot" in the brain' (pp. 91–112). They discuss it when arguing that one element of psychopathology is 'spiritual Intelligence', 'the intelligence with which we address and solve problems of meaning and value' (p. 3). The 'god spot' is the term lightly given to an isolated module of neural networks located within the temporal lobes, which, when artificially stimulated with magnetic field activity, produce experiences that correlate to those commonly portrayed and described as mystical/spiritual experiences. Moreover, they describe research that shows that heightened temporal lobe activity is induced when an individual is exposed to evocatively spiritual words or topics of conversation. One inference of this could be that the phenomenon of transpersonal/religious belief could have a biological/neurological explanation, and not as previously posited be only a consequence of consciousness or belief system.

They also recognize that the temporal lobes are linked to the limbic system and hippocampus. This strongly suggests that increased temporal lobe activity will have an effect upon emotion and memory. This, they posit, could explain why spiritual experiences are often described as 'life-transforming', because they are commonly accompanied by an 'impactful' and long-lived emotional element.

Exploring neurological functioning, Zohar, a physicist, has focused much of her research upon understanding consciousness from the perspective afforded by Quantum Physics. I return to and discuss in more depth this viewpoint when considering the works of thinkers such as Wilber (1990), Tart (1975), Grof (1976), Washburn (1988) and Pribram (1971).

Nelson (1994) also examines the brain and neurological system from a vantage point that incorporates the transpersonal perspective. As a practising psychiatrist he also includes an examination of the influence of pharmacological agents. He concentrates on the use of neuroleptics and psychedelics. This I found not surprising as he focuses upon the psychotic spectrum, including conditions such as schizophrenia that can be confused with transpersonal phenomena (I will explore this further when discussing 'Spiritual emergence'). Furthermore, he writes before the widespread use and popularity of selective seratonin re-uptake inhibitors. I would have valued finding a discussion of their effect from a researcher who encompasses the transpersonal, for since the mid-eighties they have become the most widespread of all prescribed psychopharmacological agents, though as yet I have not found one.

## Research and transpersonal psychology

Transpersonal psychology, despite having gained academic and clinical recognition, does not have a great body of research when compared to many other psychological schools. Most studies, however, that have been published, endeavour to follow academic protocol and look towards qualitative and not quantitative methodologies. With this qualitative bias it comes as no surprise that for many scientists situated within traditions that rely upon quantitative analysis the field cannot meet their rigorous classifications of validity. Moreover, orthodox 'scientists' may jump to conclusions, and tar transpersonal psychology with the same brush of un-scientificness they use when looking at fields such as religion, philosophy and parapsychology. Whilst many may claim to not have a pre-existing bias when looking at any phenomenon or body of knowledge that is not encompassed by their rules, my experience leads me to think this may not be the case. Thus, with an un-scientific label often already affixed, transpersonal thinkers who do not make claims utilizing orthodox scientific constructs are going to naturally find it more difficult to gain academic respectability than their colleagues in fields where 'scientific' constructs are utilized, for instance behavioural psychology.

The notion that transpersonal psychology has not yet fully gained 'academic respectability' may be a useful idea when thinking of its place in the wider field of psychology. Friedman (2002) recognizes this and is keen to differentiate between the larger area of transpersonal 'studies' and the discrete discipline or transpersonal psychology, which he sees as being situated within the field of 'scientific' psychology. With the potential for confusion of the two being one and the same, he is keen to point out that, whilst sharing many areas of equivalence, a common though misleading assumption would be to see transpersonal studies and transpersonal psychology as analogous. A position he makes clear when stating that,

> ...transpersonal studies and transpersonal psychology are not equivalent. The former is a broadly defined domain of inquiry that can legitimately include a diversity of methods ranging from those of the humanities to those of a variety of scientific endeavors. Psychology, on the other hand, is defined by most psychologists as a scientific discipline; except for a few humanistic and transpersonal adherents who insist that including alternative, that is, nonscientific, approaches is important for the discipline, science is widely accepted as the mainstay of the discipline. A preliminary conceptualization of transpersonal psychology that I see as useful is to place it as a field of study and applied practice positioned at the intersection between

the broader domain of inquiry known as transpersonal studies and the scientific discipline of psychology.

(pp. 179–180)

Taking the foregoing as a springboard, and recognizing it may be important to find a taxonomic home within the broad scope of science, in the following chapter I discuss transpersonal psychology's relationship to the philosophy of science. Now, though, I will once again concentrate upon the place of research into transpersonal psychology. To my mind, within transpersonal psychology research methodologies have received considerably less attention than the subject/phenomena that have been the focus of research. And whilst the field has been gaining increasing recognition over the last 40 or so years, it has only been within the last 20 or so that research methodology has taken a more prominent role. This may not be surprising considering the nature of the transpersonal with its basic assumptions differing to those of the greater number of orthodox areas of scientific inquiry. There is now, however, a greater degree of attention that in the present academic climate is being directed towards research and research method suitable for studies of transpersonal psychology.

The greater interest in research methods is, I think, not solely confined to transpersonal psychology and could equally well be seen in a great many other psychological disciplines – a view, however, that is only based upon anecdotal evidence and my own experience within the academe of the United Kingdom. Following this line of thought, I have noticed in my academic work that there appears to be a greater onus upon finding acceptable measures for academic soundness, a state of affairs that is increasing as many clinical trainings, that are not based upon the medical model, have now become validated by mainstream universities with graduates receiving degree equivalent qualifications as well as degrees themselves. Quite naturally, to this end the training bodies and university departments are creating alliances that have to adhere to academic protocol. Perhaps, as well as needing to speak the same language, the accrediting body, the universities themselves can only maintain their own academic standing by adhering to academic protocol and ensuring that their partners do likewise.

I welcome the challenge that this brings as well as recognizing that, although transpersonal psychology places human experience in the widest possible context, academic respectability brings an intellectual rigour to bear on the justification for transpersonal psychology that may have not been needed in the early days of the field. Before moving on, however, it may be useful to recognize that it may not just be academia that is influencing the need for the field to account for itself in terms that are understood by the prevailing scientific orthodoxy. In the present political climate, whole of the counselling/psychotherapy profession is been urged to show that it can meet acceptable measures of validity. Though not the case globally, the profession in the United Kingdom is under increasing pressure to meet legislation that is being called for by the government and medical professions. The idea behind this tightening upon the psychological professionals is the establishment and policing of protocols that ensure clinical accountability.

Regardless of why research method may be taking a more obvious role in the whole field of psychology, the transpersonal therapies will have to do the same if they want to be accepted in the prevailing political and scientific milieu. The challenge here is that, for no other reason than transpersonal psychology's acceptance of models that accept transegoic functioning, modes of inquiry will be required that are necessarily quite different from those that may be better suited to some other areas of psychology. Yet, whilst recognizing that researching within the whole field of psychology may require a multimethod approach, transpersonal inquiry could be regarded as being a field that is no less suited to methods of observation and experimentation, a position that is similar to many other areas of psychological inquiry. For example studies exploring the relationship between a sample population's self-reports of the benefits of transpersonal functioning and well-being and another population's self-reports of the benefits of ballroom dancing and well-being may use the same methods of data collection and outcome analysis. Although the example here is obviously made up, it highlights that empirical focus can be directed towards areas that can measure such things as altered states of awareness. And just because transpersonal psychology proffers realms and ways of functioning that may not have been subject to recognized methods of inquiry before, it does not mean that these areas cannot be approached with valid and academically robust methods, even if the empirical data take the form of subjective experience. Even the briefest of reviews of the transpersonal research literature will reveal that most serious transpersonal researchers favour qualitative methods, a methodological paradigm that is also commonly employed in many non-transpersonal psychological studies.

Although there may be much care and consideration of appropriate method in research design, transpersonal psychology, like all fields, needs a critical evaluation of method. From a quantitative standpoint this would be seen as validity and would be questioned in both the design and execution of any project. Even if validity is a term that it is not so commonly used by those who take a quantitative approach to research, it is an important concept and consequently deserves both naming and ensuring in any piece of transpersonal research so that the findings can be clearly seen to stand up to careful scrutiny. The need for the inclusion of validity in all research is also recognized by Winter (2000), who suggests that it is the principles that underpin the concept that need to be included in both qualitative and quantitative research.

> Some qualitative researchers have argued that the term validity is not applicable to qualitative research and have at the same time realised the need for some kind of qualifying check or measure for their research. As a result many researchers have espoused their own theories of 'validity' and have often generated or adopted what they consider to be more appropriate terms, such as 'trustworthiness', 'worthy', 'relevant', 'plausible', 'conformable', 'credible' or 'representative'... [For] Unlike quantitative research, there are no standardised or accepted tests within qualitative research and often the nature of the investigation is determined and adapted by the research itself.... Instead the 'validity' of the research resides with the representation of the actors, the purposes of the research and appropriateness of the processes involved. The only similarity between the two research methods is that, at some point, questions will be asked and data will be collected. Likewise, commonalties within definitions of 'validity' only exist within its concern for the research process and its appropriateness to the phenomena investigated.
>
> (Winter, 2000 online serial).

In quantitative research the inquirers could be considered as standing outside the field looking in, unlike their qualitative cousins who often are 'closer' to the phenomena being viewed. And in my examination of the works of students undertaking research in transpersonal psychotherapy this is the one area that repeatedly brings challenges when accounting for their work's validity. Namely it is the effect that the researcher may have on their research and conversely the effect of the data upon the researcher themselves that needs to be accounted for so as not to confound any conclusions drawn.

The effects upon the researcher are simply summed up by Stuhlmiller (1996), '...qualitative data collection methods change the investigator. He is "never the same again" ' (1996, p. x). Patton (2002) concentrates upon the qualitative researcher's impact on all areas of a study. He terms it the researcher's 'voice', and is keen to point out that it needs to be recognized in all areas of a research project.

> The qualitative analyst owns and is reflective about her or his voice and perspective; a credible voice conveys authenticity and trustworthiness; complete objectivity being impossible and pure subjectivity undermining credibility, the researcher's focus becomes balance-understanding and depicting the world authentically in all its complexity while being self-analytical, politically aware, and reflexive in consciousness.
>
> (pp. 484–495)

All the foregoing leads to the conclusion that, whilst innovative methods are being explored, they still need to show 'scientific rigour', and it may come as no surprise that as research into academically acceptable methods is being explored within all the humanities, transpersonal psychology is no exception with thinkers such as Braud (1998), Braud and Anderson (1998), Heron (2000), Barber (2004, 2006) and Valle (2006) who are all taking up the challenge of identifying methods suitable for transpersonal inquiry. Braud and Anderson's is perhaps the most well-known work. They identify five-method groupings suitable for transpersonal research:

- Integral inquiry
- Intuitive inquiry
- Transpersonal awareness in phenomenological inquiry
- Organic research
- Inquiry of exceptional human experiences

Although I agree with many of the arguments concerning the appropriateness of the application of these methods, I also agree with Hiles (2001) who recognizes that all five can be considered as variants of heuristic research (Moustakas, 1990) and phenomenological inquiry (Giorgi, 1985, 1997; Moustakas, 1994). Heuristic inquiry was developed by Clark Moustakas (1990) and requires the researcher to immerse themselves in their field of study, a method that requires reflexive skill, a tool that many psychological clinicians hone in their training and use daily in their work. Heuristic inquiry itself could very easily be considered to be a phenomenological method, and Moustakas (1994) places it as one of five main variations, the other four being ethnography, grounded theory, hermeneutics and Duquesne University's phenomenology.

Within the last 10 or so years there has been an ever-increasing body of literature exploring qualitative methodology within which the work of John Heron (2000) will be found. He is another who looks towards innovative research methods. His perspective in addition to being experientially biased also takes a very relational perspective and is one that he claims to be suitable for the investigation of transpersonal psychology. This is not surprising considering that he was the founder and then director of the Human Potential Research Project at the University of Surrey, United Kingdom, for many years. The Human Potential Research Project claims to be the earliest academic centre for both humanistic and transpersonal psychology and education in Europe.

Barber (2004, 2006), too, was a University of Surrey academic, and his views display the influences that Gestalt psychology and Taoist philosophy can bring to research method as well as a social constructivism/co-operative inquiry flavour.

The collaborative stance in some qualitative methods is not some brand new concept, as many in the field have considered, for many years now, that it is preferable to deem the researchers and research subjects as being co-researchers, an idea that would raise more than eyebrows in quantitative circles. Reason and Rowan (1981), for example, maintain that, 'true human inquiry needs to be based firmly in the experience of those it purports to understand, to involve a collaboration between "researcher" and "subjects" so that they may work together as co-researchers' (Reason & Rowan, 1981, p. 113).

To complete this short exploration of how research in transpersonal psychology is approached, I look (naturally in a reflexive manner) to my own experience of supporting students as they design research projects that explore various aspects of transpersonal psychology, and also give a brief description of the bare bones of one of Braud and Anderson's five transpersonal research methods.

Here, as in other areas of all things transpersonal, it would be easy for the misinformed to claim that the discipline lacks discipline, with an anything goes, lets wait and see, wishy-washy, laissez-faire attitude to research protocol. This may be because researchers utilize innovative methods to reveal data that are gleaned from aspects of reality that simply cannot be described or revealed through more traditional methods. Yet, concepts such as the contention that the object/focus of research can suggest appropriate method are a valid position from many quantitative and qualitative traditions, and thus an idea that can also be claimed to be true of research in the transpersonal sphere.

For as long as data are collected or identified in an appropriate way and likewise analysed with a suitable tool, as well as measures of validity given and well argued for, regardless of how they are termed, credible results can be revealed. This may be enough for myself and colleagues situated within a discipline that relies more upon subjective accounts than hard evidence; however, for many, this may not be enough because the phenomena often of interest to transpersonal researchers themselves are subjective, value laden and at times best described as ineffable. This in turn means that the use of any methodology, particularly those that fall within the qualitative camp, cannot be a quantitative recipe for 'baking a perfect pie every time'. Especially if the subject of research dictates that the researcher places themselves in a 'fertile void' in order to utilize all their senses, including those other than the common five such as intuition, to capture the potential richness and depth that is hoped will emerge.

To my mind all the foregoing can suggest that research can be considered to be a stance from which the researcher is willing to be, if necessary, the research instrument. With an attitude such as this Braud and Anderson's transpersonal research methods may make sense. For example, looking at 'Intuitive Inquiry' (Braud & Anderson, 1998, pp. 69–95) in this light will make sense even of ideas that can seem strange at first glance, ideas such as this method's understanding of data collection as 'Setting The Stage for the Experience under Investigation to Show Up' (p. 90) as well as their proposition concerning an analysis stage,

> data analysis should accommodate the data that present themselves, rather than being immutably established at the outset of the study. If the data appear to be organized in key concepts and themes, qualitative content or thematic analysis applies. If the design allowed for focused descriptions of the constituents of one particular experience, phenomenological analysis applies. If the data are quantitative, various statistical procedures apply. If interview data resulted in long narrative or storytelling sessions, narrative and discourse analysis applies. If participants or the researcher suspects that thematic analysis would alter the unique voice(s) of those in the study, interviews or narratives can be presented act to parallel the analysis. If

data are deeply personal, reflective, and gathered from many sources, heuristic and hermeneutical analyses may apply. Many researchers blend the analytic procedures with beneficial results.

(pp. 91–92)

With much potential for misconstruing the aims of the field and an increasing body of research, it may behove any commentator to find the means to explore the field with an inquiring attitude that is open to innovation, as transpersonal psychology is only going to be able to hold its head up, as a legitimate area of research and consequently a valid body of knowledge and area for further research, if its research method becomes to be seen as more mainstream and thus gain acceptance, perhaps leading to it being more widely known and used.

Although transpersonal psychology in the present academic climate may be looking more towards being able to account for itself and explore further by means of methods that are still being developed and tested, as the next chapter shows not all the myriad fields that have supported and fed into the development of the field as a recognizable body of knowledge can claim to have done likewise. However, just because something has not yet been the subject of valid, critical and recognized research cannot mean that it in itself is not valid as a constituent of a larger body. Therefore I invite my reader to endeavour to remain open to putting aside any pre-conceived notions as they carry on reading the next chapter.

# 3
# The Philosophical Underpinnings of the Transpersonal

## Introduction

Thus far I have given a somewhat brief working definition of transpersonal psychology, and begun to explore its place in the whole field of psychology.

Before moving on to recount the various best-known theorists, it would be useful to deepen this investigation through an exploration of the philosophical – in its widest sense – and theoretical heritage of transpersonal psychology to reveal the rich and divergent fields of knowledge that have influenced the development of the school.

With the foregoing in mind this chapter is intended to give a broad view of the theoretical underpinnings of the transpersonal approach and to shy away from a discussion of transpersonal theory itself. Thus the focus is more upon what has informed the field rather than the field itself. By doing so I trust that the reader will be supported in understanding the work of the various blatantly transpersonal theorists that are presented in the next chapter.

In addition to placing transpersonal psychology in the wider context of general philosophy and sciences, I turn my attention to many prominent 'psychological schools', in order to show how transpersonal thinking is to be found in the greater majority of all the 'four forces' of Maslow's (1971) psychological taxonomy, whilst concurrently also showing how some schools explore themes that at first glance seem transpersonal, yet they are not. At the same time as looking at how transpersonal themes are explored by differing psychological schools, the influence that transpersonal psychology itself has had upon divergent schools of psychological thought will also be revealed.

However, whilst exploring psychology, many other fields of knowledge or disciplines will be discussed, for instance neurobiology and philosophy, as transpersonal psychology draws upon such a wide range of them. Yet, if in order to offer a greater insight and further illuminate their influence I was to give an exhaustive account of all the fields that go to support transpersonal thinking, this work would end up as an encyclopaedia. Therefore, with so many strands to tie together, some get a deeper level of discussion than others, though reference is given to influential works or theorists to enable the reader to explore their own interest.

In planning this work I started off with both a fairly logical and systematic idea of what content to include and a coherent sequence, in which one school or field was discussed, summed up, to then lead onto the next body of knowledge. However, as the work progressed and more and more complexity emerged, I then chose a more 'splateral' rather than lateral stance, where the competing and complimentary theories were discussed in a less-rigid order. At first I found myself fighting the emergence of a structure that did not follow my previous plan; yet, surrendering to the nascent flow lead to a deeper appreciation of the complexity and divergence that transpersonal thinking offered. This also pointed to a conclusion that perhaps, when exploring a field that is considered to have been of interest to peoples from ancient to modern times, from all parts of the globe, some licence in not following too rigid a sequence was permissible. If this were not enough, orthodox scientific thinking provided a poor means by which to discuss, explore or validate transpersonal phenomena, as this field seeks to elucidate what is often regarded as the unexplainable or ineffable. To add to this already rich theoretical stew, a brief outline of the place transpersonal psychology holds in the philosophy of science is also presented. In conclusion, this 'splateral' melange of conjectures, models, assumptions, hypotheses and the lived experience of many offered a field that could be seen to provide a whole which was greater than the sum of its parts.

Moreover, for those who would rather read a synopsis of the fields that generally support and create the transpersonal view and its inclusion in psychological thinking, a précis of all the fields discussed, without recourse to in-depth explanations, is provided at the end of the chapter.

Whilst some may prefer this condensed version, a few words of warning to the hasty would be wise, for although a general summation may include a discussion of the underpinnings of transpersonal theory, it cannot offer enough to follow the claims in the next chapter that the transpersonal theorists make for their view of the world and clinical praxis.

## The transpersonal viewpoint: is it psychology, philosophy or perhaps naivety and fancy let loose?

With the transpersonal offering such a wide theoretical base to choose from, it can be hard to decide from which angle it could be useful to select as a starting point. If one were to look, say, at the contribution that religion in its various guises has offered the field, those clinicians or thinkers who, for instance, look more towards the cognitive sciences or show specialized interest in fields such as psychiatry or neurobiology may rightly want to offer their vantage point as an important place of embarkation. The foregoing is a contrived example of the dilemma I had in deciding were to begin, which was based upon my own experience of asking those in the field what was the most important aspect of the transpersonal that was addressed or explored in other fields. Almost as many differing answers as the number of times the question was asked lead to the conclusion that it was the interest and/or life experience of the individual that informed their own view. However, what has emerged in my repeated asking of the question was that, although differing individuals and indeed populations had their own interpretations of what underpinned the transpersonal, they all without fail suggested that it was a transhistorical and transcultural ontological reality that was available to be experienced by all sentient beings. The foregoing is not only based on anecdotal evidence compiled by a clinician firmly embedded in the field, but it is also confirmed by the literature.

Whilst speaking with the converted – professionals who claim to include the transpersonal in their work – may bring disagreement regarding which is the most important field to start this exploration from, it is also useful to bear in mind that for a great deal of practitioners and theorists within the psychologically biased caring professions the transpersonal is not an ontological reality. For them, instead, its existence is either some form of misinterpretation of another field or some form of psychological defence, a mechanism created to defend against the onslaught of unwanted psychological material. With this in mind what is not the transpersonal will also be included within this chapter. So, for instance, the common misconception that transpersonal psychology in its various guises is a school of philosophy may be as good a starting point as any.

In conversation with other psychotherapists, both experienced clinicians and those new to the profession, I have needed, on countless occasions, to defend the contention that transpersonal psychology can rightly claim to be a psychological school, and not some form of naïve philosophy that seeks to spiritualize psychopathology. Thus I feel it important to briefly explore this area.

To begin with, it is necessary to recognize that both psychology and philosophy share many similarities and a common epistemological heritage. Untangling the roots of these fields is a gargantuan task, as both philosophy and psychology are immense fields that offer an overabundance of complex views of the world that can be both heterogeneous and at oft times complementary.

If this were not enough, looking towards transpersonal theorists will reveal that, like many traditional psychological thinkers, they turn their gaze upon the ideas of others in order to build upon their predecessors' thinking, or use their theoretical constructs to validate their own unique views. This is a common method utilized by most philosophical enquirers who also often look towards the ideas of other philosophical schools in order to further a philosophical debate that offers explanations for the human condition.

Wilshire (1968) acknowledges a good example of this. He recognizes that Hursserl was influenced by the work of William James, particularly in the overcoming of 'psychologism', specifically the idea that mind and thoughts are not inseparable or conceived independently from the world that appears to mind. From this perspective the world as phenomenal can only be formulated through a philosophical investigation of the world's structures ('Essences' in Hursserl's terms) that are revealed to the mind, as well as the workings of the mind itself.

This would also be easily recognized by transpersonal psychology, as it too could be seen as the seeking of a worldview that endeavours to make sense of and account for consciousness and reality. And as such, this making sense is not novel or in any way unique, for it could be likened to representing the 'meat and potatoes' of many philosophical debates. In this light we could view philosophy as a discipline which has created a body of knowledge, accumulated over several centuries, that offers a plethora of worldviews all of which claim to present a window through which to view reality.

However, 'transpersonal' is a term that cannot be commonly found in the body of literature associated with traditional academic philosophy. Regardless of this omission both fields share a common epistemological lineage, in that they can only claim to validate a view of objective existence with the information supplied by the senses, an individual's 'subjective frame'. Thus, like academic philosophy, transpersonal theory can only be verified by the limitations inherent in our self-referential experiences. Therefore, we can only try to base our knowledge of consciousness and reality through the means of our self-referential experiences. A concept firmly established in philosophy.

The above position, as I show later, is being challenged by developments in neurobiological research and academic philosophy. However, in the present scientific climate worldviews that conceive 'truth' as unearthed through direct observation are commonly regarded as the norm. With this in mind I also present in this chapter theories that offer competing epistemological approaches positing that reality can exist alongside the consciousness that seeks to realize, know or observe it. These alternate worldviews are non-empirically testable and employ methods of knowing such as intuition, insight and illumination (the 'meat and potatoes' of transpersonal research).

Returning to the philosophy and underpinnings of transpersonal psychology and with all the above in mind, I was aware that an in-depth exploration of the whole field of philosophy is not within the remit of this work. Therefore, in order to be concise, whilst offering an insight into the philosophical heritage of transpersonal psychology, I referred to well-known theorists such as Heidegger, Wittgenstein, Nietzsche and Popper without discussing their thinking in great a detail.

As I began exploring the extensive literature that influences the transpersonal, I became conscious that, when exploring material that was overtly philosophical, I was embarking upon an area of study that included much that I was not familiar with. This was in spite of the extensiveness of my professional training that had only explicitly addressed philosophy when speaking of the psychopathology engendered by existential crisis, with a focus upon the range of possible interventions and praxis. This is also true of all the professional psychotherapy, psychiatry and counselling trainings I am aware of, both within the United Kingdom and abroad, with the exception of those offered by existential therapy schools.

This was not the only personal insight that this aspect of my research provided. Another was the cementing of the realization that I customarily viewed my world, and consequently I was regarding philosophy, through the lens of psychological constructs and thinking. This included both how I viewed philosophical theories themselves and the psychological make up of their originators.

A clear example of the first is Heidegger's concept of the relationship between Being (the primordial 'ground') and beings (the entities that exist in the world). I found that from my 'dasein' (the specific world I inhabit and identify with, namely psychology) I was quick to compare and contrast this concept with theories I was more familiar with, for instance those espoused by psychologists, such as Perls et al. (1994) figure ground model and Assagioli's (1990) identification/disidentification model.

The second bias – my proclivity to view philosophers themselves in psychopathological terms – was highlighted, for instance, when thinking about Foucault's life. I found it natural to speculate about the psychology of his personality, and how psychological disturbance can be obscured or excused in a society which values and applauds high intellectual functioning. In Foucault's case my wondering focused upon how his views/experience of society and peers influenced his own behaviour and thinking, particularly those practices such as self-mutilation that are commonly seen as non-ego syntonic.

Before turning my gaze towards other fields of knowledge that inform transpersonal psychology, I feel it important to recognize that a great majority of the whole field of psychological and psychotherapeutic thinking deals with areas of the human condition that are not empirically testable, such as consciousness, emotions and values. Thus many psychological schools could be interpreted as philosophical inquiries, and psychology could justifiably be conceived as a branch of philosophy rather than a stand-alone scientific domain. Moreover, psychology as a discrete discipline, being less than one hundred and fifty years old, is, in relation to philosophy, a relative newcomer to the world of theories of human nature.

As a distinct field psychology could be conceived as having sprang from the medical model, with its therapeutic praxis as psychotherapy and psychiatry. On the other hand, philosophical enquiry in itself is sometimes regarded as therapeutic for both writer and reader. A view that is certainly held today by some, such as Mace (1999) who reminds his reader that Wittgenstein suggested that the essential function of philosophy is therapeutic.

This is an argument supported by others such as Heath (2002), who strongly argues and gives justification for the inclusion of the study of philosophy in psychotherapy training. His portrayal of philosophy as offering a means to '...ask questions which are intended to go under the surface of accepted views and common-sense assumptions (...) which, without such testing may never surface as assumptions and may simply be believed (assumed) as being the case' (p. 29) speaks to me as a basic postulate of most therapeutic approaches andpsychological schools,  and is certainly at the heart of much transpersonal thinking. Although Heath is at pains to make a distinction between philosophy and psychotherapy, he does recognize that philosophical methods and problems are sometimes addressed in the course of psychotherapy, though often unwittingly so.

Some thinkers go further when regarding the importance that philosophical enquiry can play in helping individuals experience psychological well-being. Perhaps the loudest and best-known proponent of this view is Marinoff (1999, 2002, 2003), who is vehement in spreading his belief that many who seek help and support from the psychology professionals would benefit more from taking heed of the insights offered by classical and contemporary philosophy. Not content with how the American Society for Philosophy Counseling and Psychotherapy (http://www.aspcp.org) was promoting this approach, he set up his own organization – the American Philosophical Practitioners Association (http://www.appa.edu). However, many in the philosophy and psychology communities criticize his approach and its application. These concerns are explored by Duane (2004), though not discussed in an academic manner.

In terms of this work, I am aware that at points I have found it hard not to speak of the reasoning and philosophical underpinnings inherent in the matters discussed. Inasmuch as at times it is hard to delineate the difference between the philosophical and psychological. Transpersonal psychology, with its at oft times focus upon ultimate reality and meaning, is out of all the differing schools of psychology, is the one most likely to be the main contender in the confusion stakes. The foregoing also includes the awareness that the existential psychology school, as discussed later, whilst openly addressing similar views as philosophical fields, clearly sees itself as a psychological school. Returning to the ease that transpersonal psychology can be confused with philosophy, it would only need the casual reader to look towards the work of transpersonal theorists such as Wilber (1993c, 1998) or Washburn (1988) who themselves are both academic philosophers, to find ideas that need careful consideration. Having established that for the uninformed it may not be easy to differentiate between psychological and philosophical thinking, it may now be helpful to look towards the main psychological schools in order to further the search for the underpinnings of the transpersonal.

## The four forces of psychology

I have already recognized that I would need to draw upon a diverse knowledge base in order to encompass many of the potentially competing and divergent voices that speak of transpersonal psychologies' underpinnings.

However, with a diverse knowledge base it would be helpful to find a framework that could help to untangle and identify where transpersonal thinking has influenced other psychological schools or conversely has informed their theoretical constructs.

To this end I examine the four forces of psychotherapeutic thinking, of which transpersonal psychotherapy/psychology is, as previously mentioned, the fourth force. I pay particular attention to highlighting the transpersonal in each of the first three forces as well as exploring theories that could be conceived of as being in opposition. Maslow describes the 'four forces of psychology' in an order of force one, equating to the behavioural and cognitive schools; force two, the psychodynamic/psychoanalytic; force three, the humanistic-existential and finally force four, the transpersonal. Although keeping to this taxonomy, I will not explore them in strict order; instead, I will first delve into the second force, as doing so will aid in teasing apart the rich and divergent strands that help to support the transpersonal viewpoint.

However, as it will be seen, the four-force taxonomy of psychological thinking, though useful to examine the underpinnings of transpersonal psychology, is not an adequate tool for the task, as transpersonal theory draws from a diverse knowledge base that is not solely situated within psychological schools. Therefore, as well as highlighting the transpersonal dimension in various approaches to psychology, I make sporadic inroads into fields that at first glance may seem far removed from psychological thinking and praxis, and also turn along the way to other traditions, such as consciousness research, biology, modern physics and neurology, in order to account for how transpersonal thinking has been influenced by and includes the insights that are offered by a diverse knowledge base.

## The second force of psychology

The second force is predominantly made up of psychodynamic thought, and is dominated by thinking that is influenced by Freudian and Jungian theory. Two major schools formed and took their names from their originators, Freud and Jung. Both of these figures could be seen to be charismatic leaders who presented ideas that challenged the prevailing scientific paradigm.

However, in today's psychological milieu, for those outside the field it can be difficult to tease apart the influence that each school has had upon the whole field of psychology, particularly so as their work has become more mainstream and much of their lexicon can be found in common parlance. With this in mind, in order to lessen the potential for confusion, I will refer to Freudian influenced thinking as 'psycho-analysis' and thinking influenced by a Jungian viewpoint as 'analytical psychology'.

In the previous chapter, I noted that Jung could be credited with introducing the term 'transpersonal' in the field of psychology (ueber-personliche). With this in mind and upon examining his thinking, it is easy to see how his worldview and the philosophy he espoused can be considered, from today's perspective, to contain much that would receive ready agreement from the transpersonal community.

Noll (1996), in his critical analysis of Jung's world and psychology, claims that Jung encouraged a personality cult to form around him, and that he based his theories upon many of the mystical ideas that were in vogue in his time. Furthermore, Noll traces the influence that 'Naturphilosophie', sometimes referred to as 'essentialism' or 'morpho-logical idealism', had upon Jung's thinking. This philosophy posits that humans can, through spiritual development, recognize divine essence by means of an intuitive function. This worldview shares many similar-ities with the 'perennial philosophy' that is prominent in Ken Wilber's earlier work. The perennial philosophy (Huxley, 1947; Schmitt, 1966; Smith, 1982) could be seen as a means to find ways to marry thinking from the spiritual traditions of both the East and West, providing a method to describe a transcultural and re-occurring esoteric worldview that can be traced throughout history. It posits that the foundation of consciousness is spiritual, which manifests through differing levels of frequency such as physical, emotional, mental, psychic and etheric. Huxley (1947) gives an in-depth exploration of this conceptualization of human existence, its place in the context of evolution and the world. His brief description of this cosmology is that it is,

> The metaphysics that recognises a divine reality substantial to the world of things and lives and minds; the psychology which finds in the soul something similar to, or even identical with divine reality; the ethic that places man's final end in the knowledge of immanent and transcendent ground of being.
>
> (Huxley, 1947, p. 1)

The foregoing would meet with ready agreement within the transpersonal community, but is, however, in stark opposition to Freud's worldview, the other dominant influence in the same force. Freud conceived a deterministic model that concentrates upon the influence that biographical material has upon an individual, such as 'hedonic principles' that favour the avoidance of pain through maximizing the pursuit of pleasure. He insisted that his theories were scientific, though from our present day perspective his use of a single-subject case study, from which he based many of his theories and the generalizations made about all mankind, would be questioned. Philosophically his work (as well as Jung's) could be seen as being influenced by the thinking in ascendance at the time, such as the works by Friedrich Nietzsche (1844–1900) who rejected conventional moral values and held the belief that all organisms live to increase their life force.

Karl Popper (1962), a philosopher from more recent times, by means of his 'falsification criterion of science' model, criticized Freud's psychoanalysis claiming that it was a 'pseudoscience'. Also Ellis, whose vehement criticism of the transpersonal I discussed earlier, claimed to use this logic set as a tool to support his attack upon the field of transpersonal psychology. Popper's critique, however, has been criticized in turn by others. Grunbaum (1984), for example, addresses psychoanalytical thinking in order to propose a differing criterion for science to Popper, whose argument focuses upon the validity of psychoanalytic interpretations being confounded by suggestion having a central role in psychoanalytic observation. Though the ensuing debate examines Freud's thinking, it may be in fact more concerned with the distinction of 'what is science'. There are others, such as Ollinheimo and Vuorinen (2001), who offer a counter-argument to Grunbaum without entering into debate about the scientificness of his thinking. Others, on the other hand, do not take a vehement stance from which to view Freudian thinking. Gellner (1985), in his study of the logical status of psychoanalysis, recognizes that it needs to be understood as consisting of a theory of knowledge that could be best described as 'conditional realism'. A view that accepts that pivotal to psychoanalytical theory is the tenet that the knowing or perceiving of 'reality' can be mediated by the interface or contents of the unconscious, a form of inner interference.

I feel that entering the debate about how, if at all, Freudian thinking fits into a recognized criterion for science would not shed further light upon the place of transpersonal psychology in the second force, regardless of the fact that the psychoanalytic school has been a powerful influence both from within and upon the whole field of psychology since near its first inception.

However, what is important to recognize is that Freud's vehement refusal to see the transpersonal as anything other than the regressive yearning and escape from existential vulnerability may in fact be influenced more by his biography and psychopathology, than anything else. This position is argued for by Rizzuto (1998), who with psychoanalytical theory makes interpretations regarding Freud's deep-seated rejection of god and his outspoken call for atheism as the outcome of his early biography which was to shape his personality and influence the adult theorist's thinking.

I would like to add that during his lifetime it would have been difficult to challenge not only the great man's viewpoint regarding the transpersonal by relating to his psychological development, but also the fact that, although Freud insisted that an analyst's training needed to be centred around their own analysis, a prerequisite and mandatory requirement that is still in force today, he himself was never an analysand. I wonder, if he had been in analysis, would his analyst have challenged his thoughts concerning the transpersonal in relationship to his biography?

Looking towards Freud's biography for keys to the aetiology of his theoretical positions, although not uncommon, is not the norm, as it is much easier to look towards his model to explain his thinking. For example, Freud thought that the need for the transpersonal was brought forth by the conflict that can arise between the survival instinct and the understanding that death is inevitable. This conclusion is not hard to reach for those who are happy to only look towards his work.

Although Freud's thinking has undoubtedly made an immense contribution to psychology as it is understood today, it has been those who build upon his thinking and look towards object-relations theory, who are more able to include a transpersonal element in their work. In this light the transpersonal represents or indeed is an important element in early object relations.

Thinkers such as Winnicott (1953) and Guntrip (1969) can make use of Freudian concepts without needing to see the acceptance of anything that may be regarded as religious, spiritual or transpersonal as a defence leading to a neurotic disposition. The Jungian perspective, instead, sees a movement towards the religious, spiritual or transpersonal as natural. This difference brings a contrast, yet overtly transpersonal theorists who include an exploration of a relational element in their developmental theories, such as Almass (1996, 1998), Washburn (1988, 1999) and Firman and Gila (1997) all take elements of both Freudian and Jungian thinking to build their models. Although both streams can be identified in their work it can at times be hard to identify where concepts originate.

For instance, Freud's position that the ego itself is formed as a result of the conflict between the id and the external world can be used as a springboard to hypothesize that internal relations with the transpersonal will also influence the structure of the whole psyche. In this case the notion of 'internal' could be used solely because the transpersonal cannot be measured and quantified in the same way that the 'external' world can.

Going back once more to the whole school of psychodynamic thought, another difference between the works of the two founding fathers of analytical psychology was their respective analysis methods. Freud's case study method of using his findings gathered through the observation of an individual from which to generalize to the collective was in stark contrast to Jung who looked more towards society and collective phenomena to explain the psychological life of an individual.

It can be argued that the recounting of the analysis of a psychological theory's place in a scientific framework may seem of little relevance. However, as I discuss later on in this chapter, transpersonal psychology, like many other psychological disciplines, makes a strange bedfellow to much of the orthodox prevailing epistemological approach to science. This is a paradigm that relies upon validation gleaned through means that are familiar to and encompassed by the Cartesian/Newtonian view of reality, which is comprised of observable truths that can be reduced and replicated.

With the foregoing in mind, the idea of 'conditional realism' could with ease be levelled at transpersonal thinking, for, like many analytical concepts, transpersonal theories could also be described as being a 'pseudoscience'. This would place the field at best on the periphery of mainstream 'orthodox' psychological and psychiatric thought.

Returning to an area that is of more apparent disparity and obviously relates to this study it is important to recognize that, when viewing Freud's and Jung's thinking, a significant difference is that esoteric thought, such as Theosophy, epitomized by the work of Blavatsky (1966), was a rich influence on Jung's thinking. His interest in what would be termed in the present era parapsychological phenomena, such as mediumship, is well known. Spiritualism according to some, such as Charet (1993), provided a significant influence upon his thinking.

Jung also differed to Freud in that he was actively interested in the then burgeoning field of Quantum Physics, and showed great interest in the work of Wolfgang Pauli. Pauli, one of the pioneers of the quantum perspective, at the age of nineteen (in 1921, i.e. only 6 years after the publication of Albert Einstein's paper, *The Foundations of General*

*Relativity*) wrote what has become to be seen as a seminal work: *Theory of Relativity* (1981).

In 1931, as Meier (2001) reveals, Pauli, following a severe break-down, consulted Jung, and their relationship moved from an analytic encounter to a close friendship and theoretical collaborators. Their friendship and thus the insights of the new physics profoundly influenced the evolution of Jungian psychology. I will explore further when looking at quantum mechanics and transpersonal theory later in this chapter.

As it has already been stated earlier in this study, classical Freudianism is clear in its refusal to place importance upon any experience seen as spiritual, suggesting that it is merely a regressive yearning for the earliest oceanic bliss of symbiosis with mother (Freud, 1930). However, the psychoanalytical school that sprang from Freud's thinking was not so dismissive of the transpersonal. Bion (1970), who is an influential thinker from this school, conceived of 'ultimate reality/absolute truth' as a concept that he termed 'o'. Bion saw the psychoanalytic relationship as a means to seek the patient's spirit or essence, their 'o'.

The view that transpersonal experience has a basis in some form of regression is in accord with my own, albeit limited, experience of psychoanalytical therapy as well as my studies of the literature. The combination of both leads me to conclude that classical Freudianism places importance upon the biographical determinants of psychopathology and personality structure. This may give some justification of why Bion is best known for his contribution to other areas of psychoanalytic thought, such as his understanding of group dynamics and not for the importance that he placed in the pursuit of 'o'.

With all the above in mind it would be hasty to dismiss all that classical psychoanalytic thought could bring to placing importance upon the transpersonal in the psychotherapeutic relationship. This, however, would be contradicting the views expressed by Freud who, whilst being one of the second force's most influential thinkers and arguably the father of modern psychology, was dismissive of anything that could be construed as religious, or not in accord with his own worldview. It would be prudent, therefore, to turn towards the Jungian influence in the second force to find the philosophies that may lie at the heart of some transpersonal thinking.

However, before delving headlong into analytical psychology as a means to find the second force embracing transpersonal psychology, care must be taken not to confuse transpersonal psychology with archetypal psychology, Hillman (1978, 1997a), a school influenced by

Jungian thought and firmly situated within the post-Jungian school (Samuels, 1990).

Therefore, in order to make clear the subtle relationship that exists between transpersonal and Jungian influenced thinking, I explore further the Jungian and post-Jungian worldview.

Before doing so, it is important to make one last comparison between the psychodynamic and psychoanalytical traditions, one that reveals a fundamental difference between the two schools, namely the distinction between individual psychology and collective psychology.

Freud posited that certain psychic events take place 'below the surface' of awareness. An idea that supports the now generally accepted idea that each individual has a personal unconscious that is particular to the individual: the 'unconscious mind'. Jung, agreeing with this model, also included the concept of the existence of the collective unconscious, which can be conceived of as being analogous to a reservoir of the experiences of mankind, and is potentially available to all.

Although this concept may be familiar to many in the present academic and popular climates, it is useful to remember that the concept of a transhistorical and transcultural collective unconscious that can be realized by all individuals underlies all Jungian thinking.

Returning to the transpersonal influence of Jungian thinking a good place to start is by looking towards some of the more esoteric influences of classical Jungian thinking, a viewpoint that suggests a developmental schema, before moving on to explore archetypal psychology and latter day interpretations of Jungian thought.

From the Jungian analytical standpoint Neumann (1973), writing in 1949, presents a model, endorsed and praised by Jung, that forges a link between psychology and mythology. He presents and argues for, in a scholarly fashion, a hypothesis that suggests that historically mankind's consciousness as well as that of an individual's ego go through a series of developmental stages.

A very brief overview of his thinking reveals that the stages he posits are archetypal and can be readily identified in universal myths. (For a contemporary account of archetypes see Stevens (1982) who offers an in-depth explanation of archetypal theory.) He posits an evolutionary journey that starts with unity and passes through stages of self-consciousness and division that progress to a higher degree of coherence and synthesis.

These stages begin and end with the Uroboros, the serpent that eats its own tail, which, in terms of consciousness, is described as 'pleromatic', representing a primordial, undifferentiated universe that is suffused with divinity. It is from this 'place' of unity that the 'embryonic ego consciousness' emerges into a world that contains experiences of opposites and polarity. This notion of pleroma can be traced back to the early centuries AD in which Gnosticism flowered. It is also reminiscent of Neo-platonic thought in which all life originates in unity, the 'one'. Hardy (1996), when perusing the philosophical heritage of psychosynthesis, recognizes that Jungian psychology like that of psychosynthesis can be conceived of being Gnosticism in twentieth-century dress.

It is easy to see the influence of this philosophical approach and that of Neumann's work upon the perspective of contemporary thinkers who draw predominantly upon mythology and Jungian thinking as a means to illuminate theories of human nature, such as Campbell (1993) and Washburn (1998), although both of them are not considered to be situated within the Jungian psychological school.

Hillman (1997a), however, the founder of 'Archetypal' psychology, though regarded as a Jungian bases much of his thinking within another philosophical lineage which he sees clearly as not being influenced by transpersonal theory. Yet, as the following shows, he could very easily be misconstrued as being a transpersonal theorist.

Whilst his thinking has a significant Jungian influence, Hillman relies less on developmental theories such as the one espoused by Neumann, still retaining at the same time a strong philosophical bias. Even though sounding as if it would fit within the loose boundaries offered by transpersonal thinking, he takes a more existentialistic stance influenced by Hiedegerarian metaphysics of presence, Heidegger (1996), and Hursserlian phenomenology, Husserl (1977). His perspective seeks to allow meaning to reveal itself in phenomena. Here phenomena include experiences that are familiar to the psychological discourse found almost universally within all models, such as death, failure and love. As well as the above, symptoms that would be pathologized and diagnosed as distinct psychiatric disorders, such as paranoia and depression, are also included as meaningful phenomena. Thus he presents a perspective that concentrates upon the imaginal with metaphor taking a central role. This view is not confined only to the individual, for he extrapolates to the collective, positing the concept of 'Anima Mundi', the soul of the world (1997). Whilst this approach places an emphasis upon phenomenology, it cannot be equated with the existential psychology school, of which I will discuss later.

With an emphasis on both the individual situated in the world, and the world as constellated by the individual, Hillman's perspective on psychotherapeutic praxis, like that of much in the transpersonal framework, differs to the empirical bias found within the orthodox clinical approach.

Archetypal psychology openly displays its philosophical bias, presenting a distinct worldview that is not solely encompassed by a larger body, such as transpersonal psychology, or Jungian analytical psychology. This is in spite of offering a body of literature that could be misconstrued as being either Jungian, because of its lexicon, or transpersonal, due to its field of study.

In fact, upon examining the philological aspect of the above it is easy to see that confusion could be provoked by the use of terms such as 'soul, soul-making and spirit', which are also familiar to transpersonal thinking. Moreover, the interest placed upon values and a strong metaphysical bias could be very easily taken to mean that it is at least allied to, or at most indistinguishable from, an existentially biased transpersonal perspective.

Hillman's own description of soul amply highlights, I think, these potential areas of confusion.

> *By soul* I mean, first of all, a perspective rather than a substance, a viewpoint towards things rather than a thing in itself. This perspective is reflective: it mediates events, and makes differences between ourselves and everything that happens. Between us and events, between the doer and the deed, there is a reflective moment- and soul-making means differentiating this middle ground. (...) However intangible and indefinable it is, soul carries highest importance in hierarchies of human values, frequently being identified with the principle of life and even of divinity.
>
> (Hillman, 2002, pp. 20–21)

As if the above were not enough to confuse the casual reader, he insists that archetypal psychology is not transpersonal because it is a depth psychology (1989).

However, clarity emerges when regarding his viewpoint concerning spirit, for he distinguishes soul from spirit. Though valuing the importance of the latter in the arts and religion, he recognizes a potential for escapism to the 'heights' attainable by spirit, positing that spiritual practices can be a means of artificially rising above or transcending the world (of soul) (Hillman, 2002).

Coming from a psychosynthesis perspective, which includes recognition of both height and depth, I find a theoretical resonance with this way of thinking. However, to me his insistence on soul-making could encourage the potential for escapism from the 'heights'. Though I do not want to digress, I would like to point out that psychosynthesis recognizes the importance of working from the bottom up, in Hillman's terms soul-making, as well as from the top down – the heights of spirit. I examine this concept further in the next chapter when exploring the clinical application of transpersonal thinking.

I have often heard Jung referred to as the 'doctor of the soul', and I am sure that he in his own historical context would have been happy to be regarded as such. Hillman, however, who was director of studies at Jung institute in Zurich for 10 years, and situated in a contemporary milieu whilst often relying on Jungian terminology in his writing, I think of as being more of a midwife to the legitimatizing of the term 'soul' in much of the present day psychological discourse.

I started this overview of Hillman's thinking and its relevance to transpersonal models by recognizing that within his work a significant Jungian influence can be found, although he relies less on developmental theories such as the one espoused by Neumann.

With the above in mind it is important to recognize that classical Jungian thinking and archetypal psychology both share an interest in the prominence of the influence of archetypes in mankind's phylogenesis, through the influence of the collective unconscious. And that this can in itself engender confusion as archetypes can be conceived of as encompassing energies that are often considered to be transpersonal.

Therefore, in my quest to recognize how analytical thought informs the philosophical basis of transpersonal thinking, a concise look at how Jungians view the importance of archetypes is important. I also include this succinct account in order to stress that it is imperative not to confuse them with the concept of 'Platonic idea', for they share common characteristics. The important difference is that archetypes can evolve and change unlike the 'Platonic ideas' that are conceived as eternal forms, existing prior to all experience, and thus inherently immutable. The similarity between archetypes and Platonic ideas is of no surprise as Jung (1974, para 275) acknowledged the influence that platonic thought had upon his own thinking.

Samuels (1990) offers a clear definition of how Jungians conceive archetypes.

Certain fundamental experiences occur and are repeated over millions of years. Such experiences, together with their accompanying emotions and affects, form a structural psychic residue – a readiness to experience life along broad lines already laid down in the psyche. The relationship between archetype and experience is a feedback system; repeated experiences leave residual psychic structures, which become archetypal structures. But these structures exert an influence on experience, tending to organise it according to the pre-existing pattern.

(p. 26)

The above, however, does not give any indication of the importance that Jung placed upon archetypes and the possibility that they can encompass elements that would be best described by transpersonal thinking. Stevens (1982) clearly states this, '... the archetype as Jung conceived it, is a precondition and coexistent of life itself; its manifestations not only reach upward to the spiritual heights of religion, art and metaphysics, but also down into the dark realms of organic and inorganic mater' (p. 29).

In the light of current scientific epistemology, 'Scientific Realism', the validation of Jungian thinking like transpersonal theory is hard to quantify. Jung himself endeavoured to explain archetypes and the collective unconscious by linking it with a possible physical correlative by positing that archetypal forms were present in the germ plasm (1959, p. 75). However, to me this idea seems somewhat far-fetched, as it is an unconvincing hypothesis that structures that fit the description of archetypal forms could be inherited through the DNA or any other physical structures.

Having explored the archetypal aspect of analytical psychology and the possibility that this could confuse those looking towards finding explanations for transpersonal thinking, I conclude by recognizing that although Jungian developmental models have clearly influenced the world of transpersonal psychology, they cannot be conceived as being transpersonal. However, with the foregoing in mind it would be unwise to not recognize the important contribution Jung brings to transpersonal psychology, and therefore he is included in the next chapter as one of the significant figures in transpersonal psychology.

If the idea that archetypal forms are somehow present in the germ plasm seems far-fetched in relationship to mainstream thinking, the next area I explore could also be seen to hold little scientific credibility, yet when taken out of a transpersonal context it is met with wide-ranging acceptance.

I am referring to the notion that individuals, and indeed mankind, have the capacity to evolve. The transpersonal community would posit that this includes a spiritual element, that some how supports, or 'is', the centre of an evolutionary direction that suffuses the universe.

Whilst this notion would meet with the full agreement from all transpersonal theorists, it is not a construct that would sit happily in the thinking of theorists from the whole field of psychology. Taking just the second force as an example Jungian thinking could be conceived of as holding a tenet that mankind is in some form of evolutionary context that includes consciousness, whereas the Freudian perspective would dismiss this fanciful naive idea and place an onus upon instinctual forces which seek to ensure the survival of the species, evolution as blind survival.

With the transpersonal community in ready agreement that evolution has a fundamental link to consciousness, it would be useful to look towards both sides of the argument to gain clarity.

Wilber upholds a transpersonal view of evolution. He addresses mankind's consciousness from an evolutionary perspective, and makes clear in *Up From Eden* (2002) that Neumann (who I recounted was readily supported by Jung) offers the psychological perspective for his study. The transpersonal is in the heart of his thinking, which presents an argument that challenges Charles Darwin's (1999) 'natural selection theory' which it could be claimed has provided a cornerstone of the Cartesian worldview. Wilber (2002) makes the bold statement that,

> the theory of natural selection, is on the verge of collapse ( ... ) Evolution is not a statistical accident it is a labouring toward Spirit, driven not by happy-go-lucky chance, ( ... ) but by spirit itself. *That* is why evolution is a progressive advancement, and why it proceeds in leaps and bounds that far outdistance statistical probabilities.
>
> (Wilber, 2002, pp. 321–322)

Wilber is certainly not the only thinker to suggest that Darwinism presents a view of evolution that is not adequate. Perhaps the best-known proponent of the organismic/holistic school of philosophy is Sheldrake (1981), a biologist who presents morphogenesis as an alternative.

Wilber is not the only thinker in the transpersonal community who discusses Neumann's work and the philosophical legacy that he represents. Another is Washburn (1988), whose developmental model I discuss in the next chapter. This is no surprise as he is a Jungian psychologist and unlike Hillman he recognizes that his model fits within a body of knowledge that is recognized as transpersonal. Washburn's, however, is not a lone voice when it comes to finding the influence of Jungian thinking alongside theories that purport to include the transpersonal as a valid area of exploration in the psychotherapeutic environment.

Mindell (2000), the originator of process-orientated psychology, is another Jungian psychologist whose work is overtly transpersonally biased. I give a brief overview of his thinking later in this chapter, as he is one of many thinkers who challenge psychological thinking to move beyond the Cartesian worldview.

The possibility that to make any sense of transpersonal perspectives will involve moving beyond scientific realism and the Cartesian worldview will become increasingly evident as this exploration of the underpinnings of the field continues. So I invite my reader to join me in being open to exploring and making sense of the world in a manner that is far removed from the view offered by many who reside within the traditional academic community; a community that is firmly entrenched within a reductionist worldview, and therefore favours the exploration of objective measurable phenomena.

Thinkers such as Williams (1996) typify the orthodox knowledge base that informs this approach. Bateson and Martin (1999) also epitomize this position, 'The processes of behavioural and psychological development that give rise to an individual's behaviour are themselves the products of Darwinian evolution' (p. 240).

This proposition could be seen as stemming from the view of development as having a basis in biological maturation, whereas transpersonal thinking, without ignoring the biological, also places importance in the development of consciousness. However, the inclusion of consciousness in evolutionary theories is a theme that is not unique to transpersonal thinking. The theoretical neurophysiologist Calvin (1997), for example, posits, by means of insights from evolutionary biology, anthropology linguistics and the neurosciences, that consciousness is the result of evolution.

This view, though, is not shared by all. Hodgson (1993), for example, presents an argument that posits that consciousness is neither matter-dependent nor matter-associated. He argues that it could have existed prior to the big bang, as physical structures are not needed in order to support consciousness. The 'prior to the Big Bang' concept could be accounted for by viewing the universe as not situated solely within space–time, thus suggesting that in fact different laws that may be better described by an alternative epistemology are needed.

Hodgson's ideas are in line with the view of consciousness that transpersonal thinking offers, though he approaches the subject from a Quantum Physics perspective, a knowledge base I discuss later on in this chapter.

The exploration of consciousness has been an area of continuing interest and study by thinkers from diverse psychological schools as well as those who would identify themselves as being philosophers. My own view (as a transpersonal psychotherapist who trained originally in psychosynthesis) that consciousness is bound by neither the ego nor biology was confirmed through my exploration of the literature, for I was to find no thinker who addressed transpersonal psychology that proposed a contrary view. With this in mind I return to the field of consciousness research from differing perspectives at a later point, as well as an exploration of psychology and Quantum Physics.

Thus far, though taking a circuitous root, I have shown that transpersonal thinking is firmly established within much of second force. However, although the Jungian influenced sphere can at first glance seem to offer a greater acceptance of functioning that is not driven by instinctual needs such as sexuality (S. Freud) or aggression (M. Klein), the inclusion of the transpersonal can be found in the work of many second force thinkers, the unsurprising exception being the now less-common orthodox psychoanalytic school. However, whilst the foregoing may be true it may be unwise for practitioners who work within a transpersonal orientation to view all psychodynamic ideas as some form of antithesis to Freud's claims regarding the transpersonal. For doing so may well limit the range of interventions available, and moreover, would offer the skilful clinician a paucity of theoretical constructs from which to address the integration of the transpersonal in clinical work.

The inclusive approach that transpersonal psychology tends to adopt may also be emerging within the psychoanalytical movement itself. A position that would fit well within the ethos of 'Relational Psychoanalysis', Mitchell and Aron (1999), an approach that has sprung from within the orthodox psychoanalytic world, in the last two decades or so, and is centred mainly in the USA. Without turning towards a Jungian view of spirituality, it could offer a contemporary perspective, a psychoanalytical movement that looks towards a progressive change in the psychoanalytic understanding of spirituality. With its emphasis upon exploring real and imagined relationships there is the possibility to move beyond gaining insight regarding the influence of sexual and aggressive drives, instead an individual's relationship with their real or imagined experience of the transpersonal can be included within the therapeutic encounter.

Within this approach well-known and highly respected thinkers are free to examine themes that traditionally would only be left to those who claimed a transpersonal orientation. Thus Sorenson (2004) can deconstruct the Freudian 'wholesale pathologizing of religion' whilst recognizing that spirituality in the present climate does not need to be confined by the religious doctrines. In addition to accepting spirituality as a valid part of life he posits that the analyst can have a greater impact on their patients' spirituality than the patients' own parents have.

His is not a lone voice; perhaps one of the best-known thinker from this school is Eigan (1998) who is free to address mysticism in the psychoanalytic world, a subject that I think could only be looked upon as being in Freud's day abnormal pathology.

Returning now to my promise to portray both sides of an argument that is centred upon the notion that evolution has a transpersonal aspect, I am aware that the non-transpersonal view of evolution has received little discussion.

In order to remedy this we can turn to a school that can offer many obvious contenders for an 'against a transpersonal view of evolution', 'Evolutionary psychology' Pinker (1998) Wright (1995), Cosmides and Tooby (1992, 1997).

## Evolutionary psychology

Evolutionary psychology had not yet emerged as a discrete field of study in the 1960s when Maslow formulated the four-force taxonomy and was one of the 'new kids on the block' in the field of psychology. Besides proffering an anti-transpersonal view, I introduce this body of knowledge at this point because it is a discipline that could be said to bridge some of the orthodox theories of evolution with insight from the next field I portray, the first force of psychology. In addition to the foregoing it, like many of the theories previously discussed, also at heart offers psychological developmental models.

Evolutionary psychology, formerly sociobiology, Wilson (1975), is a field that has emerged over the last 20 or so years, and is gaining rapid academic respect and credence as a distinct school in its own right. It endeavours to present a complete and scientific account of human nature by primarily combining evolutionary biology (Cronin, 1992) and cognitive psychology (Skinner, 1953, 1974), with additional support from anthropology, primatology, archaeology and linguistics. Although it has gained academic respectability, it is a field that is concerned with pure conjecture and unlike the greater majority of disciplines I discuss it is not, as far as I can ascertain, as yet applicable in the consulting room, solely because of its focus upon conjecture and a transhistorical/transcultural bias.

Regardless of this, Cosmides and Tooby (1992), who are commonly regarded as leaders in the field, make bold claims regarding how they see its future significance to psychology,

> Just as one can now flip open Gray's Anatomy to any page and find an intricately detailed depiction of some part of our evolved species-typical morphology, we anticipate that in 50 or 100 years one will be able to pick up an equivalent reference work for psychology and find in it detailed information-processing descriptions of the multitude of evolved species-typical adaptations of the human mind, including how they are mapped onto the corresponding neuroanatomy and how they are constructed by developmental programs.
>
> (2004 online serial)

With their emphasis on tracing how evolutionary forces have shaped biology, it comes as no surprise that evolutionary psychologists place little if any importance upon the transpersonal aspect of mankind, favouring instead to address biological and societal functioning. An example of the former is the nature versus nature debate, genetic determinism versus environmental determinism. A field of study that endeavours to find a means by which to address phylogenetic versus adaptationist explanations of mankind's psychological as well as biological make up.

With the latter, the interest of evolutionary psychology in societal functioning is evidenced by the importance that is placed upon hypotheses that address factors like what could be the possible effects that group size plays in areas such as the evolution of reason and the intellectual functioning?

With the foregoing in mind looking for evolutionary psychologies view of the transpersonal is not overly fruitful, considering the reductionistic framework that it views the world through, this is a position that will not be found surprising. However, the field does hold an interest in the place that religion may have played in mankind's successful evolution as dominant species. Kirkpatrick (1999), Boyer (2001) and Sloan Wilson (2002) all offer hypotheses regarding the significance that religion has played in human evolution. All do not take a view that the transpersonal may be a valid sphere and that it may be anything other than the creation of the human mind. Sloan Wilson presents a typical argument in which he posits that religion can be regarded as providing a 'bio-cultural' cohesive force that could unite individuals, thereby forming coherent groups that provide mutually beneficial co-operation, thus offering optimum evolutional chance.

With tongue in cheek, I wonder if the foregoing could also be applicable to the various schools of psychology I am presenting, including the fourth force and evolutionary psychology. A view that is supported by having attended many conferences situated within one school, where I have come across many, including respected academics who, whilst not always openly declaring so, see their own field as providing the most important/valid maps of the human condition.

All the above could lead to the conclusion that evolutionary psychology and transpersonal psychology would make strange bedfellows. In terms of worldview this would be hard not to dispute. However, the means by which their academic credibility are/were developed share similar traits in that hypotheses cannot be tested and confirmed by means of test re-test principles and methods. Moreover, because of their respective methods of theory generation, each could be accused of being non-scientific whilst being situated at opposing ends of a reductionistic spectrum.

Another similarity that could be noticed is the way that both fields can be regarded as perspectives from which to view psychological life. A viewpoint succinctly stated by Cosmides and Tooby (1997),

Evolutionary psychology is an *approach* to psychology, in which knowledge and principles from evolutionary biology are put to use in research on the structure of the human mind. It is not an area of study, like vision, reasoning, or social behavior. It is a *way of thinking* about psychology that can be applied to any topic within it.

The very same could also be said of the transpersonal in that it too could be conceived as a *way of thinking* about psychology that can be applied to any topic within it.

With both fields being able to be regarded as an approach to psychology, it is not surprising that both share a common epistemic tendency in that they generate theory utilizing a wide range of disciplines.

Moreover, both fields can be seen to share similarities in their heritage. Cosmides and Tooby (1997) trace the psychological roots of their discipline back to the works of William James (1842–1910), as did I when introducing transpersonal psychology. However, evolutionary psychology chose to take his views regarding instinct as its major focus. Transpersonal thinking, on the other hand, without dismissing the importance of instinct, took from his work the need to include the 'spiritual self'. Thus, the transpersonal elements of our being when regarding psychology were also included.

Whilst having stated that both fields share a common epistemic tendency, another difference could be seen in methods of theory generation. To my mind evolutionary psychology could be accused of pursuing 'greedy reductionism' (Dennett, 1991). This is a term that is applied to theories that appear to provide overly simplistic and neat answers to complex problems. This accusation could not be levelled at transpersonal thinking, for it would be hard-pressed to be seen in the light of reductionism at all. And yet, from the reductionistic standpoint transpersonal thinking would be accused of endeavouring 'to provide overly simplistic and neat answers to complex problems'.

However, unlike transpersonal psychology, evolutionary psychology has been more readily accepted by scientific orthodoxy, despite having a lack of empirical validation, as I think it has been amply shown. This, I think, is due to its reductionistic stance. Unlike transpersonal psychology it gains academic respectability, because it promises to focus upon finding correlations between physiological functioning (matter) and psychological phenomena through the means of reductionistic methodologies, and thus whilst the fields of study may be on the edge of 'proper scientific thinking' the means of study do fulfil many of the tenets accepted as being valid science.

To bring this section to a close I distill the foregoing into a couple of sentences. It would be easy to claim that whilst transpersonal psychology and evolutionary psychology as approaches to psychology sprang from a similar epistemic and theoretical heritage, the fields take a very different view upon evolution, with the latter looking more towards instinct and survival of the most well-adapted. In addition to, or perhaps because of this, it relies upon a reductionistic framework, a set of models that are more in accord with the practices and theories of the schools that fall under the umbrella of the first force of psychology.

## The first force of psychology

It is now time to move on to the first force of psychology, the behavioural school. Thus far we have seen that there appears to be an ebb and flow regarding the acceptance of the transpersonal in psychological thinking. William James and the forerunners to analytic thinking include the transpersonal, Freud does not, Jung most certainly does, and evolutional psychology swings back to the no position, a stance that is further highlighted from the behavioural schools perspective, which sees transpersonal phenomena and indeed the whole transpersonal realm as deserving little, if any, credence or thought.

At first sight one could be forgiven for asking why give account of the behavioural school within a work that aims to explore transpersonal psychology, for one is presented with two schools of thought that could be construed as coming from vastly differing views of the world. Besides, in relation to this work standing solely in the behavioural schools' philosophical context and viewing transpersonal concerns solely from this perspective would prove a fruitless task.

Yet, by viewing the behavioural school from the transpersonal perspective, the insight and understanding of human behaviour that this field brings to psychological thought would be accepted as one of many components that go to create a larger picture that seeks to illustrate the whole of the human condition. This inclusiveness could be regarded as typical of transpersonal thinking and is in stark contrast to the exclusive interests typified by the behavioural school.

Though there are numerous complex and competing theories within this school, for the sake of convenience I recognize four influential thinkers who could be said to characterize this school's approach. They are:

- Beck (1979), who placed emphasis upon a cognitive triad (thoughts about the Self, the Future and the World), and the 'errors of logic'.
- Seligman (2006), who initiated the concept of learned helplessness, and its relationship to attribution theory (Both Seligman's and Beck's theories focused originally on depression).
- Albert Ellis (1975), the father of 'Rational Emotive Therapy', which focuses on the irrational beliefs that lie at the heart of individual's belief systems. And finally,
- George Kelly (1969) who developed 'Personal Construct Therapy', which suggests that humans can be likened to scientists, actively construing events by means of bipolar constructs.

A discussion of the work of these four thinkers would reveal an overview of the philosophical bias of the behavioural school that offers scant regard for transpersonal phenomena. For the second force perspective brings a viewpoint that regards that mankind could be likened to a machine, albeit a highly complex one, in which Cartesian/Newtonian principles, such as that of cause and effect and the influence of conditioned reflexes, dominate an individual's actions. This leaves little room for the enquiring attitude that philosophy demands; it does, however, encompass ethical and moral concerns, both of which have been addressed by philosophers from ancient Greek and Roman times up to the present day.

For brevity's sake, instead of discussing in detail the work of several thinkers, I choose to portray the influence that Skinner (1953, 1974), one of the founding fathers of this school, brings, as he could be said to epitomize their philosophical bias as well as being influential in the theoretical foundations of first force thought.

I have purposely chosen B. F. Skinner as an example of a theorist from the behavioural school because he is perhaps the best-known thinker whose work is regarded as influential in the rise of popularity and regard of behavioural psychology. However, although important, it is not the only reason for my choice. In fact, his work spanned and integrated theoretical constructs from what I would term the 'old behavioural school' to the work of more contemporary thinkers such as the four previously mentioned.

The tradition that I am terming the 'old behavioural school' had its roots in physiology and not psychology, and the most widely known figure from this tradition is Ivan Pavlov (1849–1936). His doctoral thesis *The Centrifugal Nerves of the Heart*, for which he was awarded a Nobel Prize in 1904, has no psychological basis and is not as well remembered as his later work in which he examined conditioned versus innate reflex. This is his later work which had a direct bearing on psychological thinking.[1]

This combing of the old and new can be seen in Skinner's work, as he moved away, in the later part of his career, from the traditional or 'methodological behaviourism' (Skinner, 1953) towards 'radical behaviourism' (Skinner, 1974). The forma situated firmly within logical positivism seeks to find answers solely to the underlying reasons for behaviour, and does not explore consciousness; radical behaviourism, however, does, and it also takes into account and attempts to explain the inner (subjective) experience of individuals.

---

[1] It is interesting to note that Pavlov left theological seminary where he was intending to join the priesthood due in part to the influence that reading the work of the father of Russian Physiology Ivan Sechenov (1829–1905) had upon his thinking. Sechenov's work could also be seen as influential in the development of Evolutionary Biochemistry and Physiology which in turn could be conceived of as influential in the development Evolutionary psychology.

Methodological behaviourism and certain versions of logical positivism could be said to ignore consciousness, feelings, and states of
mind, but radical behaviourism does not thus 'behead organism'; it
does not 'sweep the problem of subjectivity under the rug'; it does not
'maintain a strictly behaviouristic methodology by treating reports
of introspection merely as verbal behaviour'; and it was not designed
to 'permit consciousness to atrophy'

(Skinner, 1974, p. 219)

From the above one might assume that Skinner and others from the
first force do indeed recognize that behaviour may at the least be mediated by consciousness, and consequently be open to the possibility
that consciousness could have a transpersonal aspect. However, though
thinkers from this tradition do not 'ignore consciousness, feelings, and
states of mind', it appears that they see them more as epiphenomena.
Thus maintaining their belief in the supremacy of responses that are
generated in relation to overt and objectively observable phenomena.
And this may account for the lack of research and consequently literature that addresses transpersonal awareness and functioning within the
first force.

This force or tradition is closest to the epistemological beliefs of
orthodox traditional psychiatric thinking. From the worldview offered
by this perspective emphasis is directed towards tasks and goals, rather
than the insight orientation that dominates many of the second (and
third) force models. It comes as no surprise, therefore, that the allopathic
medical model readily embraces and accepts much from this force. This
could be explained by the fact that many of the theories are described in
familiar terms, and many concepts fulfil criteria that are best-suited to
the test re-test principles of quantitative research methodology. Which
are also accepted as providing the only means to test and create pharmacological research, as well as being utilized by all the fields that go to
make up the field of human biology.

Nowadays, the behavioural viewpoint is not as prominent as it was
in the early 1960s, when psychology began to be thought of as falling
within the four distinct categories (forces), and has been eclipsed in the
present era by cognitive behavioural therapies (CBT).

Like behaviourists, the greater number of thinkers from the CBT
school, for instance Padesky and Greenberger (1995), share similar theoretical beliefs with their predecessors, such as that the world is comprised
of verifiable truths that can be identified and codified. This worldview can also be identified in 'Constructive therapies' (Hoyt, 1994), an

umbrella-term that is often used to include solution-focused therapy, brief therapy and time-limited counselling, all of which share similar ideals and practices. Their task and goal orientation, like CBT, 'is not to "understand" the cause of a given problem, but to find fertile ways of thinking about it and practical ideas to deal with it' (Furman & Ahola, 1994, pp. 41–42). This approach to therapy gives precedence to 'which' not 'why' phenomena occur; this focus leaves scant time (no pun intended) for philosophical deliberation nor transpersonal functioning unless it has a direct and observable bearing on a considered and desired result.

I found it difficult to find an author from the first force who gives an explanation of the philosophical component of their work. A notable exception was in Clarke (2001), where a chapter is devoted to explaining how unconstrued experiencing can be admitted by accepting a phenomenalist approach, particularly participative views of reality.

Moreover, in relation to this study, Clarke (as my discussion of her thinking in the following section shows) is also the only thinker I could find who identifies themselves as being situated within the first force and who addresses what are often described as transpersonal phenomena with an openness and willingness to accept their validity as part of commonly construed reality.

This accounting for a philosophical heritage and an open acceptance that reality can be viewed from various vantage points is at odds with the greater number of thinkers within the first force. This comes as no surprise, however, as the thinkers who constitute the greater majority of this force could be conceived of primarily striving to uphold 'Scientific Realism'. A good example can be found in the work of Albert Ellis whose vehement criticism of transpersonal psychology I discussed earlier.

## Neurolinguistic programming and life coaching

Before completing an exploration of the first force and moving onto the third force, or humanistic psychology, it is worthwhile to note that presently there are a number of approaches to personal growth and well-being that are not commonly considered to be counselling or psychotherapy. Indeed, the rise and popularity of CBT in the present psychological climate is also mirrored by the explosion and popularity of various coaching models. Like CBT and solution-focused theories they tend to not need a clinician who has studied psychology in depth in order to practice and effectively work with clients. For example, no developmental theories or psychopathological constructs are needed to be understood.

Another similarity to the solution-focused approach is the reliance upon a goal orientation that is directed towards behaviour modification. Behaviour, however, is recognized to be the tip of the iceberg, and it is acknowledged that the associated beliefs need to be explored, with behaviour in-the-here-and-now being a useful signpost to the material that drives it.

The best-known coaching model is perhaps neurolinguistic programming (NLP). NLP began in the early 1970s at the University of California, Santa Cruz, when Richard Bandler, a graduate student of psychology and John Grinder, an Assistant Professor of Linguistics, began working together. Much of early NLP was based on finding a means to model the effective elements in the work of psychological clinicians Virginia Satir, a family therapist; Fritz Perls, father of Gestalt therapy and Milton H. Erickson (1901–1980) the hypnotherapist. The work of anthropologist Gregory Bateson was also influential. This emulating is a core concept of NLP and is termed 'modelling', and simply means the building of models of how people perform or accomplish something. Interestingly, a model does not have to be 'true' or 'correct' or even perfectly formed, it only has to be 'useful' when applied to what it is designed for.

A brief aside to mention that the four figures that Bandler and Grinder modelled would recognize that, although the transpersonal was not a major focus of their work, all four pursued an active interest in transpersonal and spiritual matters. The inclusion of Zen thought has already been recognized in the work of Pearls. Virginia Satir, recognized as a pioneer in family therapy, was also a Director of Training at the Esalen Institute, in Big Sur, California, a workshop and training centre where nearly every influential figure in the transpersonal and humanistic schools had taught or lectured.

Although Erickson (1901–1980) did not comment upon transpersonal concerns, he posited that the unconscious mind has its own awareness and is creative, solution-generating and often positive, not merely a psychic rubbish dump for unwanted or unacceptable psychological material. This view would meet the approval of many transpersonal theorists, as would Erickson's idea of the 'consensus trance'. This last postulate is similar to the work of transpersonal theorist, Charles Tart (1987). Also Bateson did not publish his views regarding the transpersonal, though he was a member of the Lindisfarne Association, which is a group of intellectuals and prominent thinkers interested in an interdisciplinary exploration of the importance of consciousness, esoteric traditions and religious and spiritual practices. NLP can be regarded as a psycho-educational tool, helping individuals understand how they create their own internal 'map' or 'world' (beliefs). This awareness-raising is accomplished through a process of uncovering unhelpful or destructive patterns of thinking based on impoverished 'maps' of the world. Once these patterns are identified, tools are offered for trans-forming or replacing them with better-suited, useful or helpful ones.

With a focus upon subjective experience and a set of tools that are designed to aid individuals in achieving their goals, NLP is gener-ally regarded by the general public as a personal development system and is commonly presented in group trainings, seminars or individual client/practitioner consultations. It is also increasingly applied as a therapy in itself or as an adjunct by therapists who claim an allegiance to another school. Although NLP is commonly used to explore the more worldly or secular aspects of human functioning, it is not surprising that also the transpersonal is included, given the era of its birth, the inclus-ivity of its interests and the wide-ranging scope of its application. This inclusion of the transpersonal is not at first so easy to find, as most of the ever-growing literature focuses upon the meeting of ego needs and interpersonal relationship. Moreover, the fact that proponents of this school often refer to themselves as 'life coaches' may convey a message that ego needs are the central area of interest.

Dilts and McDonald (1997) are two influential NLP practitioners who recognize the transpersonal as a valid arena of exploration. They acknowledge that individuals seek 'a state of authenticity'. Their descrip-tion of this state is in accord with many other descriptions of the transpersonal and suggests similar goals to those posited by psychosyn-thesis: an increased sense of personal freedom, a greater appreciation of the individual's place in the greater whole as well as the fostering of a relationship to something greater than themselves. They accept that 'Traditional Tools of the Spirit' such as prayer, meditation, song and ritual are all methods that can be used to support an individual in this endeavour, though they consider NLP to be a kind of 'meta tool', one that can be employed to create other 'tools of the Spirit'.

They are not the only well-known figures in the coaching world. O'Connor & McDermott (2001) and Whitmore (1997, 2002) are others in the field who also consider that the transpersonal is an important realm of functioning. O'Connor and McDermott bring the insights of McDermott's many years of meditative practice to NLP. In 'The NLP Coach' the six logical levels are described as 'a way of identi-fying underlying structures and patterns in thinking about ideas, events, relationships or organizations. They help us understand what's involved, or what's going on' (McDermott & Jago, 2001). The logical levels are hierarchically structured, and at the top of the structure is the spiritual level where it is possible to relate to others as well as 'to that which is more than your identity... being one with humankind the universe or God' (O'Connor & McDermott, 2001, p. 6).

Undoubtedly NLP has had a significant if not primary influence upon the whole field of coaching, it is also important to remember that it is not the only model employed by life coaches. Not all well-known figures claim an NLP stance: a good example of an influential figure who does not is Whitmore (1997, 2002). He is one of the thinkers who have been instrumental in the success of psychological coaching in the world of sport and business, and he makes no bones about the importance of the transpersonal, and those familiar with psychosynthesis will not fail to see its influence in his work.

I have purposely chosen to give a brief account of coaching because, to my mind, it has become, in the last 10 or so years, for an ever-increasing number of the general public, a well-known and accepted approach to psychological problem-solving. At present like counselling, it is not regulated in the United Kingdom. A state of affairs that enables it to be marketed or sold as whatever anyone wants. In my limited experience, it is often sold as a panacea for all ills by individuals who can market themselves well, though only have one or two days training in the model. This is unfortunate for the whole school, as not all individuals claim to be experts when they are not, though both the skilled and unskilled alike are armed with powerful transformational tools which can and do stir up psychological material from the depths of the psyche, and thus dismantle or shore up defensive mechanisms that whilst limiting an individual keep them safe from the overwhelming onslaught of their own psychological material.

The conclusion I draw from looking towards the first force for evidence or at least acceptance of the transpersonal is that from this vantage point mankind could generally, as stated earlier, be simply likened to a machine, a physical, chemical, genetic mechanism. A viewpoint that is in accord with the claim of scientism fitting in with the restriction that only scientific knowledge is genuine knowledge. Which can then legitimately uphold the notion that man is no more than a machine (Sellars, 1963). And although this perspective excels at exploring the mechanisms that may be used to make sense (understand) transpersonal experiences, it offers an inadequate means by which to integrate the transpersonal, due to its focus upon goal orientation and need to place the human condition within a framework that places high regard upon cognitive functioning by way of concluding an examination of the first force.

For me, situated outside the field and looking in, I find that this point of view offers a very limited account of the complexity and range of experience that permeates the whole human condition, though it clearly excels in its focus upon cognitive functioning and instinctive response. In my opinion from the transpersonal perspective this fuels the conclusion that this force offers paucity in its view of the understanding of human nature and reality. This claim certainly could not be levelled at transpersonal psychology and the next force I examine is the third force or humanistic psychology.

## The third force of psychology

Before examining the thinking that illuminates this force and its relationship to transpersonal psychology, it is important to note that the whole sphere of humanistic psychology is encompassed by a different philosophy of science than the first and much of the second force of psychology. The yardstick by which to measure this field's validity is radically different, as 'Scientific Realism' is not considered to be of uppermost importance. Gone is the need to deconstruct and examine the constituent elements of functioning, with more emphasis now placed upon wholes and larger pictures (though not exclusively so). In lay terms, it could be said that the thrust of exploration and the account of mankind's 'doing' – how we act in the world (though still important and worthy of exploration) – has been replaced with an emphasis upon 'being'.

With this emphasis upon 'being' within the third force – humanistic psychology – it comes as no surprise to find that philosophy and transpersonal thinking have had a direct and apparent influence upon psychotherapeutic practice and theory. This influence permeates the whole of this force to a lesser or greater extent. In fact, one school 'Existential Psychology' (Binswanger, 1963; Boss, 1963; Bugental, 1980; Condrau, 1998; May, 1969; Spinelli, 1997; Van Deurzen-Smith, 1997; Yalom, 1980), which is situated firmly within this force, endeavours to address how a client's own life philosophy interfaces with all areas of their lived experience. This would include their intra-psychic world as well as their relationship to the world perceived outside themselves.

As at first glance existential psychology and transpersonal psychology can appear to be one and the same; because of this I explore the existential approach latter in this chapter.

Returning to the whole of the third force it is possible to find with ease concepts, principles and areas of concern that inform transpersonal thinking, such as the fact that both forces pursue an active interest in consciousness. This is evidenced by the importance placed upon 'intentionality', one of the philosophical tenets of all third force approaches to psychology. Intentionality is a concept that suggests that all consciousness, and therefore action, is imbued with meaning and intent, a concept that is also familiar to the transpersonal worldview. However, we must be careful not to confuse intentionality with other philosophical concepts. A good example of potential confusion could be the Freudian psychoanalytic principle of 'psychic determinism'. Though psychic determinism and intentionality may be related, the emphasis within intentionality is not relegated solely to unconscious drives. Taking this as a theoretical assumption in the consulting room would reveal a praxis that encourages clients to recognize their own part in what life presents them with, and to actively engage in the authorship of their life, an outcome of which may be the discovery of how they view and, perhaps more importantly, create their world. This could be seen as concordant with creating an environment where an individual is able to experience Heidegger's (1889–1976) concept of 'being-in-the-world'. From a philosophical stance intentionality would also concur with Hursserl's (1859–1938) paradigm that sees intentionality as an integral aspect of consciousness. Together, being-in-the-world and intentionality could be conceived as a means by which to overcome the subject–object dichotomy that philosophical epistemology has grappled with since Descartes (1596–1650).

Whilst the foregoing may seem overtly simple, it may be helpful at this point to unpack this bold statement, particularly so as at first glance the foregoing seems somewhat simplistic.

Intentionality can be conceived as the fact that consciousness is always conscious of something that is not consciousness itself, but a meaning for consciousness. Thus human meaning and encounter establish a connection between an individual and the world, and it is this that gives rise to the formation of relationship with the 'in between', the loosening of separation of subject from object.

Though I discuss intentionality in one short paragraph, it is in fact a complex subject whose philosophical history can be traced back to the medieval philosopher St Thomas Aquinas (c. 1225–1274). In the present era, Crane (1995) gives an overview of the philosophical components of this complex subject, whilst Dennett (1999) concentrates more upon how we describe phenomena and the possibility that intentionality can be directed towards both the 'real' and the 'believed'.

Aware that this study is not just concerned with psychology as an abstract theoretical construct, I turn to the thinking of Martin Buber to shed light upon how philosophical insight can be put into practice in the psychotherapeutic relationship.

Martin Buber (2002), philosopher and Hasidic (Jewish) theologian, most certainly saw the transpersonal as a valid field, although he is best known for his philosophy of dialogue, the 'I–Thou relationship'. His hypothesis that human existence was based upon the premise that existence is experienced through encounter was originally discussed in German (Ich und Du) in 1923, and although not widely known about until the 1960s his original thesis remained unchanged.

The concept of I–Thou relating highlights that it is possible, indeed preferable, to perceive you (another) not just as an object or 'it', for you are in fact, from your point of view, a 'subject' (of your world). This may at first glance seem simplistic or obvious. However, when applied to the psychotherapeutic relationship, it has far reaching implications. First, it emphasizes that you are not a fixed thing but in fact a 'process'. Still, I turn you into an 'it' (a passive object) each time I use you for my own purpose, such as needing your admiration to prop up my view of my importance, or needing for you (the patient) to recover in order for me (the therapist) to feel competent and professional, or at the least of help. You of course can also turn me into an 'it' in order to meet your needs.

Although Buber was not to explicitly address the transpersonal when positing the importance of the I–Thou relationship, as a Hasidic scholar he felt that the transpersonal can be experienced in daily life and is not some discrete separate realm.

In Chapter 1, I related how Gestalt was influenced by Eastern thought such as Zen Buddhism. Here though, I point out that with its emphasis on experience Gestalt is one obvious theoretical approach that is also influenced by Buber's thinking. In fact Laura Perls, Fritz's wife and collaborator, studied with Buber as well as the philosopher and Christian theologian Paul Tillich (2000).

We need not only look towards the roots of Gestalt to find Buber's influence, for recent theorists such as Hycner (1993) have also turned their attention towards the 'I–Thou relationship' to create a 'dialogical model of psychotherapy'. He also recognizes that, 'It is difficult to think of an existentially-orientated therapist who did not incorporate an understanding of the I–Thou relationship into therapy' (p. 106). In addition to examples of thinkers who are seen as existentialists, such as May (1969), Yalom (1980) and Bugental (1980), he also gives examples of the importance of the 'I–Thou' relationship in the thinking of other schools: Rogers (1961) and Maslow (1971) from the humanistic, Jacoby (1984) the Jungian, Guntrip (1969) the object relations, Atwood and Stolorow (1984) and Kohut (1971a) from the analytical school.

Yalom is perhaps the most widely recognized and influential humanistic orientated theorist and practitioner of the last three decades. His book *Existential Psychotherapy* (1980) has become a classic within the psychotherapeutic literature. It makes clear the importance that 'I–Thou relationships' can play in therapy. He recognizes that it is more than the psychoanalytical transferencial relationship, a theoretical construct that suggests that the object of the transference is used as if they are dummies upon which feelings and attitudes from past relationships are projected. He sees that inherent within 'I–Thou relationship' the 'I' when 'truly' relating to another opens up to both, the other and themselves. In this relational mode the patient learns that they have the potential for the full range of the human condition – such as love, rage, joy, passion and peace – that in fact has existed within themselves even if they have been dissociated from or lain dormant.

As I will recount it is often very difficult from today's perspective to differentiate the third and fourth forces when looking for a purely transpersonal approach. This is because the whole of the humanistic movement tends to be inclusive of and hold an interest in the transpersonal. However, the subtle difference is that within the third force the transpersonal is recognized though not given a place of importance, a position that is reversed in 'logotherapy'.

Logotherapy (Frankl, 1967, 1984) is commonly regarded as belonging to the existential school (Cooper, 2003; Graham, 1986), although its theoretical orientation is overtly transpersonal. However, because of the insistence that there is a realm of spirituality – the noetic – that is beyond both the psychological and the physiological, I place it firmly in the transpersonal school. Therefore, I give a brief exploration of logotherapy in the next chapter. However, it is easy to see how logotherapy is often seen as an existential/humanistic approach as Frankl its founder was keen to insist that mankind is drawn towards seeking meaning and purpose in life, a position that would fit with ease in the thinking of the humanistic practitioner, and is one of the central tenets of all third-force approaches.

The majority of the thinkers who have been influential in the humanistic school came to prominence in the 1960s, an example being R. D. Laing (1959) who experimented with an approach to the healing of schizophrenia, which came to be known as 'radical therapy', that was at odds with the prevailing types of treatment regard as the norm. He is considered to be from the 'British Existential School' (Cooper, 2003; Graham, 1986). The 'radical therapy' and the 'anti-psychiatry movement' that he is commonly associated with also have their historical roots firmly embedded in the 1960s and the advent of the counterculture. However, these views of the theories of psychology and praxis, like Buber's work, are hard to fit solely into any one of the four forces.

Formulated in the late 1950s Laing's approach to the care and understanding of individuals suffering from mental illness was critical of the prevailing medical model. He was at odds with its practices of routine institutionalization and the hasty use of surgical procedures and electrical or drug therapies as a means of cure, without regard for the social context the individual was situated within. He saw mental disease in another light: for example, his understanding of schizophrenia, which he regarded as a metaphor for alienation and despair. His first book *The Divided Self: An Existential Study of Sanity and Madness* (Laing, 1959) presents and argues for a theory that he termed 'an Ontological theory of schizophrenia' which offered a radical alternative to the prevailing thinking and practice of the psychiatric profession.

He posited that psychologically individuals may experience internal splits and divisions, a fragmented self (a familiar concept in psychoanalytic and psychodynamic thinking). They '(...) may not posses an over-riding sense of personal consistency or cohesiveness' (1969, p. 52). He saw this fragmentation developing as a response to an early family matrix that did not foster the experience of developing the experience of self as a unique being who has a relationship with the world. This aids unendurable social pressures that are experienced as 'ontological insecurity'. This contrasts with the 'sane' that experiences 'ontological security', which is typified by the experience of having a distinct psychological identity (a 'self') that is also confirmed by the reactions of those around them.

Mental illness was in fact the individual's attempt to maintain coherence and reintegration of 'self' in the world. He contended that what is needed from clinicians is for them to view the world through the schizophrenics eyes. This would then enable them to comprehend that the patients' behaviours are in fact natural responses to the impossible situations they experience themselves to be in.

He and colleagues were to experiment with lessening the dosage of anti-psychotic drugs that patients received combined with existential analysis, a treatment plan that may receive wholehearted approval from a transpersonal clinician. Unfortunately, Laing's contribution to psychiatric thought has been eclipsed by the popular image he has been labelled with as a 1960s counterculture prophet. This may not be surprising, as he became a familiar voice and spokesman for many of his generation that espoused the belief that a radical change in moral codes, such as the legalization of cannabis, was needed.

Working within the present orthodox psychiatric model clinicians may question the wisdom of purposely inciting altered state of consciousness. Clearly, the rationale for this is that symptom reduction leading to 'normal functioning' is regarded as paramount for this approach.

Returning to thinking about the 1960s and the advent of the counterculture, it was in this period that an academic philosophical perspective can be easily seen applied to psychology. Foucault (2002), for example, can be seen to be a thinker who amply speaks for much that Laing and his colleagues strove to practice. Foucault traced the European historical attitude towards, and the care (or lack of) of, those deemed to be mentally ill or insane. As well as interested in history, he was also a commentator upon political science and explored what he saw to be some of the social determinants of madness. He, unlike most thinkers who address such issues, was to pay scant interest to psychopathology. It was this and the influence of the thinking of his tutor and close friend Georges Canguilhem (1904–1995), who questioned the scientific basis of psychological thinking, that lead to his questioning of the psychology of his time, which was typified by orthodox psychiatry.

Like Laing, Foucault was also seen as an influential figure in the 1960s counterculture and both were certainly aware of each other's thinking. In fact my copy of Foucault's *Madness and Civilization* (2002) includes, in the flyleaf, a glowing recommendation for the work by Laing.

I include this brief mention of Laing and Foucault here not just because their thinking was at odds with the prevailing academic orthodoxy. I do so because they typify how, within this period, with the advent of the human potential movement, humanistic psychology as the third force came to be recognized, with transpersonal psychology seen as the fourth force.

Concurrently in the Western 'first world' it could be said that within this era, 'the swinging sixties', it became possible for many young adults to experiment with greater levels of autonomy from parental and orthodox societorial norms by addressing standards such as moral and religious issues. This freedom of thought and deed also became the laboratory where the prevailing psychological theories of human nature, psychiatric and analytical thought, could be scrutinized. It also brought about the possible introduction or inclusion of ideas and concepts from other cultures and knowledge bases. If musicians such as the Beatles could introduce Eastern influences such as the sitar into popular music, it comes as no surprise to find that the inclusion or synthesis of such things as Zen philosophy or Vedic thought took place in the psychological atmosphere of the time, adding fuel to the increasing popularity of the human potential movement and a fledgling transpersonally orientated view of psychology.

During the same period it was not only the easier access to the insights of Eastern religion that could permeate psychological discourse. With all dogma ripe for examination, or cementing firmly in place, the role and function of traditional Western religious and spiritual views and their interface with psychology was also up for grabs. With the foregoing in mind at the end of this chapter I will discuss the 'Psychology of Religion', a school that, although not fully fitting the taxonomic criterion of either the transpersonal or humanistic schools, could be wrongly construed of as transpersonal psychology because of the thrust of much of its areas of exploration.

First though, as promised, I return to exploring existential therapy (Binswanger, 1963; Boss, 1963; Bugental, 1980; Condrau, 1998; May, 1969; Spinelli, 1997; Van Deurzen-Smith, 1997; Yalom, 1980). Like all humanistic schools it is an approach that tends to focus upon the-here-and-now of the lived experience of the patient. Generally there is a shying away from exploring the biographical aetiology of symptom, thus the developmental theories familiar to first-force therapies and the behavioural responses favoured by the second are not given as much precedence.

## Existential psychology

The existential school could be split into two rough categories:

- Daseinanalytic psychotherapy (Binswanger, 1963; Boss, 1963; Condrau, 1998) and
- Existential psychotherapy (Bugental, 1980; Laing, 1959, 1969; May, 1969; Spinelli, 1997; Van Deurzen-Smith, 1997; Yalom, 1980).

Both schools look towards revealing and exploring the experience of the client as the creator of their life.

Daseinanalytic psychotherapy follows two similar streams, one following the work of Ludwig Binswanger (1881–1966) and the other the work of Medard Boss (1903–1990). Both seek to imbed Martin Heidegger's philosophical ontology within a psychotherapeutic model that concentrates upon the phenomenological aspect of the human condition within a psychotherapeutic praxis. Simply put, and losing the psychobabble, this could be seen as creating a context in which to invite a client to engage in an exploration of all that inhibits (closedness) or supports (openness) them fully participating in life.

Binswanger is considered to be the initiator of Daseinanalytic psychotherapy, formally 'phenomenological anthropology', in the early 1930s. Although a close and life-long friend of Freud (Binswanger & Freud, 2000), he disagreed, however, with the psychoanalytical premise that emphasizes a reductionistic model that concentrates upon mechanistic, deterministic and instinctual mechanisms, preferring instead to place emphasis upon the patient's suffering from a philosophical perspective by looking towards their experience of 'being-in-the-world' through the lens of primarily Heidegger's and Hursserl's philosophical models.

Medard Boss had been one of Binswanger's most ardent followers; however, Heidegger disagreed with Binswanger's interpretation of his thinking and favoured his friend Boss's application of his philosophy in psychotherapeutic praxis. For many years they were to work closely together and Boss, with Heidegger as his mentor, wrote one of his seminal works, *Existential Foundations of Medicine and Psychology* (1979).

The Daseinanalytic clinician is not interested in what psychoanalytical therapists would regard as intra-psychic conflict; they favour the view that internal conflict points instead towards some form of 'closedness' to the world.

Moreover, gone is the idea that some form of unconscious must be brought to consciousness, as only that which is experienced is held as important to work with. In addition to a radically different way of exploring the life of the patient from the view held by psychodynamically orientated therapists, this view also negates the widely held belief of many transpersonal clinicians that there is some form of spiritual, noetic or transpersonal a priori realm that, though at times hidden from experience, is always nevertheless available.

Binswanger and particularly Boss hoped that the Daseinanalytic approach would be widely accepted and take centre stage in the field of counselling and psychotherapy. Whilst this has not happened, the training of Daseinanalytic psychotherapists is thriving in Europe, yet this particular branch of the humanistic school is by and large unknown. The existential approach is however widely practiced or incorporated by a large number of clinicians, yet it is the next form of existential psychotherapy I portray that has a much wider following and is also more familiar to many more counselling and psychotherapy clinicians outside of the existential school.

Here the use of German words, such as dasein, mitwelt and eigenwelt, to explain mankind's lived experience, are replaced with terms familiar to every day English vocabulary. As most of the field's main proponents work in England and the United States, it comes as no surprise that the English language is used.

However, it is not the change of mother tongue of the main theorists that holds the greatest difference; it is that there is also less reliance upon utilizing existential philosophy as a central theoretical principal. In some ways it could be seen as a form of 'dumbing down' existentialist philosophy, yet many central themes are similar, if not the same: for example, meaning and meaninglessness, purpose, death, freedom and the unknown.

Without needing to study what can be difficult philosophical texts, the existentially biased clinician can support their clients to meet the vicissitudes and triumphs of the human condition without recourse to a thorough understanding of the field's literature, nor its theoretical arguments. Whilst a lack of knowledge of more than basic assumptions can be an obstacle for those that practice in other disciplines, such as psychodynamic or cognitive behavioural therapy, this is not true for both existential therapists and those that practice transpersonal psychology.

Exploring existential themes and their attendant anxieties leads not to seeking answers regarding the aetiology of behaviour. Instead the focus is upon finding the means to come to terms with the dilemmas that existence presents in order to address challenges. For example, faced with anorexia nervosa a psychoanalytic therapist would turn to psychopathology as a context, whilst looking towards the patient's intra-psychic world, the past and developmental impediments for clues. Whereas, a clinician whose praxis is cognitive behavioural, would look towards symptoms as clues to learnt behaviour and maladaptive responses to unhelpful beliefs and personal history. Existentially orientated clinicians, however, would not only encompass the foregoing, but also seek to look towards how the symptoms support the client in not facing the dilemmas and associated anxieties that being fully alive engenders in the here and now.

In relation to transpersonal therapy the existential approach does not have the same spiritual orientation, yet will not marginalize nor discount the transpersonal experience of a client, nor a worldview that incorporates the transpersonal.

Although the transpersonal does not hold a central place in existential practice, there is recognition that it can be a fruitful area of exploration. Van Deurzen-Smith (2002) recognizes that for many a spiritual dimension (ueberwelt) which cannot be proven is a part of their lived experience. And she maintains that this dimension is a valid area of exploration in the therapeutic context, whilst not suggesting any form of self-actualization, as a life or therapeutic goal. As a leading existential philosopher as well as therapist, care must be taken when exploring her work as her use of terms, such as spiritual, need to be considered in an existential light. Thus when she refers to spirituality it is not the same concept as this work and many others are referring to. Her view is that it is more of a system of meaning and value at the heart of one's being, a fundamental making sense of the world. And as such she claims it can be a useful healthy mechanism, 'a place to dwell in', as well as a place that is sought as a means to defend against the vagaries of life and what is commonly regarded as existential anxiety.

In addition to not discounting spiritual experience and functioning, like the transpersonal school, existential psychology became better known and flourished during the counterculture revolution of the 1960s. Rollo May is generally considered to be one of its chief exponents and was the mentor of perhaps the most influential figures in the field: James Bugental, Irvin Yalom and Emmy Van Deurzen-Smith. May in turn was a mentee of the philosopher and existential theologian Paul Tillich (1886–1965) and regarded him as his spiritual father (May, 1988).

As it can be seen, with its focus upon existential themes, and particularly meaning, it is not surprising that existential psychology is often confused with transpersonal psychology. Once again we can turn to Van Deurzen-Smith (1997) for a clear explanation of the remit of the existential school, and she makes no bones about where she sees the school's place in the whole field of psychology as well as spiritual thinking.

Although existential thinking is often seen as essentially atheistic, it is in fact merely secular. Within its secular brief it is concerned with all matters of human existence and therefore inevitably investigates the realm beyond the purely visible. Most therapeutic ideologies do not leave room for such a meta-level of experience: everything is explained in psychic terms instead. The only notable exceptions are transpersonal psychology, Jungian psychology and psychosynthesis. These approaches are, to my taste, often too fanciful and undisciplined, raising the supernatural to mythical status.

(p. 125)

Here it may be useful to remember that the existential approach is not the only strand within the humanistic approach and looking at the whole school both transpersonal and existential themes can be found.

As both strands permeate the whole of the third force I include a discussion which encompasses the whole of the humanistic school and not just the existential orientation, as it will reveal much that could be conceived of as belonging to both the third and fourth forces, two schools with subtle yet distinct differences.

An examination from today's perspective will reveal that numerous well-known theories can be very hard to differentiate when examining philosophical assumptions and underpinnings of both the third and fourth force. A good example of this can be seen in the work of Carl Rogers (1961) who is customarily seen as one of the influential thinkers in humanistic psychology, and Abrham Maslow (1971), who is credited with coining the term 'transpersonal'.

Early on in his research into effective psychotherapy Rogers posited that in the human being there is some form of natural growth tendency that he saw as a healing factor. 'Therapy is not a matter of doing something to the individual, or of inducing him to do something about himself. It is instead a matter of freeing him for normal growth and development' (1942, p. 29). Later on in his exploration he refined his thinking and formulated the concept of the 'formative tendency' (1980) that he saw as the directional tendency in the universe towards the realization of potential. He termed this 'formative tendency' in an organism such as human beings the 'actualizing' tendency and is the basis of the theory of client-centred therapy. 'In client-centred therapy, the person is free to choose any directions, but actually selects positive and constructive pathways. I can only explain this in terms of a directional tendency inherent in the human organism – a tendency to grow, to develop, to realize its full potential' (Rogers, 1986, p. 127).

This proposition is similar to some theories from thinkers who are commonly seen as being situated firmly in the fourth force (transpersonal), such as Maslow who proposed the tenet that humans strive for self-actualization. And to confuse matters more, it is fully in accord with Assagioli's (1990) transpersonally biased view that mankind is in a process of evolution. With the potential for misunderstanding closer scrutiny is called for. A careful consideration of Rogers' and Maslow's theories of actualization will reveal how they are often mistakenly equated and how both can be mistaken as being transpersonal theories. Rogers defined the actualizing tendency as the sole motivational force, and thus included the motivations conceptualized by Maslow (1971) as 'deficiency needs', that is, basic physiological needs, such as safety, belonging, love and esteem.

Maslow hypothesized that only through meeting these needs can one proceed in a hierarchical manner to self-actualization. Here it is easy to equate Maslow's self-actualized person with Rogers' concept of a 'fully functioning person'.

However, Rogers' concept of a 'fully functioning person' does not represent a state of being nor a class of person as in Maslow's actualizing personalities. Rather, Rogers is suggesting a facet of directionality that he believed is inherent in human beings which becomes obvious and accelerated under propitious psychological conditions, which he termed the 'necessary and sufficient conditions for constructive personality change' (1961).

The proposition that there is some form of force, drive, need or consciousness that seeks actualization within the human psyche is not unique to the thinking of Rogers, Maslow and Assagioli. Others who place importance upon the transpersonal approach share similar views that can further confuse this melange of theory and the ensuing implications for practice. Clarkson (1996) would be a good example. She sees herself as not practising from within or relying heavily upon one school or tradition, instead she chooses to be referred to as an 'integrative' or 'eclectic' clinician.

She frames the concept of *formative tendency, self-actualisation* and *the process of evolution* by returning to classical Greek thinkers – the pre-Socratics – who considered that Physis, the creative process of growth and change in the psyche of both the individual and the collective, permeated the whole of creation. 'Physis antedates Eros and Thanatos. It (…) represents the evolutionary impulse inherent in every cell. It is also viewed as more spiritual since it implies that it is in the nature of the person and the planet to evolve creatively' (Clarkson, 1996, pp. 262–263).

My own experience of professionals within the humanistic school, although being confined primarily to the British Isles, is that eclecticism, 'integrative psychology', is on the increase, with many clinicians finding a means to look towards several schools to supply the theoretical underpinnings of their praxis. I have also recognized that a great many training bodies within this school mirror this and teach their students a broad range of theories. Although I have not found confirmation in the literature that this is so, or that it is either increasing or decreasing, talking with many senior practitioners who identify themselves as having trained as humanistic clinicians has supplied much anecdotal evidence that this could well be the case.

The possibility for confusion regarding where or to whom theoretical constructs can be attributed is easy to see in an eclectic approach and in much of transpersonal thinking. In fact, this is something that applies to a broad range of psychological disciplines, as in most psychological schools, be they orthodox or innovative, a multitude of philosophical and clinical strands from over 100 years of psychological debate can be hard to untangle, as each of them in turn can offer a complex discourse comprised of theories which have been influenced by, and been woven into thinking from diverse bodies of knowledge. The foregoing highlights how difficult it can be to place many prominent thinkers solely in one force. This is particularly so in the third force, as it tends to have a philosophical bent towards including insights offered by differing schools. This may speak of the openness and willingness to experiment that was in ascendance in the era of its birth, as well as the fact that by the late 1950s and early 1960s psychology had become a recognized field of knowledge and study in its own right, which had accumulated a rich and diverse knowledge base.

Utilizing Maslow's four-force taxonomy 40 odd years after its inception to explore the place of the transpersonal in psychological discourse has also highlighted that, whilst it can be a useful means to illuminate the inclusion of the transpersonal, not all psychological schools can be found to fit into one category. Evolutionary psychology is a good example of a school that cannot be placed in one force, and as previously mentioned, it is an approach that at the least discounts the validity of transpersonal experience. Another school that also does not fit into one force, yet readily accepts much that is considered transpersonal, is the 'Psychology of Religion'. Although it is not transpersonal and does not fulfil the criterion of a humanistic school, it could be wrongly construed of being transpersonal psychology because of the thrust of much of its areas of exploration.

## The psychology of religion

Though not situated solely within the context of the third-force paradigm, the 'Psychology of Religion' is a school in its own right that came into being in the USA and Europe in the early 1920s. I discuss it at this point for, like much in the third force, the psychology of religion examines, as its name suggests, areas such as meaning and faith, though in the context of religion. As well as the interface of religion and the individual it also addresses the social relevance of religion, its effect from and upon social systems and communities.

In my definition of transpersonal psychology I pointed out the variance between the various schools of pastoral counselling/therapy and transpersonal psychotherapy. The forma are often linked to the psychology of religion; however, as Wulff (1997) points out, contemporary thinkers within the field are increasingly in favour of using the terms 'spiritual' and 'spirituality' to replace religion and religious, finding them more apt in the present milieu. (This, I would suggest, could engender confusion regarding the field's classification within psychological taxonomy.) He also recognizes that post-modern thinking influences the psychology of religion, and it is this that allows for competing views.

Moreover, from within the field itself there is no agreement concerning where it belongs: is it a sub-field of psychology or does it in fact sit more securely within religious studies, or a branch of theology? This confusion or disagreement is highlighted by the fact that exploration has taken place within both fields; however, developments within one may not be known or are inaccessible to the other.

Although some scholars such as Kelly (1991) and Bidwell (1999) recognize the important contribution that transpersonal thinking can offer those who are situated with the psychology of religion, the inclusion of, or reference to transpersonal theorists is scant, because the majority of theorists and researchers who identify themselves as working in the field, such as Charet (1993), see the psychology of religion as not needing the insight that transpersonal models bring, instead focusing upon other areas such as the study of the psychological origins of the religious beliefs of individuals who are explicitly religious.

The above, however, as I have shown, is not a position held by all in the field, therefore I am keen to make clear that whilst the psychology of religion differs from transpersonal psychology they both endeavouring to explore some similar areas, such as the seeking of meaning and ultimate values. With the foregoing in mind I include a brief overview of the psychology of religion in order to further explore the differences and similarities between the two schools.

Like transpersonal psychology the psychology of religion is an immense field with an extensive literature; I found Wulff (1997) and Fontana (2003) give good though contrasting accounts of the field, its interests and scope. Fontana (2003) brings to my mind a more contemporary account and explores areas such as mystical experience that many with a transpersonal orientation are also interested in. His approach to exploring the subject is influenced, I am sure, by being a Professor of transpersonal psychology. Wulff (1997), on the other hand, takes a more traditional approach to portraying the field; as well as offering an in-depth definition of the psychology of religion, he gives an overview that spans the works of thinkers from the beginnings of the twentieth century, such as William James (1902), to the present day. He includes the work of well-known theorists, such as Gordon Allport (1897–1967), a devout Episcopalian, and Rollo May (1909–1994), who served as a Congregational Minister before he studied for his doctorate in clinical psychology.

The importance of May's contribution to existential psychology as one of the founding fathers of the American Existential Psychology School has already been stated, as has the recognition that his contribution is considered to be of major influence in the whole of humanistic school.

However, the claims that influential thinkers belong to one school or another are common throughout the whole of the psychological literature. And it is not too uncommon to find schools competing through claims that the thinking of individuals belongs to their discipline. The work of Rollo May is not a good case in point although his work is recognized and claimed to be influential by the existential/humanistic schools it has also undoubtedly offered the psychology of religion the means to explore the relationship between religion and constructs such as meaning and motivation.

In my own examination of the psychology of religion's literature I found that for many from this school an important task was/is to find methods and procedures by which to 'measure spirituality' (Gorusuch, 1984; Hodge, 2001; Piedmont, 1999; Slater et al., 2001). By far the most commonly used approach is by means of qualitative methodology, with some form of questionnaire being utilized. Slater et al. (2001) recognize that the number of assessment tools (psychometric tests) are increasing. Their own search of the literature recognize accounts of the use of over 125 tools; they also identify that these predominantly rely upon the distinction of intrinsic versus extrinsic religious orientation, a model developed by Allport and Ross (1967). Exploring this work myself I was to find that they were concerned with finding a means to identify two differing religious outlooks that they placed within two different personality structures: 'Extrinsic' and 'Intrinsic' religious orientation.

Extrinsic religious orientation designates a personality structure that is characterized by an individual who is prone to use religion as a means to meet other personality needs, such as security, status or self-justification.

Intrinsic religious orientation designates a personality structure that is characterized by an individual who 'lives his religion' (p. 434). Although the meeting of the aforesaid needs are given more importance, this does not mean that other needs are ignored, because they are of less significance, and can be harmonized with religious beliefs and practices.

With the foregoing in mind I question claims that studies which rely on the measures of intrinsic and extrinsic religious orientation can measure nothing other than religious orientation regardless of the validity or provenance of the methodological approach employed. Furthermore, my own assessment of many of the studies that seek to measure 'religiosity' is that the conclusions drawn are ambiguous, and this is so regardless of the measurement tools used.

Whilst my conclusions are those of a researcher who is not an expert in this field, I concur with Zinnbauer et al. who recognize that scales which seek to quantify meaning in the religious and spiritual realm can provide dubious data due to there being a '... multiplicity of religious and spiritual meanings, self ratings of religiousness and spirituality are likely to yield uninformative and ambiguous data' (Zinnbauer et al., 1999, p. 914).

Moreover, further confusion may be engendered by those in the field, such as Slater et al. (2001, p. 17), who claim spirituality is a post-modern offspring of religion. This I think is an interesting position to take that may in fact highlight the use of linguistic convenience, for spirituality, though commonly linked to religious practice, cannot be placed solely within a religious framework, as religious traditions cannot claim to have a monopoly upon how individuals experience the spiritual/transpersonal, although history is scattered with religious traditions, both orthodox and innovative, that openly profess to do so.

Monopolies, however, as I suggested earlier, do not only surface in religious circles, as they can also be found in the claims of psychological schools. A good example of this is how Rollo May's taxonomic position in psychological classification can be claimed by proponents of the Psychology of Religion Humanistic Psychology and of Existential Psychology. As well as reminding us that psychologists are also human, this may further highlight the complex philosophical and clinical strands that are woven into each force. A state of affaires which can make it difficult to place various 'founding fathers', such as May and Carl Rogers, solely into one force. In fact from today's perspective Maslow, the originator of the four-force taxonomy, would be hard pressed to place as situated within any one school.

Of course thinkers themselves cannot be divorced from the theoretical positions they champion or create. And this is no less true today than in any other era. Therefore, regardless of the field one is situated within, the recognition that post-modernism will influence transpersonal thinking (like all positions) needs to be acknowledged. With this in mind, spirituality will need to be recognized as not exclusively being an offspring of religion, nor the specialized interest of one or two psychological schools. Thereby refuting any claim that the transpersonal can be exclusively the domain of any one school, or be of interest to only one particular body or theoretical cartel that have sole rights to this area of research.

The idea that divergent schools can be utilized to view what this book calls the transpersonal can be found in the literature, and is concordant with thinkers such as Young-Eisendrath and Miller (2000), who do not claim to be situated within one field. Though obviously situated within Jungian analytical theory, they make their influences apparent. They bring together thinkers from developmental psychology, depth psychology (primarily Jungian thinking), religious studies and theology to view the psychology of what they term 'mature spirituality' that is beyond humanism and theism. They posit that mature spirituality is comprised of integrity, wisdom and transcendence. Integrity they see as not only ethical commitment; it also refers to the ability to 'be integrated', the ability to bring together multiple meanings whilst bearing ambiguity and paradox. Wisdom from their perspective is not exclusive to intelligence nor sets of truths. It is, however, sustained and sustaining and not obtainable solely from one source. Transcendence, a familiar theme to Jungian thinkers, refers to expanding the limits of ordinary consciousness with experiences that connect the individual with an expanded symbolic or phenomenal reality to that which is commonly experienced daily. Transcendence they point out is something that is sought by many individuals today through the use of mind-expanding practices. My own experience of addressing the psychological needs of mature students in a large university suggests that mind-expanding and transpersonal phenomena can often be induced through the use of natural entheogens such as *Amanita muscaria* and Psilocybe (Psychedelic mushroom) and illegal class A drugs, such as methylenedioxy-N-methylamphetamine (ecstasy or MDMA) and lysergic acid diethylamide (LSD or Acid), and is explored further in the next chapter.

Having discussed my exploration of the psychology of religion which recognized the potential for confusion that, being seen as either or both a transpersonal approach to psychology or a distinct school in its own right, brings to current psychological discourse, I return to my exploration of the transpersonal in relation to the four forces of psychological taxonomy with a brief summation.

## Widening the net, moving beyond psychology

As it can be seen I have found it fruitful to look towards the first three forces for clues to the philosophies that inform the transpersonal perspective, for each has offered something of worth and value. This I see as supporting Wilber's definition of transpersonal psychology that I quoted earlier, which acknowledges the inclusion of a wide knowledge base drawn from all psychotherapeutic traditions.

> It [transpersonal psychology] fully acknowledges and incorporates the findings of modern psychiatry, behaviorism, and developmental psychology, and then adds, where necessary, the further insights and experiences of the existential and spiritual dimensions of the human being. We might say it starts with psychiatry and ends with mysticism.
>
> (Wilber, 1994, p. x)

Thus far in this section I have primarily concentrated upon revealing how transpersonal psychology makes use of and contributes to the first three forces of psychology. However, to deepen the examination of the theoretical underpinnings of the field will require exploring more than just psychological discourse.

I could argue that Western Orthodox philosophical enquiry is comfortable and familiar with placing its gaze upon 'the modern psychiatry, behaviourism, and developmental psychology' aspects of transpersonal thinking. It is also recognized as providing an academically legitimate means by which to seek an understanding of meaning and existential ontology.

However, the search for and understanding of the 'spirituality' aspect of transpersonal thinking is an area that has not received as much attention, though other disciplines such as religious studies have spent considerable effort in the exploration of spirituality. Eastern philosophical thought on the other hand has a long history of including spirituality within metaphysical enquiry.

With the above in mind it makes sense that transpersonal theory, as we know it today, began to be popularized in the 1960s. This era bought the possibility of global travel for many, whilst the teachings of Eastern philosophy also became available, if not in vogue in the West. Up until this time Eastern thought was only studied by a few intellectuals and not widely understood or known about. Earlier in this chapter I recounted how changes in cultural attitudes made possible the advent of the human potential movement and Humanistic psychology. I would like to suggest here that concurrently with changes in social mores there was also a flowering of interest in Eastern philosophy. This interest also brought a growing interest in and a more widely recognized acceptance of philosophical traditions such as Vedic and Buddhist thought. Up to this point in time such foreign ideas had only been explored by an elite few in the West. Moreover, this popularizing of what were then alternative traditions also brought a flowering in the practising of numerous spiritual techniques such as meditation, tai chi and yoga.

As I was not an adult in the late 1950s and the 1960s I can only imagine how cultural changes such as those I recount above could have influenced popular thinking.

My own experience of Eastern culture has certainly broadened my mind (maybe in 1960s parlance, they could be described as mind-expanding experiences). I have, in fact, had the privilege of working and travelling extensively, spending long periods in countries such as India and Thailand as well as others that are also considered to be in the East, such as Mongolia and Siberia. Commonly I have found that in the East, religious (spiritual) practice is more evident in daily public life, within all socio-economic strata, than in the West. Moreover, the endeavours to include spirituality in daily life are more apparent.

This acceptance of spirituality as an aspect of reality, or even reality itself, that brings forth acceptance of phenomena which are considered spiritual and incorporated in daily life, is concordant with the understanding of all the transpersonal theorists that I have discussed.

## Bringing together East and West

In the previous chapter I recounted how the inclusion of Eastern philosophical traditions, such as Buddhist thought and attitudes, Sufic thought, the Hindu Vedic system and the Kabala, has influenced and shaped transpersonal psychology. And how many influential thinkers such as Perls et al. (1994), Nelson (1996), Walley (1996), Epstein (1996), Almass (1996) and Vaughan (1985) turned to Eastern philosophy in order to create theories of human nature which were consequently included in their psychological models. Moreover, no one school or tradition can claim to have been 'the' major contributor to transpersonal theory. Though each is distinct and unique, bringing its own heritage often spanning thousands of years, all however share a similarity in that they all contend in differing fashions that reality and therefore mankind's make up is purely defined by materialistic dualism, a viewpoint that is unable to accept or recognize anything which cannot be measured by physical means. The influence that each of the above Eastern philosophical traditions has contributed to the philosophical underpinnings of transpersonal psychology as a whole field has offered beyond doubt a rich and varied perspective from which to view mankind's psycho/spiritual make up. However, another influential field is the Western esoteric tradition, Blavatsky (1966) and Bailey (1970), which to the casual observer may look as if it is an Eastern philosophical tradition. This worldview is most evident in the work of transpersonal thinkers, such as Assagioli (1993) and Wilber (1990, 1993b,c, 1997, 2002).

Without elaborating further I think it is clear that this inclusiveness has also supported and given rise to much of the philosophical basis of transpersonal thinking, whilst also influencing the Jungian, humanistic and existential schools.

## Mysticism's contribution

Though Eastern philosophy and the Western esoteric tradition have influenced transpersonal thinking, I feel it important to recognize that there is another field that has also influenced transpersonal thinking, namely mysticism, which can without careful scrutiny be confused with Western esotericism and Eastern philosophical thought.

Zales (1978) recognizes that mystical experience is distinct from magical, visionary, metaphysical, occult or esoteric experience. Mystical practices can be regarded as offering the potential of a direct relationship with ultimate reality, and it is this that separates the mystic from individuals who subscribe to institutional religions and various esoteric practices that offer the promise of the mediation of ultimate reality through others.

He posits that mysticism serves psychic needs, though he is not clear on which needs these may be; he does point out, however, that mystics could be conceived as undergoing what could be misinterpreted as schizophrenic breakdown, a concept I discuss in depth later on when exploring the concept of spiritual emergency. His reasoning argues that psychotic breaks and mystical states both present symptoms that could be seen as a retreat from outer to inner reality. He contends, though, that they differ in three important ways. First mystics seek inward retreat in a facultative not obligatory manner (Vaughan's (1985) inward arc); secondly, for the mystic this journey is partial and not complete and thirdly mystics often find it desirable (and are able) to associate with others who share similar experiences and worldviews.

Forman (1998) too looks towards mysticism for answers to transpersonal experience, though he concentrates upon mysticism in relationship to consciousness. He speculates that mysticism may in fact represent a simple form of human consciousness, a pure consciousness event or PCE.

He identifies three distinct types of pure consciousness events.

- A wakeful but contentless (non-intentional) experience, where an individual remains awake and alert, emerging with the clear sense of having had an unbroken continuity of experience.
- A dualistic mystical state (DMS), where an individual has a sense on a permanent or semi-permanent basis of being in touch with their own deepest awareness. He likens this experience to 'a silence at one's core', whilst remaining conscious of the external sensate world. In this 'state' awareness itself is experienced as silent and as separate from its intentional content.
- The last is a state where an individual experiences becoming unified with external objects, a connection with things or lack of boundaries between consciousness and object.

The above three descriptions of mystical experience share many similarities with instances recounted and emphasized in the patients' notes of numerous of my clients who have been referred from psychiatrists. These as symptoms in orthodox psychiatric thinking which could very easily be construed as evidence of some form of psychotic episode.

Before moving on, I think it important to note that Forman is keen to emphasize that phenomenology is not science, and describing experience will not offer 'hard scientific proof'. However, he does point out that though phenomenology cannot serve as the sole basis for any theory of reality, it can point in a fruitful direction for metaphysical hypotheses to be generated from phenomenological descriptions.

Zales and Forman are not alone in distinguishing between mysticism and esotericism. Underhill (2001), who I recounted in the previous chapter, provided what is regarded as a seminal inquiry into mysticism and was also keen to distinguish between mystical practices and occult or magical ones. She saw mysticism as a means to surrender gracefully to the transpersonal realm, and the occult and magical practices as an attempt to harness transpersonal energies by means of the will.

From a contemporary perspective this difference may not mean much; however, at the turn of the twentieth century intellectuals in the West were exploring differing traditions that claimed to reveal competing rationales and approaches to transpersonal experience. Arguably the most well known are Aleister Crowley (1998), who offered a perspective that focused upon 'Magic', Alice Bailey (1970) 'Esotericism' and Underhill (2001) 'Mysticism'. Though they are three distinct approaches, they all share similar languages and methods. It is therefore not surprising that this can give rise to confusion.

Moreover, with what can be conceived of as arcane bodies of knowledge, such as mysticism, esotericism and Eastern philosophical thought, contributing to transpersonal psychology, I find it of no surprise that it is a field that the academic community struggles to fit into traditional scientific paradigms. Taken as a whole one way of conceptualizing transpersonal thinking is that it is firmly rooted within a paradigm presenting an epistemology that has moved beyond that of the traditional or orthodox view of science, thus presenting transpersonal psychology as a 'Metapsychology' – a philosophical study of those aspects of psychology that cannot be examined experimentally.

Consequently, transpersonal thinking could be perceived as springing from a philosophical lineage that includes a diverse heritage that does not stand up to the scrutiny of the present day orthodox scientific community, and indeed may be seen as a simple means by which to account for a philosophical position that can justify and include the possibility of transegoic experience. It would be easy, or at the least convenient, to justify this with the claim that, as transpersonal psychology fulfils the criterion of 'Metapsychology', it could just be accepted as a valid body of knowledge on face value.

This could offer the uninformed the potential to see transpersonal thinking as overly simplistic in relation to hard science. This line of thinking, as I have shown, does not present transpersonal thinking as Dennett's 'greedy reductionism'. However, it could be possible to dismiss transpersonal psychology from an orthodox standpoint with the accusation of it being merely greedy metaphysics. An argument that could be hard to refute considering the ease with which most if not all transpersonal theorists and clinicians claim mystical experiences to be one of many valid realms/states of functioning.

To counter this (I think valid) argument, I present a short overview of exploration of consciousness research. Whilst this will not address the justification of the inclusion of mysticism and esotericism within transpersonal psychology, it will illuminate research undertaken in the West that seeks to move beyond everyday functioning without looking to arcane bodies for answers.

Moreover, transpersonal psychology itself could be considered an attempt (like much in the field of psychology) to be an endeavour aimed at understanding consciousness.

## Consciousness research

As previously mentioned in this chapter transpersonal psychology has held an active interest in the field consciousness research, which is an area that over the last 20 or so years has gained recognition as a legitimate field of enquiry. However, the major thrust of this research has been focused upon looking more towards every day consciousness, not into 'altered states of consciousness' – a corner stone of transpersonal psychology.

One obvious thinker from the transpersonal school, who has spent a great deal of effort exploring consciousness and its relationship to the transpersonal, is Wilber (1997), as he draws together with all his work a wide range of disciplines in order to offer 'an integral theory of consciousness'. His model seeks to establish a transpersonal worldview, which includes the whole spectrum of human experience that encompasses the insights offered by 12 distinct disciplines: cognitive science, introspectionism, neuropsychology, individual psychotherapy, social psychology, clinical psychiatry, developmental psychology, psychosomatic medicine, non-ordinary states of consciousness, Eastern and contemplative traditions, quantum consciousness and subtle energies research. He sees each of them as offering an important essential contribution, each of which he incorporates within the whole field. He discusses these disciplines in all his works; however, for a succinct overview of his 'integral theory of consciousness' model I would recommend the article of the same name.

Whilst Wilber's model offers an in-depth exploration of consciousness, he is not the only transpersonal theorist who seeks to 'make sense of' consciousness.

The approach that the transpersonal perspective seeks to explore tends to focus more upon 'altered states of consciousness' with influential thinkers such as Tart (1975) and Grof (1985, 1988). Although transpersonal psychology is less well known than some of the fields in this chapter, and has not built a large research base, thinkers such as Tart and Grof can certainly claim to pursue an active interest in finding methodologies that would be acceptable to the prevailing epistemological orthodoxy despite the subject matter under investigation.

Although I have started by bringing attention to the obvious place that consciousness research holds in the transpersonal field, I am aware that the purpose of this chapter is to investigate the theoretical underpinnings of the transpersonal approach and not to discuss transpersonal theory itself. Therefore, I will concentrate more upon how research into consciousness has informed the field rather than the field itself, as doing so may support a deeper understanding of the work of the various transpersonal theorists who are presented in the next chapter.

Consequently, for a discussion of the insights that consciousness research can bring to bear on making sense of the claims of the transpersonal movement, I would like to quote Chalmers (1995, p. 200), one of the best-known figures in the field. I do so as he makes a profound, though simple statement, 'Consciousness poses the most baffling problems in the science of the mind. There is nothing that we know more intimately than conscious experience, but there is nothing that is harder to explain'. He (1995, 1996) can also be credited with originating the claim that there are two distinct areas of questioning in consciousness research, 'Hard and Easy problems'. Easy problems are typified by seeking answers to processes like vision and memory, whereas hard problems relate to feelings and phenomenal consciousness (quilla). This, however, is not a position that is acceptable to all. For instance Dennett (1996), another 'big gun', sees this form of categorization as not being a useful contribution to research.

In relation to this study I, instead, find it a useful vantage point, though the delineation between the easy and hard problems would certainly place transpersonal thinking beyond both the easy and hard problem category, simply because it focuses upon transegoic functioning.

Therefore, to my mind I would need to create a third set, that of very hard problems. Having added in one brief sentence to the already complex field, I feel it necessary to at the least explain my bold assertion that some aspects of consciousness, particularly transpersonal phenomena, are not adequately described using prevailing orthodox epistemology, which is currently by and large already preoccupied with the gargantuan task of grappling with everyday consciousness.

With the above caveat I feel a closer inspection of the whole field of consciousness research is helpful, particularly so, as it consists of a mind field of conflicting views that stem from a plethora of epistemological strands. As in my portrayal of other areas of research allied to the transpersonal thinking, I am aware that I could be accused of gross oversimplification, for I have placed my findings for the sake of ease in three broad categories: Biology/physics (Neuroscience), Philosophy (particularly Metaphysics) and Quantum Physics.

Having begun to explore in the previous chapter the relationship between the transpersonal and neurological system functioning, I return to neurobiological research in order to explore the relationship between consciousness and physiological functioning. If this is successful as a direction of enquiry, it offers the possibility of establishing connections between consciousness and physiological functioning. This may help in the legitimizing of transpersonal psychology in the traditional academic community. It could do so by explaining many of the phenomena such as mystical union and other altered states of consciousness that many transpersonal thinkers posit as valid constituents of reality.

However, for me exploring neuroscience as a means to understand how consciousness arises brings epistemological conflict. For I would be viewing consciousness solely within the present epistemological orthodoxy and therefore could only conclude that as all contemporary neuroscience is based on classical physics. I could only view consciousness as phenomena governed by the brain enslaved by a set of mechanical laws. The logical outcome would be that I would be unable to explain how consciousness arises, since there is no consciousness in classical physics.

Simply put, within present Cartesian methodologies and epistemology – the prevailing mind-set – it is eagerly accepted that the science of classical physics defines for us what is meant by the term 'physical reality', readily agreeing that anything that cannot be physically measured is treated as not having physical reality. Therefore, if it is not possible to physically measure something such as consciousness, then it either does not exist, or must be treated as being non-physical.

To me it suggests that this approach is fundamentally methodologically flawed for it is seeking to look at consciousness using a tool that does not accept consciousness as a valid concept.

Nevertheless, as I show there is considerable advancement being made in the measurement of brain function and many hypotheses created.

However, these are speculations regarding correlates of consciousness and brain activity. Crick and Koch (1990) typify this field of research, which is termed 'the neuronal correlate of consciousness' or 'NCC'. The hypothesis being tested is that NCC is likely to consist of particular neurons in the brain and particular patterns of activity. The eventual outcome of such research would be the ability to predict phenomenal states based on physiological states.

Crick and Koch are not lone figures in some obscure branch of science, as Solms and Turnbull (2002) and Fenwick et al. (2001), whom I mentioned in the previous chapter, are also researchers who are interested in the interface of consciousness and neurobiology, a field that includes well-known respected 'brain theorists' such as Baars (1988).

He sees the brain as a large group of separable, very specialized systems that are unconscious for much of the time during which they operate. His work, however, seeks answers solely to the cognitive aspects of consciousness without mention of qualia, qualitative experience.

His 'global workspace theory of consciousness' suggests that the brain is composed of many different parallel processors (modules), each of which is capable of performing some task on the symbolic representations that it receives as input. The modules are flexible in that they can combine to form new processors capable of performing novel tasks, and can also reform and subside into smaller component processors. In terms of this study I see his work as another attempt to explain how something is made conscious, 'the mechanics', not the key question of 'what' is consciousness. However, his theory in relationship to transpersonal experience could account for how phenomena are recognized as awareness.

Dennett (1991), yet another well-known figure, offers a view of consciousness that is at odds with transpersonal thinking, and his approach is clearly situated within a reductionistic view to science. His 'neurophilosophy' posits that consciousness and subjective experience are solely the function of neural nets (groupings of interconnected neurones).

Having given a brief account of the work of thinkers who do not recognize, or at the least ignore, phenomena that are routinely considered transpersonal, I now turn to others who do include the transpersonal and phenomena that are commonly regarded as 'non-ordinary states of consciousness' as a valid area of research.

Fischer (1978, 1986) is another neurobiological researcher, yet his thinking is not situated solely within a reductionistic deterministic paradigm. The thrust of his theory is not towards general consciousness, for he explicitly explores the interface between transpersonal experience and neurobiological functioning. He presents a theory that offers the argument that the mystical and ecstatic states of consciousness familiar to transpersonal thinking have a direct link to sub-cortical arousal. He presents a schema that places mystical and ecstatic states in a circular continuum that present two ways to the attainment of 'Self' (his description of which concurs with my use of the transpersonal). Within this model movement from individual 'I' consciousness towards universal consciousness 'Self' can be possible in two directions. The first, 'Ergotropic Arousal', brings increased activity of the sympathetic nervous system. He sees this as characteristic of creative, psychotic and ecstatic states. Movement in the other direction of his circular continuum is seen as 'Trophotropic Arousal', hypoarousal (reduced stimulation) that he sees as occurring in and characteristic of meditative states such as those promulgated by many of the differing yogic schools and world's religions. Placing the continuum within a circular framework accounts for the concept that direct experiencing of 'Self' (transpersonal) can be achieved as the outcome of both extremes of 'Ergotropic' and 'Trophotropic Arousal', even though they represent opposing physiological processes.

Still keeping within the neurobiological framework Fischer is not alone in his interest in consciousness including aspects that fall outside of normal experience.

Newberg et al. (2001) claim to have found correlates of mystical or religious experiences in the brain through employing single positron emission computed tomography (SPECT). Their findings reveal significant changes in the activity of numerous areas in the brain in subjects who were studied whilst reporting that they were experiencing peak experiences that had been engendered and reached through meditation.

Though their findings reveal hard evidence (it is commonly accepted that radioactive isotope do not lie, borrow theoretical constructs from others for convenience, nor fudge results), I consider their findings to have a basic methodological flaw, one that concerns 'scientific' validation. A challenge that I think besets all studies that explore higher consciousness, namely 'how do we really know the subjects are experiencing higher consciousness?'

Their research identified changes in the brain activity of subjects (Tibetan Buddhists monks and Franciscan nuns) who through self-report claimed to be experiencing what this study has identified as transpersonal consciousness. Their findings confirmed that the subjects were highly skilled in doing something that required the use of parts of the brain not used, or not used as much, when not experiencing phenomena not reported as being transpersonal.

They assert that their findings proved that the transpersonal experience of the subjects was 'real' and not simply delusional. I would like to agree with this conclusion as providing a means for transpersonal experiencing to be recognized by the traditional academic community. However, I cannot, for scientifically detectable changes in brain physiology cannot be regarded as reliable indicators of higher consciousness or any other transpersonal phenomena. Though they do give hard data confirming that changes in brain activity are correlates to self-reported transpersonal phenomena, thus confirming that something (yet not to sure what) is going on, and is not the product of a delusional mind.

Having looked towards the literature regarding neurobiological research and transpersonal consciousness, what emerged was that in today's neurobiological research climate techniques that employ 'cutting edge technology', such as SPECT , seem to be the 'flavour of the month', and that these cutting-edge, high-tech methods have eclipsed simpler, older and less high-tech measurement tools, such as simple machines that measure the electrical activity of the brain by placing electrodes on the scalp, such as Electroencephalography (EEG). However, as Austin (1999) points out, though now considered a simple brain activity, EEG is one of the easiest brain parameters to measure, and is still the most commonly studied correlate of higher consciousness. Indeed it has been the tool of choice for much of the research regarding the affect that meditation has upon cerebral functioning.

Whilst brain function correlates for transpersonal experience may be revealed by the use of low- or high-tech means, this is not the only avenue employed by those who look towards the neurobiological for answers.

Ornstein (1992), for instance, presents a model that offers a rationale for a wide range of the experiences, ones that range from everyday functioning to the transpersonal. He developed the now well-known and commonly accepted proposition that human beings have a 'Bifunctional' brain (Gazzaniga, 1970; Hoppe, 1978; Zdenek, 1986) which comprises two distinct modes of knowing that employ different mechanisms and functions in differing ways: one is related to the functioning of the left cerebral hemisphere and operates primarily through a rational–intellectual mode. This functioning mechanism is concordant with the orientation to science, enquiry, and knowledge acquisition that I equated with the Cartesian/Newtonian stance, the positivistic.

The second distinct mode is related to the functioning of the right cerebral hemisphere and operates in a primarily intuitive–holistic mode. Unlike the first, this functioning mechanism is concordant with non-empirically testable methods of knowing such as intuition, insight and illumination, all of which, transpersonal researchers such as Braud and Anderson (1998) claim, can offer ideal mechanisms by which to explore the transpersonal.

These two modes of knowing can be seen as two distinct forms of consciousness or, as Ornstein suggest, a 'Bimodal Consciousness'. Though this consciousness operates in differing ways, he makes clear that to view the two modes of consciousness as completely separate and distinct from one another is limiting, for they do not compete. Yet, for the sake of clarity it can be useful to examine each independently, particularly for our rational–empirical mode of knowing. However, relying solely on the rational–analytic mode of consciousness can lead to creating conceptual boundaries that are too firmly set, potentially obscuring interrelationship, the heart of intuitive–holistic ways of knowing. Consequently bimodal consciousness is best–viewed through the lens of bimodality.

With this entreaty in mind, examining the first mode (modus operandi) will reveal a paradigm that is familiar to orthodox Western ways of thinking that conceive 'truth' through direct observation or hypotheses that are testable by rigorous forms of logic and the use of methodologies that prove or disprove them.

Pivotal to this mode is that things are expected to have a beginning, middle and end, a linearity and sequentiality. A good example is the importance that is placed upon the structuring of time as having a past, present and future, and the use of an analytic mode of verbal discourse. This aspect of bimodal consciousness is adept at comparing and contrasting, measuring one variable/aspect with another.

We move now to the other mode (modus operandi) of bimodal consciousness – the intuitive–holistic – that can be conceived as involving 'reality' being experienced as timeless and not readily communicated through verbal representation. In this mode the linear and conceptual characteristics of language are a poor means by which to depict lived experience. In this mode the symbolic and present-centredness (immediacy) is focal, allowing patterns to be comprehended as entire wholes and not discrete elements that create wholes. Moreover, the possibility that paranormal phenomena such as extrasensory perception exist can be accredited to this mode of consciousness as well as the concept of 'being'.

Ornstein reviews numerous studies in order to account for a substantial body of evidence as empirical confirmation for a bifunctional brain. All of which supports the contention that it is the left cerebral hemisphere that supports a rational–intellectual mode, and the right cerebral hemisphere an intuitive–holistic mode, recounting how injury to the left hemisphere often results in language disturbance and impairment; whereas injury to the right hemisphere will have little effect on language though can hinder spatial–relational sense as well as kinaesthetic abilities and awareness.

Having briefly described Ornstein's two modes of knowing, it could be easy to take Clarke's model, as described in the following section, and speculate that the propositional subsystem of logical cognition and thinking processes can be linked to the left cerebral hemisphere, with implicational cognitive functioning the right.

Ornstein concentrates upon how the two cerebral hemispheres function, the bifunctional brain. And whilst offering potential explanations for mechanisms that may function with transpersonal energies, his work, however, does not concentrate upon any form of consciousness, instead choosing to focus upon mechanisms employed by consciousness. We may need to turn, therefore, to an allied field to look for answers if, as suggested by many transpersonal theories, reality is comprised of some form of continuum of consciousness.

First, though, it may help to turn towards the work of Jaynes (1976), who is another thinker who looks towards the bifunctional brain, though his perspective stems from consciousness research, and not the mechanisms that consciousness employs.

Jaynes started the concept of mankind possessing bimodal consciousness (not a bifunctional brain). He posited a theory that at first was greeted with scepticism by the philosophical community almost 40 years ago. Now, however, his work is receiving growing recognition by well-regarded researchers such as Dennett (1991). He proposed the theory of the 'Bicameral Mind', a theory that posits that what is now referred to as 'consciousness' is in fact a recent development in mankind's evolution. Consciousness according to this theory may have only developed as recently as 3000 years ago. And he claims that before this period human mentality was distinguished by auditory and sometimes visual hallucinations in which the voice of the Gods issued instructions. Only when this process became internalized and recognized as in fact coming from the individuals' own mind did modern consciousness arise.

A split or dissociation between the lateral hemispheres, the bicameral mind, could account for the consciousness of preconscious peoples he suggests. However, a theory such as this cannot be put to the test, and we may never really know if there was some sort of shift in the consciousness or the functionality of ancient people's brains. This notwithstanding he does though give a reasoned argument by examining historical evidence, particularly from Ancient Greece, Mesopotamia and the Old Testament.

The above, with a methodology based on conjecture and circumstantial evidence, mirrors the methodological approach used by evolutionary psychology. From this vantage point theorists posit that the brain's architecture is the result of adaptations that arose in order to solve specific environmental problems. These adaptations consist of dedicated neural mechanisms (modules) that operate primarily unconsciously and upon specific realms of human experience and function. However, though genetically determined, they require input from the environment for their maturation.[2] Ornstein building upon his earlier work also follows a line of reasoning that is more in accord with those used by evolutional psychologists and conceives that our minds have evolved through adaptive response to help us survive, not to reason.

As my brief exploration of neurobiological research has shown, there are numerous competing theories that are emerging. What I hope is evident from my portrayal of the literature is that though neurobiological research may not offer concrete proof of the existence of transpersonal consciousness, it may offer a deeper understanding of how the brain works. And, as our understanding of neurobiological functioning increases, whether or not it is aided by the advent of progressively more sophisticated technology, it appears to me that at the least it will only offer explanations regarding correlates between consciousness and brain activity. This may not aid our understanding of what has been uptil now, and continue to be, the existence of non-empirically testable theories, the 'meat and potatoes' of much transpersonal thinking.

This leads me to conclude that neurobiological research is unlikely to be the ideal avenue in which to place hope in finding answers that contribute to the validity of transpersonal functioning. Therefore, there is a need to look towards another field to find answers.

---

[2] The concept that genetic determination requires input from the environment is one of the many competing theories that are used by biologists discussing the nature nurture debate. This position is also used by many Evolutionary psychologists when building their theories.

## The new sciences

With rare exception, a reductionist approach to consciousness is the norm in neurobiological thinking, as with many of the fields explored so far. However, the next field I present is situated within the so-called 'new sciences', and as the term suggests there is not just one scientific domain that makes up this area, though I concentrate upon Quantum Physics. I do so as it offers a view of the world that repeatedly suggests that phenomena often described as being transpersonal are beyond Newtonian and Descartian/Cartesian views of the philosophy of science, or that at least they are poorly described by them.

New sciences are, however, better described by, and understood in relation to the likes of Quantum Physics, which has replaced mechanistic/positivistic outlooks with a view of the universe that is more fluid and relativistic. These commonly embrace at the least unpredictability and the acceptance that boundaries can be permeable or elastic, and culminate in the view that matter is suffused with consciousness. This as a basic tenet also means that fields which I have already accounted for can be once again explored from a different perspective.

For example, Walker (1998) could be seen to look for a bridge between neurobiological research and the worldview offered by Quantum Physics. He asserts that quantum mechanical processes are associated with the brain's functioning, and specifically with synaptic activity. His is not the only voice to make similar claims. Jibu and Yasue (1995) posit that the brain functions as a unified system and base their thinking on the properties of quantum field theory. Another who recognizes that classical, algorithmic neural dynamics are insufficient for understanding the operation of the brain is Penrose (1994). He, however, comes to this conclusion by positing that consciousness must be a quantum phenomenon because neurons are too big to account for consciousness. However, the thinking of Karl Pribram (1971), who posits brain functions utilize holographic properties, may offer the most convincing postulate for a brain functioning being best-described by Quantum Physics. Therefore, I am going to explore his contribution to the field in greater detail after recounting how the universe, both seen and unseen, is perceived from the Quantum Physics perspective.

## The quantum perspective

Before investigating the contribution that the quantum perspective can bring as a field that underpins or supports transpersonal theory, it is valuable to recognize that, when viewing the world through the lens that quantum mechanics offers, it is important to bear in mind that, whilst 'Observer-dependant theories' are the most prevalent and well known, they do not present the only quantum perspective.

Simply put, observer-dependence suggests that 'reality' only 'exists' when 'observed'. Thus, from this perspective, if the transpersonal realm does in fact exist, it could only do so if an individual or group of individuals were to observe it. A position that would be at odds with the common transpersonal contention that the transpersonal is a realm that, as an integral aspect of reality, exists independently of any consciousness that experiences it. However, the positing of 'modal interpretations', which are observer-independent theories, has increased since the 1970s. Vermaas (1999), describing modal interpretations, recognizes that they ascribe quantum mechanics as providing,

> ...a universal theory of nature. Quantum mechanics thus applies not only to elementary particles, but also to macroscopic systems like measurement devices, planets, cats and elephants... modal interpretations give rules to ascribe properties to systems at all times. This property description depends on the states of systems and applies regardless of whether or not measurements are performed. States of systems thus have a meaning in terms of properties possessed by systems and not merely in terms of outcomes of measurements.
>
> (p. 23)

The above then gives rise to the possibility that reality offers the potential of including the likelihood that an observer functions as a participator. This will then offer the possibility that they will affect reality. This in turn leads to the assumption that if the observer is aware of their effect they could in principle be able to change it, or in some way compensate. This viewpoint is in stark contrast to classical physics where the observer sits outside the system, as well as the view offered by traditional quantum mechanics where the observer is a participator whose presence in the system *will* perturb it.

In relation to the transpersonal, all the foregoing could then support the idea that the transpersonal realm is not some form of static thing that can only be experienced as 'something' outside oneself. Instead, it can be conceived of as being more like a field and experienced as a 'part' of oneself, whilst concurrently being outside of oneself, an apartness/inclusion that cannot be conceived of using the confines of subject–object separation. This then places reality and the consciousness that perceives reality as being in some form of relationship that cannot subscribe to Cartesian laws.

## The quantum self

Although it is not common to find discussions that include both Quantum Physics and transpersonal psychology, Zohar (1991) is one thinker who looks towards a quantum mechanical view of consciousness that includes the transpersonal as an integral component.

Simply put, Zohar conceives reality as being a field of potential and that consciousness is created. Whilst this may seem at first glance somewhat impractical or implausible, she presents a well thought out argument for her claims. Taking the first – reality is a field of potential – offers the view that reality is a co-created process of interaction which is constantly unfolding. This perspective recognizes mankind's consciousness as being both particle-like and wave-like, thus having a relationship to reality that is separate (particle-like) and also interrelated (wave-like). This view mirrors the central concept of quantum mechanics that shows that light and matter exhibit properties of both waves and of particles, wave-particle duality.

However, the contention that humans demonstrates quantum effects at first would be discounted by anyone with a rudimentary understanding of Quantum Physics, simply because quantum effects only become apparent on a macroscopic scale in supercooled conditions, temperatures near absolute zero ($-273.15°C$), and the human being is unable to survive such conditions. In order to account for her claims she turns towards the work of Herbert Frohlich (1905–1991), a pioneer in 'superstate physics' who examined how quantum coherence can exist and play a role within biological functioning.

Zohar relies upon his work to give a possible explanation for her contention that consciousness is created and is best described in terms of Quantum Physics. At normal (body) temperatures, when energy is pumped into electrically charged molecules, a threshold of excitation is reached beyond which the molecules begin to vibrate in unison as they

> ...pull themselves into the most ordered form of condensed phase possible – a 'Bose-Einstein condensate'... (and) that the many parts which go to make up an ordered system not only behave as a whole,

but *become* whole – their identities merge or overlap in such a way that they lose their individuality entirely.

(pp. 65–66)

This she contends creates a backdrop of consciousness/coherence that also supports the idea that consciousness does not originate in matter. Moreover, it also points towards reality being relational.

It is easy to liken these highly condensed phases to descriptions of higher or transpersonal consciousness that many transpersonal theorists talk of, a good example being Wilber's (2000a) transpersonal band, which he posits is the most ordered (coherent) polarity of his spectrum.

Having claimed that reality is a field of potential in which it is possible to find that atoms and individuals can lose their individuality, Zohar also builds into her model explanations concerning partness/separation. She reasons that internal conflict within systems (less coherence) will lessen the overall amount of energy available to the system. The obvious outcome is that those systems that contain the least energy are less likely to be able to achieve or maintain a condensed state. With this contention it is also easy to find parallels with many transpersonal theories; turning once again to Wilber's model (1990, 1993a) this viewpoint would give credence to the notion that pathology or development arrest/failure can occur within any fulcrum.

Until introducing the quantum perspective I have primarily given account of consciousness being in some way connected to the individual, particularly the brain. Though, with the introduction of the quantum perspective we can now speculate that consciousness, including transpersonal consciousness, could have a universal character and not be bound to individual sentience.

## Jung, post-Jungians and quantum effects

The foregoing would be in accord with transpersonal thinking as well as explain the Jungian concept of the collective unconscious (1959). Previously I recognized that from the early 1930s Jung's thinking was influenced by the work of his friend Wolfgang Pauli, and although Jung was not to utilize a physicist's vocabulary the influence of quantum thinking can be found in much of his work. A good example is the possibility of the existence of non-local, acausal quantum fields that could only be explained by phenomena such as synchronicity, an abiding interest of Jung's.

Care here must be taken though, as Jung was not interested in synchronism – the simultaneous occurrence of two events, a simple chance or happenstance. His interest was in meaningful coincidence, for instance that of a physical state, or event, and a psychic event where there is no causal relationship of one to the other. A good example would be when an inwardly perceived event such as a dream, or premonition, has a correspondence in external world; simply put, the inner image of premonition has 'come true' with no hope of causality offering an explanation. Jung (1974) claimed that these phenomena could only be put down to the activated archetypal processes in the unconscious and thus subject to laws that transcend time and space.

From this vantage point gone are the rules of Cartesian effect. For instance, movement is no longer something quantifiable that measures matter travelling at a calculable speed through space, in an in-between, from a point of departure to a point of arrival. Reality, from a quantum perspective, does not recognize the concept that movement can only happen if there is a 'between' and time interval. Instead movement can be considered to be instantaneous, as electrons do jump from one energy state to another, depending on the amount of quanta (energy packets) they have absorbed or released.

The influence of quantum perspective in Jungian thinking is still very much alive today with post-Jungians such as Mansfield and Spiegelman (1989) looking towards the transferencial relationship as an interactive field condition displaying quantum phenomena.

They are not, however, the only thinkers who are influenced by both Jungian thought and Quantum Physics. Another theorist whose work is influenced by both is Arnold Mindell (2000), the father of process-orientated psychology, POP. He trained originally as a physicist and looks towards both Quantum Physics and psychology to explain how psychological processes inform and create what we experience as reality.

He builds upon the thinking of an eminent physicist Hugh Everett (1930–1982). Everett (1973) posited a theory (the Everett relative-state) that offers an interpretation of the 'collapse of the wave function', one of the cornerstones of Quantum Physics, in which something exists in many states but then collapses into one state when observed. His premise is that reality is in fact comprised of many parallel realities (worlds), all of which exist and are equally valid. This then offers us and Irwin Schroedinger's cat the mind-twisting thought that it could be *both* alive *and* dead before it is observed, and that reality (say a wave function) does not actually collapse but that you slip into, or participate in, one of the realities while the others continue to exist simultaneously.[3]

Mindell (2000), building upon this, suggests that as we begin to focus on something we see its most *probable* state, the one that most corresponds to the observer's culture and consensus reality. According to his thinking all reality is an aspect of a multitude of other possible realities (all of which exist simultaneously); however, we choose one and *marginalize* the others. Bluntly put, as soon as I recognize or interpret something as 'a' or 'b' all of its other possible states have been marginalized (c, d, e, etc.). Nevertheless, though other states cannot be recognized, it does not mean that they do not exist just because I am not focusing upon them.

The above position in relation to the question raised by this study could suggest that transpersonal phenomena are just one of many competing constituents of reality. The logical outcome being that individuals engaged in these 'worlds' could be well served by therapists who inhabit or at least are not hostile to the same world.

As shown, quantum theory offers possible interpretations for the mind–body problem. Stapp (1996) made the very clear statement that 'Quantum theory is essentially a rationally coherent theory of the interaction of mind and matter, and it allows our conscious thoughts to play a causally efficacious and necessary role in brain dynamics'. Taking this as possible, I would posit that mind and/or matter that includes transpersonal energy would equally affect brain dynamics, and thus deserve exploration in the therapeutic environment.

However, whilst the 'quantum perspective' may offer a vantage point that provides a useful means from which to understand or at least accept transpersonal phenomena, it may not be an ideal perspective for the majority of practicing psychologists. This is not because the field is unable to offer scientific validation and hard evidence, unlike many of the bodies of knowledge I have discussed such as mysticism, for as a branch of physics the 'quantum perspective' uses the tools of empirical science. Nevertheless, it can be difficult for those of us without a post-graduate grounding in the hard sciences to make sense of the mathematical formulae that validate this field, and thus find it no easier to decipher than ancient Egyptian hieroglyphs.

---

[3] Though this position can at first sight be seen as inhabiting the further reaches of science fiction it in fact is held in high regard by many prominent physicists such as Stephen Hawking and Murray Gell-Man.

Although the foregoing may put many lay readers off, the 'holographic model', or 'holographic paradigm', as it is sometimes referred to, may be more accessible to a wider population. Like Zohar's model of the quantum self, it too claims that reality is participatory, a co-created universe, and also springs from the quantum perspective and consciousness/neurobiological research. It offers a model that whilst having academic creditability/respectability is a perspective that could claim to be able to portray a transpersonal element in accounts of reality that are easier understood by the layman, and may make more sense to psychology graduates whose studies have commonly been situated within the humanities.

## The holographic model

The holographic model is attributed to the work of two respected scientists, the eminent quantum physicist David Bohm (1980, 1987) and the renowned neurophysiologist Karl Pribram (1971). Interestingly, whilst working from two very different directions, these two researchers independently, and from differing fields, came to the strikingly similar conclusion that reality has holographic properties.

Whilst both came to similar conclusions, Bohm is perhaps the best known of the two. This may be in part to due to his research spanning several fields and directed towards 'reality in general', as opposed to Pribram, whose research is more confined to one field, neurophysiology. With this in mind, I will explore more of Bohm's thinking, though by doing so I do not want to overlook Pribram's important contribution, which is summarized below.

Pribram from the neurophysiologist stance became convinced, through his research into consciousness and brain functioning, that the brain stores memories in 'non-specific areas' and that memories are in fact distributed throughout the brain as a whole. This can be evidenced in practice by observing a rat once it has been taught to negotiate a maze and then having differing portions of its brain surgically removed received wisdom would suggest that its (pre-surgery) memories of how to run the maze would be destroyed; yet research shows this not to be the case, thus refuting the idea that memories are somehow stored in specific areas of the brain. This experiment and its baffling outcome had stumped neurologists since the 1920s, and it was not until the 1960s that Pribram became the first researcher to realize that distributed memory resembled a holographic record, and that this could then account for the brain's memory store to not need to be localized, as well as the ability to quickly retrieve whatever information is needed from the vast amount of information held, as well as offering a mechanism for the ability to make ordered use of, or translate, the incessant deluge of data it receives via the senses into the concrete world of our perceptions. It takes no big leap then to suggest that if memory is not stored in cells, but rather in wave interference patterns, the brain as a whole may well operate according to the same quantum mathematical principles as a hologram.

However, the importance of the foregoing pales in comparison to the ramifications to our understanding of the brain and the mind when it is put together with Bohm's theory. Doing so will reveal that 'reality', as we perceive it, is in truth a holographic blur of frequencies which are selected by the (holographic) brain which in turn transforms them into the sensory perceptions that we know as objective reality. To put it even more bluntly, what is being suggested is that right now and always your brain is constructing what you know as objective reality, and is doing so by interpreting frequencies that are ultimately projections from an unseen and unmeasurable dimension that is beyond both space and time.

Statements such as the above can be for many bewildering to say the least and in extreme sound utter rubbish. Therefore, to unpack and make sense of such statements requires that we now turn towards Bohm's understanding of the universe in order to not immediately relegate the holographic paradigm to either the waste bin or the mutterings of a deranged mind.

Bohm's conviction that reality has a holographic nature came after many years studying Quantum Physics. His interest was originally fuelled by the contradiction that arises when exploring physics from the vantage points offered by the 'new physics', such as quantum mechanics and the classical perspective of relativity theory. The contradiction is fundamental as each view offers a diametrically opposed explanation of the universe. In simple terms quantum mechanics requires reality to be discontinuous, non-causal and non-local, whereas relativity theory requires reality to be continuous, causal and local.

In search of answers to this fundamental dilemma he looked towards the common attributes that each share, namely some form of undivided wholeness. This in turn led him to focus upon the inter-connectedness of all matter, a position that Quantum Physics can demonstrate, yet cannot explain. Viewing the universe as holographic, however, offers, Bohm claims, an explanation by recognizing that it is an illusion that things are separate, and that instead all constituents of matter are in fact a part of a continuum.

Bohm's interpretation of the nature of physical reality, the 'Implicate Order', is both highly complex and paradoxically exceptionally simple. My five-and-a-half-year-old daughter may well be able to grasp the basic theory with more ease than an average Western adult, as she has not yet been conditioned to understand the world through the lens of Cartesian science. Bohm claims that through the 'lens' of quantum mechanics and relativity theory the world as we know it, regardless of how we measure it, is not a collection of separate objects, but rather an undivided whole that is in perpetual dynamic flux in which all parts merge and unite in one totality. This undivided whole, which is in a constant state of change, can be likened to a kind of invisible atmosphere from which all things arise and into which all things return. He terms this flow the 'holomovement' (on the purely conceptual level this idea has much in common with Neumann's concept of the 'pleromatic' which I discussed earlier in this section). Teasing apart the term 'holo-movement' reveals that he purposefully chose it to denote that 'movement' refers to the two primary features of reality as being in a constant state of change and flux, whilst 'holo' signifies that reality is structured in a manner that can be likened to holography, in that each part of physical reality contains information about the whole. This can be seen in the holographic images that became popular in the last 30 or so years, in which each small portion of the hologram contains information about the entire image. This is in direct contrast to a 'normal' photograph where each small portion of film contains its own unique and correspondingly small part of the total image. It is the bringing together and simultaneously marrying the holographic structure of reality with its perpetual dynamism that begets the holomovement. Bohm, though, whilst proposing that the foregoing explains reality, is aware that it cannot be observed. So then, in order to make sense of this, he offers a *basic postulate* that reality consists of two fundamental features, the explicate order and the implicate order, and that there exists in the universe a hidden sequence, or order, that is present in what to us appears to be chance or randomness.

Exploring the universe from this vantage point reveals that what we look upon as matter is in fact only the apparent manifestation of one of the fundamental features, the explicate order, which in itself is merely the surface appearance of a much greater (in Bohm's terms enfolded or implicate) order most of which is unseen. As it is not measurable it is therefore not recognized by the fields of science I have termed as classical, traditional or orthodox, for they only recognize the explicate order and its attendant structures. This in relationship to this work explains why traditional science, with its focus upon the explicate order is unable to adequately explain transpersonal functioning whilst being able to recognize transpersonal correlates. The foregoing is at first glance a simple theory; yet it has far-reaching implications as it turns on its head all that the Cartesian worldview has striven to uphold. Particularly so if it is recognized that the implicate order is not some form of subtle level of reality that is subordinate to the explicate order. However, my explanation thus far is Bohm's basic postulate; refining his thinking further, he predicted (1987) that, in addition to the implicate order, there is also a superimplicate order. Now the implicate order is likened to a field, with the superimplicate order being a more subtle and complex implicate order, and the explicate order (all that we can see and measure) is created by the effect that is exerted by the superimplicate order on the implicate order.

Although the holographic paradigm can be used to explain 'normal' or everyday phenomena, it may come as no surprise that transpersonal theorists such as Wilber, Nelson and Grof recognize that it can also be used to elucidate the mechanisms behind many of the phenomena that are seen to not fit in the confines of traditional science and are therefore seen as paranormal or mystical experience.

Grof (1985, 1988), in particular, is keen to recognize that traditional neurophysiological understanding of the brain needs to embrace the holographic model, an attitude which would then create a mainstream position which could accept with more ease such phenomena as the collective unconscious, and the archetypal realm, as well as the myriad phenomena which are met during altered states of consciousness.

Nelson (1994) is another transpersonal thinker who also claims that a quantum mechanics perspective is needed in order to explain transpersonal phenomena. He too recognizes that brain functioning can only be described by the holonomic model, 'Data are stored (...) neither in neat rows of boxes, as in the anatomical model, nor in complex circuitry and feedback loops, as in the chemical model, but in *phase relationships*' (p. 155).

Wilber (1990, 1993c), on the other hand, acknowledges that the holographic paradigm, whilst being important, as it reveals the interconnected (interpenetrating and interdependent) structure of all mater (the material plane), merely offers a one-dimensional interpenetration and cannot be applied to all aspects of reality. He questions the assumption that if the inter-connectedness of the material plane is recognized, this then also means that the non-material, the non-physical, constituent of reality, namely the myriad levels of consciousness, will also be similarly connected within the whole. He also aims this concern at non-holographic paradigm theorists who look towards Quantum Physics to answer questions regarding the place of consciousness in reality. These are both those who, like E. P. Wigner (1979), have earned 'orthodox' credibility and those who are considered to be on the 'academic fringe', such as J. Sarfatti (1998).

Wilber considers that just because the mystic and the modern physicist may use the very same words to describe their understanding of reality, this does not mean that they are in fact describing the same reality. For him the mystic is able to encompass a multidimensional reality that includes the physical universe, but only as one of many planes of existence that interact with each other; whereas even the most contemporary physicist is bound by the confines of their field, the investigation of the material world.

The foregoing, however, is not in accord with many who look towards the holographic paradigm to offer answers regarding the possibility that there is some unseen relationship between matter and consciousness. Bohm's own thinking regarding this changed over time. At first he was to shy away from commenting upon a possible link, while later on he postulated that material and informational processes are inextricably entangled and at some fundamental level matter and consciousness are indivisible (Bohm, 1987, pp. 185–186).

In conclusion, it is clear that the holographic paradigm is well able, on a theoretical level, to offer potential answers to the questions regarding the nature of reality, and is able to make use of Quantum Physics on levels other than the sub-microscopic and sub-atomic. However, like much in the transpersonal realm, the mainstream scientific community has not readily embraced the holographic paradigm, even though its originators are well respected, and are considered to be leaders in their respective fields.

Once again, as in the other fields that I have suggested underpin much transpersonal thinking, validation is unable to be met through the means accepted by a Cartesian worldview. And as it is often the case, many instead make correlations between their theories and how the world's religions understand what the 'stuff of reality is'. The holographic paradigm is no exception, and whilst Bohm tends not to explicitly comment upon possible parallels between religious philosophy and the holographic theory, Pribram (2006), however, states that '...spiritual experiences seem to parallel the descriptions of quantum physics' (http://twm.co.nz/pribram.htm). Therefore, it comes as no surprise that there are many who make significant links that they use to confirm that the holographic paradigm proves that spirituality suffuses mater. Arguably the best example of a writer who uses this line of reasoning is Talbot (1992), who looks towards Buddhist, Hindu and Sufic thought to account for this position.

Before concluding with the quantum perspective in its various variants as a means to account for and view reality, I want to point out that with the advent of quantum mechanics the scientific view of the world has changed dramatically from less than a century ago. Nonetheless, human thinking (including the hallowed halls of academe) seems to be still deeply rooted in a cosmology that was being considered at the same time that the prevailing worldview was staggering under the implications of the shocking notion that the world may circle the sun.

This state of affairs is more common in the hard sciences, such as physics and biology, though is not the only perspective available from which to understand the visible world. Whilst the researchers with various forms of measuring tapes claim to be able to tell us what is and is not real, the next field that I portray as having an interest in the study of consciousness, namely philosophy, has also made the same claim and has been doing so for far longer than such upstarts as modern physics and biology.

## Philosophy

As my reader will have undoubtedly noticed, when reviewing the different approaches to consciousness research, as in other areas of this work, there can be considerable overlap and commonality between the findings of the differing and discrete approaches employed to account for theoretical positions.

This is no less true for philosophy, which could be seen by its very nature to be an effort to address the 'whys' of reality as opposed to looking at the 'what is' reality, which may be better served by disciplines such as physics, including quantum views, and biology which focus upon measurable analysis and empirical observation.

However, for fields other than the hard sciences, there is no unified theory or set of principles that all adhere to. This leads to the creation of complex arguments with thinkers fighting for their view.

To add further to the potential for confusion, philosophy by not being confined by empirical observation is free to move beyond 'materialistic dualism', the term that some academic philosophers use to denote what

I have called up to this point the epistemological approach to reality offered by orthodox, classical or traditional science – 'Scientific Realism'. Scientific realism is underpinned by the assumption (recognized as validation) that physical matter is 'reality'. From this viewpoint it is very hard to refute that this assumption is not the 'truth' and therefore this makes it difficult to not use this position to shore up the basic tenet that consciousness can only be regarded as separate from, but dependent upon, reality, the material world.

With the above in mind, and though I have yet to give account of a purely philosophical approach to consciousness, it may come as no surprise that I have already quoted and referred to researchers who consider themselves (and are consensually seen as being) professional philosophers, such as Penrose (1994), Dennett (1991) and Jaynes (1976), in my account of the biological/neurological approach. Their approach to explaining consciousness through creating models and theories that have the possibility of receiving acceptance and academic credibility, makes, to my mind, pragmatic sense, as they relate their findings to concepts and conditions familiar to scientific realism, such as neural nets and neurological functioning.

However, although correlates can be deemed to be important, the assumption that scientific realism adequately describes human nature has already been shown to be in contrast to much that transpersonal thinking promotes.

Nevertheless, it is not just studies and projects lead by those who claim a transpersonal orientation that refute that the present scientific paradigm is an inadequate means to represent human nature, as one can find respected thinkers from the hard sciences who also question this.

Goswami (1995) for instance, is a good example. He is an academic physicist and argues for 'monistic idealism' – a position that recognizes that matter is an expression of consciousness and not separate from it. His thinking sees reality as consciousness manifested

materially, a viewpoint familiar to Platonic thought as well as being in accord with classical Hindu and Buddhist teachings. He also speculates that consciousness could have properties describable as universal, thus explaining phenomena that are of interest to transpersonal psychology and often described as unitary states, such as the experiences of individuals experiencing inter-connectedness, a common theme in transpersonal thinking.

Goswami is not alone in positing that consciousness is the underlying constituent of reality and that space and time are structures within consciousness; others, such as Avery (1995) also take the view that ultimately matter does not exist outside of consciousness.

However, although the viewpoint that suggests that consciousness somehow creates the material would be met with interest, if not acceptance, by many transpersonal thinkers, it is in opposition to more orthodox and better-known theories. For instance, Searle (1992), a well-known and respected theorist, offers a less radical and thus mainstream viewpoint.

His view on consciousness studies also takes a philosophical standpoint, one that agrees with much that neurobiological research uncovers. Although he suggests that the brain causes conscious states, he considers that any identification of conscious states with brain activities is unsound. This potentially confusing position recognizes that correlations can be evidence for causality though are not evidence for identity. Moreover, he states that consciousness differs from other biological phenomena in that it has subjective or first-person ontology.

The work of thinkers such as Searle, Penrose and Dennett are good examples of thinkers situated within the orthodox knowledge base. Others, for example Williams (1996), Calvin (1997) as well as Bateson and Martin (1999), though claiming to be a part of mainstream thinking, explore similar themes approaching the field from differing vantage points. Their thinking, although not situated within the evolutionary psychology school, takes a more 'evolutionally influenced' stance as they seek to illuminate aspects of consciousness such personality and intellect.

## Consciousness research method or madness

It does not take delving too deeply into consciousness research from a philosophical stance to find that it is a field that is full of competing theories. If this was not potentially confusing in itself, in addition to debates that seek to explain what consciousness is, others endeavour to look towards 'research method': how best can consciousness be explored? This is a question that is by no means applicable only to consciousness research, as it also pertains to much transpersonal theory.

Needlman (1993, p. 4) is one thinker who has looked for answers to the methodological challenges that consciousness research begets, and he calls for the need for 'Inner Empiricism as a Way to a Science of Consciousness'. By this he is suggesting that intellect alone is insufficient as a tool for the exploration of consciousness. What he sees as needed is the inclusion of experience. Yet, in the present scientific paradigm, there is a danger that rigorous methodological standards could stifle the very experiences that are open to investigation.

His thinking points towards a philosophical methodology that advocates that to gain knowledge of the outer world one must look within, to our own experience, a theme familiar to transpersonal thinking and central tenet of many Eastern philosophical/religious practices. He recognizes that this approach is contrary to the prevailing philosophical and scientific tradition in the West, which is shaped by the philosophy of Kant. In fact he sees both positivism and scientism as two of the more recent manifestations of the Kantian overestimation of the cognitive capacities of the human psyche. Furthermore, he perceives the Kantian bias of intellectual functioning to have been perpetuated by Freud. A claim that I think could apply to the greater majority of western psychological schools. In contrast he posits that 'great' metaphysicians, such as Plato, certainly based their metaphysical claims regarding reality upon discoveries made by examining their own internal experience. This self-observation, 'Inner Empiricism', would be familiar in many cultures as the practice of meditation. The application of this inner quest as a research methodology will lead the researcher, he affirms, beyond the acquisition of knowledge, beyond theory or explanation, to an experience that is deeply meaningful, which in turn can lead to profound personal transformation.

Even though claims that Freud was biased towards intellectual functioning could offer the opportunity for greater debate, I think it important here to note that 'the founder of modern psychology' in fact endeavoured to explore his own psyche in order to extrapolate his findings to a larger population. And that, by doing so, he formulated much of his theoretical work, which he saw as applicable to the human condition in general and not just one individual or group.

This way of viewing reality, as already mentioned, is regarded by transpersonal thinking as more the norm than some novel or unique approach. It clearly sees mainstream orthodox science as providing an inadequate view of the entire natural world in that it includes only objective phenomena, whilst excluding the subjective phenomenon of consciousness altogether. As this is a view that meets hearty agreement from thinkers who are sympathetic to the transpersonal perspective, it is not too hard to find proponents of alternative research methods to those generally employed.

Wallace (2000), for example, recognizes that objectivism, monism, universalism, reductionism and physicalism have lead to a scientific materialism that has impeded the development of a more integral science of consciousness that treats subjective experience seriously as the complement to third-person research. He questions the prevailing scientific paradigm that claims science can provide an adequate view of the entire natural world that includes only objective phenomena. He calls for the need for a 'Noetic Revolution' that challenges science. However, he speculates that the 'epistemic authority' that relies upon an ideology of scientific materialism and physicalism will resist any attempt to put consciousness and subjectivity into science, fending off efforts that call for at the least a participatory worldview, and certainly one that draws on both inner and outer perspectives.

Wallace is a former Buddhist monk and his views, therefore, may not come as a great surprise; however, his is not a lone voice. In fact, it is not just those who can be seen to support the transpersonal viewpoint that assert that an integral science of consciousness is necessary. Singer (2001), for example, a psychologist and academic, reasons that, as humans are both cognitive agents and sentient experiencers, both areas deserve equal credence in research. However, she points out that man, as cognitive being, is favoured in present intellectual circles, with the exception of existential and phenomenological philosophy and humanistic and transpersonal psychology. Thus cognitive functioning is seen as the core definition of humanity, with scant research of sentience. Sentience can be regarded as the aspects of consciousness that are termed 'Quilla', the intrinsic first personal and non-quantifiable. It is the combination of quilla and cognitive functioning that go to make what ancient Greek thinkers termed psyche. However, Singer points out that ironically it was they who first placed reason at its core. Moreover, she argues that the study of quilla needs to be broad enough to include an entire spectrum of consciousness that would include both the conscious (the awared) and the non-conscious. The latter is an area that is a familiar proposition of the analytic and transpersonal schools.

My own search of the consciousness research literature was to confirm that, outside of existential and phenomenological philosophy and humanistic and transpersonal psychology, research in cognitive functioning is pre-eminent. This may account for the paucity of literature exploring quilla and the inclusion of unconscious/non-conscious factors in consciousness. In fact I found it easier to find material that spoke of philosophy and consciousness by looking for studies and theories that were identified as examining the 'science of mind'.

As in other areas of this work when exploring consciousness I have repeatedly stated that transpersonal thinking is but one of many disciplines that have emerged claiming to be 'good science' that challenge the orthodox worldview of science. And consciousness research in all its forms is a good example of a field that suggests that alternative methods of theory generation are needed. Particularly so as the field of study is not solely focused upon a 'thing' or the resultant phenomena of the interactions of 'things', but it can also be the lens through which things are studied. And, thus like the transpersonal, the field can be considered as a perspective as well as the panorama that the perspective affords. This way of thinking though, is diametrically opposed to how present day science is commonly regarded. With this in mind it will not be surprising that any study that addresses either the transpersonal or 'everyday' consciousness will need to address what exactly science is.

Care, however, must be taken when exploring what science is, as in the present intellectual climate science has offered a mindset which has successfully provided the material comfort familiar to the 'first world', whilst supplying understandable answers to how the observable world functions.

If the foregoing were not enough, orthodox science is a self-sustaining entity as it supplies its own foundations and raison d'être, the benchmarks that support its validity. Thus a container has been created in which all observable and non-observable phenomena can be placed, albeit only if they can be proved to meet the rules of scientific rigour. Therefore, to question this, and consequently the way of thinking that has been instilled in a person since their early schooling, would understandably be seen as questionable to say the least.

## The philosophy of science

Although the view that the transpersonal is a perspective may bring sufficient creditability for many, there are still others, such as Nelson (1996), Wallace (2000), Singer (2001) and Needlman (1993), who need to see, at the least, the inclusion of the transpersonal within a valid scientific domain if not even a transpersonal valid scientific domain in its own right.

However, to be able to claim any credence or be offered the least chance of academic plausibility other recognized means of arguing for validity will be required. In order to do this, it is fruitful to take a very brief look at the philosophy of science: the branch of knowledge that seeks to recognize how theory and knowledge is generated, whilst also exploring how the development of concepts, terms, propositions and hypotheses can explain natural phenomena and thus predict natural occurrences.

Before investigating this field, in order to avoid possible confusion, I would like to briefly mention the philosophical concept of the 'post-modern'.

Although post-modernism is a philosophical postulate, it is not, however, one that is commonly used within the philosophy of science, as it refers to a movement as well as a historical period, which a set of ideas are situated within. And although it is a postulate that can be found in the humanities and social sciences, it includes, unlike the schools studied by the philosophy of science, a large range of fields that are not scientific such as art, literature and design. Thus, post-modernism could be better thought of as a term that speaks more of an interpretation of history and culture than one that examines concepts that seek to reveal scientific truth, such as the philosophy of science. However, for psychology, commonly seen as situated within the humanities, post-modernism can be regarded, without care, to 'be' the prevailing scientific system.

Returning now to the philosophy of science, the principal scientific construct of the present era is termed 'logical positivism'. It's norm, when exploring the world, tends to rely upon reductionism and scientific realism to offer the most perspicuous account of reality through endeavouring to make use of Ockham's razor to explain the world around us as well as mankind's inner world.

Thus, unlike many aspects of transpersonal theory, thinking is explored and then discussed through a lens that needs subject neutral language. This is required so as to be able to describe phenomena (if you prefer 'the laws of nature') in terms that are unambiguous and imprecise. However, this is not solely a linguistic device, as from this stance only the observable can be used to validate theory. Consequently, a valid theory (a true scientific postulate), both linguistically and in reality, can only be entirely defined by observation, and the term used to describe these observations is 'Correspondence-rules' (C-rules). Therefore, any proposed theory that does not contain C-rules can only be seen as a pseudoscience at best.

Whilst C-rules are the norm in the hard sciences, they are also recognized as being important in the humanities. Perhaps the most obvious place in the whole field of psychology to find C-rules is in the use of 'operationalism'. This is particularly so in schools, such as cognitive behavioural therapy, which look more towards the cognitive sciences, for answers regarding the human condition.

Operationalism here refers to utilizing some form of test or process in order to reveal either a C-rule or specific phenomena. The use of standardized tests to confirm or create psychopathological diagnoses is a good example of operationalism, and is a far cry from the diagnostic praxis employed by the majority of transpersonal clinicians, when looking at symptoms that could be transpersonal in nature. However, as operationalism is used to 'define the state of a system in specific terms' it offers the possibility that the influence of transpersonal energies upon the psychology of an individual or group could be codified, and thus present a recognizable set of (transpersonal) C-rules.

The foregoing might make naïve sense to many, as it proffers the temptation to assume that if psychometric tests, for example, can reveal the inner workings of the mind, it would be possible to create transpersonal-psychometric tests to reveal the effect of the transpersonal upon all elements of human functioning. Yet, as the next chapter reveals, healthy transpersonal functioning can be misdiagnosed by the clinicians who may misconstrue the findings that traditional psychometric tests reveal as evidence of disturbing psychopathology. The obvious reason for this is that orthodox clinicians take no account of the possibility of the existence of anything that does not fit their own set of C-rules. Consequently for the clinician/school that has either no awareness of transpersonal functioning or discounts its validity there will be no mechanism that can be employed to recognize its effect upon an individual. Thus any symptom or state can only have a basis and aetiology in non-transpersonal material.

A good example of the use of alternative C-Rules operationalized by utilizing psychometric tests can be found in the psychology of religion. Slater et al. (2001), as I pointed out earlier, found over a 125 tools that have been employed to explore the distinction between intrinsic and extrinsic religious orientation.

Although competing theoretical postulates can be put forward by various fields, they could be reconciled by claiming that this state of affairs represents an 'undertermination of theory'. This is a term that philosophers of science use to denote a situation where competing theories could account for the same phenomenon. In this case, instead of regarding this as an epistemological impasse, it is recognized that a 'TOE', or theory of everything, as mentioned in my exploration of consciousness research, is unlikely to be a viable proposition, particularly so in psychological schools that subscribe to seeing themselves as situated within the present era's post-modern perspective.

Yet, even though this is possible, in the present scientific climate transpersonal theories are still likely to be considered at best little more than pseudoscience, as they are unable to be described by the

C-rules recognized by the dominant epistemological hegemony logical positivism.

If the foregoing were the only position available from which to explore transpersonal functioning, it may be seen as foolhardy or pointless continuing to claim that transpersonal psychology is a valid field of research and praxis. However, this can rightly be claimed not to be the case, as in the early 1960s, the same period in which transpersonal psychology flowered, the philosophy of science was undergoing a revolution. The central hypothesis was the well-known suggestion that mature scientific models and domains are organized in paradigms (Greek for pattern). And a scientific paradigm, it is suggested, is not a fixed state that once established continues ad infinitum, as instead it is able to rise and fall in both its popularity and credibility.

From the present day perspective this idea is considered fairly mainstream and is based on the work of the historian and philosopher of science Thomas Kuhn (1996), whose influential work *The Structure of Scientific Revolutions* was published in 1962 and was the spring board for this viewpoint. He built a convincing case that criticized the positivist's stance and offered the proposition that alternative models could be used to explain the universe and that 'scientific revolution' is possible. A scientific revolution is seen when an established scientific paradigm has become 'normal science', yet it is successfully overthrown by another that questions and replaces the former fundamental principles before becoming the established norm, or prevailing paradigm. Thus there is the possibility that the positivist's stance that reality is a pre-existing objective state that can only be revealed through empirical observation can be seen to not be an eternal fact.

With the publication of *The Structure of Scientific Revolutions* 'Kuhnian' philosophy of science became popularized; however, like many theories that readily receive mass acclaim, its complexity and depth are commonly not recognized. In the case in point the popular misconception appears to be that somehow when two competing paradigms clash one will easily supersede the other and take centre stage. Kuhn, though, suggests that a transition from one paradigm to another is not so straightforward, and as competing paradigms clash their originators and proponents may resort to all sorts of underhand means to uphold their own perspective/position.

It is accepted that a paradigm conversion is a non-rational process, and thus, if successful, contributing factors and methods are likely to not follow conventions such as fair play and upholding the nobility of science. For example, the practitioners of the new paradigm, if skilful, are able to effectively shut down research in to the superseded paradigm, as they now have the institutional power and are able to create the next generation of text books, academic journals and so on, and thus cement their position, which in turn leads from a period of scientific revolution to one of normal science.

Kuhn posits that 'truth' does not somehow evolve over time, that periods of normal science do not always preserve the 'truths' of earlier periods of normal science, and that it is possible for later periods to be inferior to their antecedents. In addition to the idea that somehow truth is not progressively being distilled or refined, he also claims that the evolution of science does not follow some form of temporal regularity.

With all this taken into account, it is possible to propose that a science that concentrates upon transpersonal functioning has the opportunity of being recognized as offering a valid realm of inquiry within main-stream thinking. This can only happen if it can be seen to be elevated beyond a pseudoscience.

Though the foregoing remains within the realm of possibility, a scientific framework that places the transpersonal centre stage could also be seen as being a vestige of a former scientific era, a scientific paradigm based upon the insights claimed by, for example, the postulates of Naturphilosophie or Neo-platonic thought, amongst others, as well as various religious tenets from both the East and West. If indeed this were the case, taking a Kuhnian view would suggest that transpersonal-focused science would not be inherently inferior to the prevailing scientific worldview that had eclipsed it.

Conversely, although the transpersonal does not follow the present era's prevailing C-rules, it could be regarded as a constituent of an as yet new scientific paradigm, one that, perhaps, looks towards functioning within the C-rules or conventions of, for instance, a holographic or quantum universe. If so, this could aid in the validation of claims that the observable and measurable correlates of transpersonal functioning are indeed evidence of a realm of functioning that is unable to be 'officially' recognized at present. However, although all this can be conceived as belonging to the realms of the possible, presently much (if not the majority) of transpersonal theory would cause anything from derision to academic disgust from many situated within present day orthodox scientific worldviews.

Indeed, I am sure that not only physicists could easily take the earlier brief discussion of Quantum Physics and find much to criti-cize; also orthodox proponents of subjects considered to be within the 'humanities', such as philosophy, could equally pass judgement upon much of the view offered of their fields.

This could be attributed to my choice of brevity, though it is just as likely to be because I have purposely looked through the lens provided by transpersonal thinking. And as transpersonal theory from the orthodox position is generally labelled a pseudoscience, any study that claims a transpersonal orientation will naturally be regulated to the academic dustbin as unable to offer academic validity. And thus any theory that dares to suggest a pseudoscience is anything else other than a pseudoscience would certainly merit debunking.

In the previous chapter I gave a brief account of Albert Ellis's open attack on the transpersonal, and although he was unable to create a convincing argument, his is not the only voice to be found that looks upon the works of others with disdain. Well-respected academics are well able to disguise, by academically astute argument, their contempt for the thinkers outside of their field who could be seen as stepping on their toes. A well-known example of an academic finding a means to deride theories that do not fit their view of science is the 'Sokal Affair', a hoax instigated by Alan Sokal, a professor of physics at the prestigious New York University.

In 1996 he published a pseudoscientific paper entitled *Transgressing the Boundaries: Towards a Transformative Hermeneutics of Quantum Gravity* (Sokal, 1996a) in a leading academic post-modern cultural studies journal, *Social Text*, published by the equally prestigious Duke University. At its heart the paper was an argument that concluded that physical reality is a social and linguistic construct of post-modern science.

On the day of its publication in the intellectual periodical Lingua Franca (Sokal, 1996b), he announced that the article was a hoax, in which he had used ridiculous quotations about mathematics and physics made by humanities academics to create a paper that was in fact outright nonsense and absurd. His rasion d'etre for conducting this so-called experiment was to show that it is possible to publish articles based merely upon who wrote them and how they looked, regardless of whether they were accurate or made any academic sense.

I would question the underlying psychological determinants that lead a respected academic to discredit the works of other members of the academic community; what is striking reading his hoax paper is that some of the theorists, he claims to underpin his false hypothesis are the same as those whose work could be considered to support much transpersonal theory: for example, David Bohm (1980), Fritjof Capra (1975) and Rupert Sheldrake (1981).

Returning once more to the philosophy of science, Sokal's paper inadvertently highlights that the hard sciences and the humanities, whilst oft times looking at the same phenomena, utilize differing concepts to explain its existence, thus highlighting the present wider philosophical/social climate, which is described by Post-modernism's central tenet that 'grand theories' – those that claim to describe reality solely from their perspective – are unable to reveal 'the' truth.

## Social constructionism

When exploring the quantum paradigm and looking towards quantum theory, the idea that reality is constructed by the consciousness that observes it was posited with an onus upon relationality. Philosophy too hypothesizes that reality has a co-constructed element, the best-known theories fall into the umbrella-field of 'Social constructionism'. Berger and Lukman (1966), the architects of modern social constructionism, bring an academically respectable perspective that differs from both logical positivism and transpersonal theory. Unlike the physics perspective, it does not claim to describe reality; in fact, it offers a position that suggests that what is recognized as reality itself is instead the creation of 'perceived reality'. Gone are the transhistorical/pan-cultural notions that anything, thus also the transpersonal, 'is' a constituent of reality, separate from and independent of the consciousness (you and me) that perceives it.

Although the transpersonal does not fare well in this light, the positivistic claim that things can be reduced to some sort of essential nature also comes into question. Social constructionism, although containing a diverse assortment of theories and beliefs, falls into two rough theoretical camps: Weak social constructionism and strong social constructionism. The difference between the two lies mainly in the extent that theory is applied.

Weak social constructionists accept the existence of some form of underlying objective elements to reality, whereas strong social constructionists see everything as, in some way, a social construction, and can neatly sidestep questions regarding the universe as an ontological non-reality, because the question of whether anything is 'real' is just a discourse, which in itself is a social convention.

Social constructionism at first glance seems simplistic, yet it convincingly claims that individuals and groups interacting together (social systems) co-create over time concepts or mental representations. These concepts eventually become habituated into reciprocal roles played by individuals and groups, which then become institutionalized. Simply put, the knowledge and the belief of what reality 'is' becomes embedded in a society, which in turn reiterates or strengthens this knowledge in a manner which can be seen as a self-fulfilling knowledge creating a circle that, when unrecognized, culminates in the position that objective reality (not its perception) is socially constructed. This position taken to its logical conclusion would suggest that perceived reality creation is an ongoing, dynamic process in which all knowledge from the humble common sense to the most complex of ideas is reinforced and made to be true.

Social constructionism opposes any form of essentialism, including those espoused by transpersonal theory; in fact, it disagrees with the belief that there are defining essences that determine the structure of reality, because they cannot be independent of the social beings that perceive them.

Although this may be the case, I must say that as a trainer and supervisor of post-graduate transpersonal psychotherapy students I have participated first hand in what could be social constructionism. Transpersonal training bodies, and those that include the transpersonal, though not as a central theoretical orientation (like all psychotherapy training bodies), draw together groups of individuals who bring their own views of reality, shaped by many factors, such as the trainees former professions, religious persuasion, socio-economic or cultural background; in sum, all their life experience.

However, in addition to the unique factors that individuals bring, it is the norm for training bodies to insist upon entry requirements that fit their own needs and theoretical persuasion. As well vetoing unsuitable candidates, in addition to a conceptual training it is common to insist that trainees also undergo personal therapy of the same orientation as their training, and that the trainee in turn only works with training clients who fit the criteria set by the training body who also recommend their own approach within prescribed theoretical confines and praxis as acceptable and necessary.

By following the official precepts the trainee is able to meet the criteria for success and upon graduation they then join as a rule the professional body that oft times regulates their continuing practice as well as the work of the training body itself. It is also common for graduates of an institution or training body to become trainers within their school themselves, thus cementing a circle of socially constructed truths that are past down to succeeding generations of professionals.

Whilst the foregoing offers a simplified picture of a system that serves clinical schools and training bodies in keeping their theoretical approach alive for future generations, it is also generally accepted that theories developed by differing bodies of knowledge influence one another.

However, even with the cross-pollination of theoretical constructs it would take a major 'Kuhnian' scientific revolution for the transpersonal to be elevated beyond the confines of pseudoscience to a position that would meet with widespread academic respectability and support.

## Coming full circle: an ending at the beginning

As it has been revealed, exploring the philosophical heritage of the field requires the willingness to encompass a broad point of view, one that will reveal much that recognizes that the transpersonal perspective for centuries has been considered to provide a valuable contribution to the understanding of the world and the human condition. Yet, before embarking upon such an endeavour, a good place to start and indeed end is to realize where in the field you already stand, and thus how your beliefs and opinions bring there own bias. For example, as a professional psychotherapist I would have the tendency towards viewing the field through my own referential frame (psychology/psychiatry). And it is not just my academic or professional interests that colour my view; my personal biography will also influence my ability to make sense of and accept or refute the theoretical postulates and praxis of transpersonal psychology.

This open accounting for one's worldview is common to many schools of counselling and psychotherapy, and indeed supports some clinicians in making sense of the experience of their client's material through the counter-transference. With the foregoing in mind it may be useful to realize that one's understanding and indeed one's own experience of the transpersonal, whether vicarious or direct, is mediated by the consciousness that views or experiences it.

## A summation of the underpinnings of transpersonal psychology

The intention of this section, the largest of the book, has been to offer an overview of the fields that underpin transpersonal psychology, whilst concurrently finding a means to explore its place in the most common schools of psychology.

To bring this chapter to a close, I feel it is useful to summarize the various theories I have explored. I am aware that, in condensed form, neat or easy answers that can be used to argue that transpersonal theory or praxis is either useful or necessary would be nigh on impossible. This is particularly so as the transpersonal is concerned with a realm which, whilst having correlates in the 'seen world', is considered to exist beyond ego functioning and thus not measurable – a feat only manageable if one is able to move beyond the traditional scientific communities' approach to the philosophy of science.

So, a transpersonal theory, and any clinical application that is fashioned by it, needs to be regarded as both a perspective from which to view the world and a valid constituent of reality. The latter, however, is not an ontological argument in any religious sense, as the debate here concerns spirituality as an integral aspect of the universe, and is not centered upon beliefs concerning a Godhead that represents a form of supreme figure or energy. Thus, in addition to offering a vantage point from which to conceptualize theories of human nature, the transpersonal is also considered a part of human nature and the whole of the universe. Whilst both views can be found within some theoretical models, they are not always described together, with some models looking more to one perspective than the other.

Although many theorists posit overtly transpersonal theories, there is a great deal of theories and psychological schools that do not profess to be transpersonal, yet utilize some of what a transpersonal perspective can bring. This is evidenced in how transpersonal thinking is found in many schools of psychology, with elements of it spanning all the 'four forces' of Maslow's (1971) psychological taxonomy.

Yet, one needs to realize that the whole field of transpersonal theory (whether it is recognized as being transpersonal or not) poses problems when traditional hard scientific methods are used to check validity, for in practice transpersonal experience can only be verified by the limitations inherent in our self-referential experiences. Consequently, we can only try to understand our knowledge of consciousness and reality as including transpersonal elements through our self-referential frame. A methodology regarded as valid in many philosophical schools. So, if the above is taken at face value, a transpersonal orientation 'may' only be regarded as being a perspective from which to view the world, a stance that is further supported by being non-empirically testable regardless of having observable and measurable correlates in the seen world.

Consequently, it would be easy, without closer inspection, to jump to the conclusion that transpersonal psychology is solely a part of the existential-phenomenological tradition, because it too is concerned with a non-dualistic vision of existence, as typified by thinkers such as Husserl, who expanded upon the concept of 'intentionality', Heidegger, who spoke of the notion of being-in-the-world, and Merleau-Ponty, with his notion of the 'intertwining'. Although all these theories may have a bearing upon transpersonal thought, they all lack, however, a central tenet that suggests that mankind has access to (or is an element of) what can simply be described as a spiritual element.

The assertion that there is some form of spiritual element either/or or both in and around us, as many transpersonal thinkers claim, takes us away from the existential-phenomenological tradition, whilst also suggesting that the transpersonal is more that a vantage point from which to view the world. Though here trouble could be seen to set in, for there is not some form of 'thing', the stuff of transpersonal, to be measured or counted in an empirical manner.

If this were not enough, the transpersonal as either a vantage point or constituent of reality has been explored and conceptualized by utilizing similar methodologies employed by the existential-phenomenological tradition, namely that theory is generated through self-exploration. Although this is not a 'scientific method', it is a familiar practice in many psychological schools, for the founders too at the least examine their own psychopathology in order to create their models. A good example can be seen in how Freud, the founding father of what we now call psychology, based much of his understanding of the human psyche upon his exploration of his own internal world.

However, in relation to his understanding of the transpersonal, as I showed, he vehemently refused to see anything that could resemble transpersonal or religious experience as nothing other than a regressive yearning and escape from existential vulnerability – a position that could perhaps be accounted for by examining how his biography created his psychopathology or self-referential frame. With Freud being commonly regarded as the founding father of psychology, and certainly a major influence right up to the present day, it may come as no surprise that as psychology became a recognized field, for many transpersonal thinking was at best marginalized and at worst pathologized, a view that is still upheld by some clinicians and schools today.

It took Jung, who regarded as important the concept of the collective unconscious, a reservoir of the transhistorical and transcultural experiences of mankind, to counter Freud's view. He did so by including in his postulates a wide-ranging interest in all things 'other worldly', not only in the idea of the collective unconscious. And whilst Jung did indeed bring a multifaceted interest in all things spiritual, many of the theories that he subscribed to and built upon would seem far-fetched to many. Some good examples are:

• Theosophy and other esoteric and arcane schools.
• Mythology: for instance mankind being upon an evolutionary journey that starts with unity in the plerorama and leads through stages of self-consciousness and division to higher degrees of coherence and wholeness.
• Parapsychological phenomena: for example, séances where beings from other realms can communicate through mediums.
• Ancient religions and early philosophy such as Gnosticism and Neoplatonic thought.

In addition to the above, which from today's perspective would all be considered to be pseudoscience to say the least, he also included a view that encompassed the then new field of Quantum Physics.

Taken as a whole, all this would bring a Jungian influenced practitioner to conceive that the Universe contains more than meets the eye, with the likelihood of a spiritual element of some kind. All of this is in contrast to those who take a more psychodynamic stance that would concur with Freud's views of the transpersonal, which make no bones of relegating any form of transpersonal experiences to being merely defences against states of internal anxiety through some form of regressive yearning for the earliest oceanic bliss of symbiosis with mother.

From today's perspective, with its post-modern adherence to the view that no grand theories exist, both Freud's and Jung's thoughts could be included in an argument concerning the experience of the transpersonal. However, conceptual disagreement may ensue as both could be correct in their view, or more likely, each hold some truth. This both/and neither/nor perspective could engender confusion, unless it is recognized that it may suggest that some individuals may seek, or experience, transpersonal phenomena as regressive yearning and escape from existential vulnerability, whilst others find the transpersonal as something that is healthy and real. A position that, depending upon which side of the theoretical divide a clinician sits, would colour their assessment of those who seek their help and support.

If this were not confusing enough, the plot thickens when regarding the work of influential thinkers from both the psychodynamic and psychoanalytic schools, as they can be wrongly considered to include or discount transpersonal elements in their contribution to psychological theory and practice. The Jungian school is a good example: the post-Jungian James Hillman, the founder of 'Archetypal' psychology, could be wrongly construed, without careful consideration, as belonging to the transpersonal school; whereas others, such as Washburn (1988), incorporate Jung's view and conceptualization of the transpersonal.

Though Jungian-influenced thinkers may disagree on the place that the transpersonal may have in the psyche, they join forces in claiming that there is a need to move beyond the theory of natural selection, as it offers, in their eyes, a poor means to account for mankind's evolution, because it does not take into account the possibility that consciousness may also be a contributing factor.

This is in accord with the burgeoning field of evolutional psychology (Cosmides and Tooby, 1992), which, like transpersonal psychology, lacks empirical validation for its theoretical tenets and likewise can also trace its roots back to the work of William James (1890, 1902). However, the field, due to its reductionistic framework, has not looked towards the transpersonal, and thus it has not been able to recognize it as either important or at the least a relevant factor in evolution. Whilst thinkers within the evolutionary psychology school have not included the role of consciousness and the acceptance of the transpersonal, religion has, although more from the perspective that it can support the formation and continuation of cohesive social groups.

The absence of including a transpersonal element as being a constituent of the world or mankind's psyche and thus lacking in a rationalization of mankind's existence is also at the heart of some schools of psychology such as cognitive behavioural therapy, and is a stance taken by most schools that reside within the first force of psychology. This is a position that naturally leads to the conclusion that reductionism and the view that regards mankind as a highly complex machine predominantly subject to conditioned reflexes, learnt behaviours and beliefs, are a logical means by which to explain all phenomena that govern or influence mankind.

Therefore, whilst looking out at the world from this tradition, an obvious outcome would be, when regarding phenomena that share similar descriptions to transpersonal experience, to marginalize or pathologize them (a categorization device), as they do not fit within the confines of validity that the reductionistic epistemic paradigm understands. One that, whilst offering complex theories, tends to try and simplify, as it reduces experience to as few basic postulates as possible. This approach places emphasis upon tasks and goals, rather than insight orientation, with attention to conditioned versus innate reflex, and brings a focus upon cognitive functioning and instinctive response.

If finding answers that are easy to understand, to codify and to explain was one of the remits of recounting the underpinnings of transpersonal psychology, I could have chosen to confine my exploration solely to those approaches that fall within the cognitive and behavioural schools, as they can be conceived of having a narrower field of interest than schools that include the transpersonal, regardless of whether the transpersonal is either a viewpoint from which to view reality from, or an integral aspect of reality, or both.

Alas! simplicity is not at the top of my research criteria, for, if it were, I would have looked towards neither the second nor the third force, humanistic psychology, for clues to the bodies of knowledge that underpin transpersonal psychology. Humanistic psychology is a large and fairly amorphous field that is more at home with a philosophy of science that has lost much of the reductionistic bias of the psychodynamic and those approaches within the first force, and thus is more able to include philosophy.

Moreover, when regarding humanistic psychology it is possible to find with ease concepts, principles and areas of concern that inform transpersonal thinking, such as the active interest in consciousness. From today's perspective, however, it is often hard to differentiate between the fourth and third forces, particularly so as the humanistic movement, like transpersonal psychology, tends to be inclusive of the insights offered by the other three forces.

This may also account in part for my lack of presenting a distinct examination of the fourth force in order to explore its own philosophical heritage. Upon reflection I realized that I had come to regard transpersonal psychology as not falling within a taxonomic category; ironically I came to this conclusion whilst using Maslow's four-force taxonomy as a means to distinguish between differing schools of psychology. This lead me to wonder if the need to place transpersonal psychology in its own distinct category speaks more of the prevailing social and academic climate at the time of its inception (the early 1960s) rather than the subject matter itself.

When claiming the above as a possibility, however, it is important to recognize that discrete differences do exist between theories that at first glance appear to share a transpersonal orientation. With this as a possible source of confusion, I would suggest that taxonomies could still be a useful means by which to differentiate transpersonal and non-transpersonal thinking. In this vein a good example of the subtle differences between third and fourth force thinking can be seen in the work of Rogers (1961), and that of Maslow (1971), who is credited with coining the term 'transpersonal' as is applied in normal usage, and how this study uses it. They are not the only theorists whose taxonomic placement needs careful consideration. With an open incorporation of philosophy, particularly Heidegger's and Hursserl's philosophical models, it comes as no surprise that existential psychology, which, although not considered a transpersonal approach to psychology, can be mistaken as being so, as it addresses some similar questions such as meaning. Yet, whilst theoretical differences do inform the heart of both fields, they can be hard to tease apart, because of their subtle nature, a fact that could well lead to the uninformed misconstruing both as being transpersonal. However, placing all thinkers in a particular school can be difficult; Rollo May (1969) may be a good case in point, as could Victor Frankl (1967, 1984), the father of logotherapy.

Even though a debate centred around which school to place influential psychological thinkers may be useful, perhaps it would be wiser to recognize that the generation that was learning to throw out the rule books in the 'swinging sixties' birthed the human potential movement in the period that itself gave birth to humanistic psychology as the third force as well as transpersonal psychology, both of which challenged the prevailing academic orthodoxy. Thus, perhaps transpersonal psychology could be considered to be the offspring of a generation that had access to bodies of knowledge that hitherto had only been the preserve of an elite few.

Within this period it was not just psychological thought that was being radically reconsidered, for many all traditional ways of seeing and experiencing the world were up for grabs, including all the sciences as well as the arts and humanities.

With the foregoing in mind it may behove us to only limit an inquiry to within the psychological field, as, although an exploration of the contribution that many psychological schools have given to the philosophical underpinnings of transpersonal thought offers rich and varied ingredients, it is clear that psychology alone cannot account for the fullness of transpersonal theory.

This will necessitate casting the researchers' net further to include a wide range of philosophical streams and spiritual practice from both the East and West. These incorporate Buddhist thought, including Zen Buddhism, teachings from the Kabala, Sufism, the Hindu tradition and Vedic scriptures, as well as mysticism and esoteric thought. Their influence is not too hard to find in theories that openly confess to be transpersonal, such as the work of Wilber (1990, 1993a), Walsh and Vaughan (1993), Boorstein (1996), Assagioli (1990, 1993) and Grof (1985, 1988).

However, confusion can ensue, as the same influence can also be found in numerous third-force schools that may not have given the transpersonal a central place in their theories and approach to praxis, such as Gestalt (Perls, 1994) and person-centred therapy (Rogers, 1961). The influence and the incorporation of philosophical streams and spiritual practice from both the East and the West in both third and fourth forces thinking will also contribute to the challenge of differentiating between the two.

Nonetheless, I would caution getting stuck in exploring the minutiae of uncovering the differences between the two, as doing so would distract from the fact that for hundreds if not thousands of years, before psychology came into being, philosophical thought and spiritual practice were the only avenues available to explore and account for mankind's psyche. Thus it comes as no surprise that psychology finds a means to integrate and critically scrutinize thousands of years of research into reality and the human condition. Yet, many could justifiably argue that in the present era it is not useful to look towards ancient understanding of the world in fields such as physics or human biology. Even so centuries of philosophical thought and spiritual practice can make a valuable contribution to a present day understanding of the psyche.

Transpersonal psychology can clearly claim to try synthesizing the old and the new. And it could be claimed that this has partly sprung from the need to synthesize the world's wisdom and mystery traditions with the modern day psychological thinking. This approach is easier to find in some thinkers' work than others'. For example, Wilber (1990) clearly states how he has incorporated the 'perennial philosophy' into his thinking, whilst it is harder to find the philosophical underpinnings of the work of others such as Assagioli (1993) where theoretical foundations are not so openly acknowledged. However, as Hardy (1996) shows, it can be traced back to fields such as Theosophy (Blavatsky, 1966), Neo-platonic thought and Gnosticism.

Transpersonal psychology cannot be regarded only as old wine in new bottles, for with the rise of scientism and a movement towards a more secularized society in a 'modern' Western world, transpersonal psychology could be said to straddle both the world of 'science' and a world where spiritual and transegoic functioning is possible. Although on one hand this may give rise to the possibility that insight and praxis can be incorporated from both fields, on the other hand it concurrently offers the possibility for individuals and groups to denounce a position that does not fit neatly into their camp.

With the inclusion of philosophical streams and spiritual practices acting as major contributing influences, one could be forgiven for assuming that transpersonal psychology is in fact a school that addresses religious concerns. Yet, this is not so, for another body of knowledge that has borrowed from many and can be confused with the transpersonal school is the 'Psychology of Religion' which focuses upon meaning and faith, the social relevance of religion and its effect from and upon individuals, social systems and communities.

Thus far, this précis of the theoretical underpinnings of transpersonal psychology has included many divergent influences from bodies of knowledge that are commonly seen as worlds apart, many of which do not offer the possibility of being recognized by the traditional and orthodox scientific community. Good examples are spiritual practice from both the East and West that naturally bring the potential for the uninformed to misconstrue transpersonal thinking as being overly simplistic in relation to hard science. An accusation that is difficult to counter.

However, with the approach to the exploration of 'altered states of consciousness' utilized by thinkers whose work has been influential within transpersonal thinking, such as Tart (1975) and Grof (1985, 1988), it is evident that transpersonal psychology can certainly claim to pursue an active interest in finding methodologies that would be acceptable to the prevailing epistemological orthodoxy regardless of the fact that the subject matter under investigation is not normally considered scientific.

Though these researchers employ 'valid' methodologies to explore transpersonal phenomena, overall transpersonal psychology does not fulfil the criteria that hard science expects, highlighting one of the difficulties that research in the field meets, a problem that is also encountered when exploring the insights that consciousness research brings to bear on the field. Thus anyone approaching a transpersonal orientation would need to keep the following in mind: 'Consciousness poses the most baffling problems in the science of the mind. There is nothing that we know more intimately than conscious experience, but there is nothing that is harder to explain' Chalmers (1995, p. 200).

With the above as a caveat, any exploration of the underpinnings of transpersonal psychology will be seen as falling within the sphere of 'hard problems' as it relates to phenomenal consciousness, quilla, a subject that has been investigated by, amongst others, biology/physics (neuroscience), Quantum Physics and philosophy (particularly metaphysics). Although these are all distinct fields in their own right, one needs to recognize, as in other areas of this study, that there is often overlap in both the methodologies employed and the theories developed.

A brief exploration of neurobiological research and its relevance to transpersonal phenomena expose that there are numerous competing theories emerging, which with rare exception pursue a reductionistic approach to consciousness.

Exploring the advances being made in recording brain function and 'the neuronal correlate of consciousness', or 'NCC', reveals that researchers such as Crick and Koch (1990) are seeking to predict phenomenal states based on physiological states. However, they do not look specifically towards the transpersonal, unlike others such as Fischer (1978, 1986) and Newberg et al. (2001).

Researchers such as Ornstein (1992), who initiated the proposition that human beings have a 'Bifunctional' brain, examine all states of consciousness including those that can be considered transpersonal. The concept of the 'Bifunctional' brain could explain some of the observable phenomena that transpersonal thinking postulates; however, before extolling this concept as holding the key to proving the existence of the transpersonal, it must be recognized that bimodal mechanisms cannot account for much transpersonal experience. Furthermore, bimodal consciousness cannot be solely accorded to Ornstein; Jaynes (1976), whose theory the 'Bicameral Mind', encompasses similar postulates.

Whilst neurobiological research, aided by progressively more sophisticated technology, may not offer concrete proof of the existence of transpersonal consciousness by means of the examination of the brain and its functioning, it may offer useful findings, even if they might be limited to the correlates between consciousness and brain activity. Therefore, neurobiological research is unlikely to be the ideal avenue in which to place hope in finding hard proof that the transpersonal even exists. Anyway it may be important to recognize that this field could provide transpersonal phenomena, as experienced by individuals, some form of validity, merely because the methodologies employed by neurobiological researchers are familiar to orthodox science.

However, orthodox science is not some fixed entity, and Quantum Physics is being increasingly acknowledged as providing a valid means to explain the seen and unseen world. It is a field, like the transpersonal, that portrays a view of the world that suggests that all phenomena are not bound or, at least, poorly described by either Newtonian physics or Descartian views of the philosophy of science. Thus they both offer an alternative to a mechanistic/positivistic outlook and proffer a view of the universe that recognizes that the world and the laws that govern it are fluid and relativistic, as well as the acceptance that boundaries can be permeable or at least elastic, a suggestion that can culminate in the proposition that matter is suffused with consciousness.

The insights that the quantum perspective brings to our understanding of the world are not confined solely to physics, as they provide a set of rules that apply to all domains of science, and therefore can be applied to many bodies of knowledge. Some thinkers, such as Walker (1998), Jibu and Yasue (1995) and Penrose (1994), endeavour to create a bridge between neurobiological research and the worldview offered by Quantum Physics. Although they are concerned with the everyday aspects of consciousness, others such as Zohar (1991) and Nelson (1994) direct their research towards the realm of transpersonal functioning and argue that quantum effects are the best means to explain how the brain functions.

The brain being subject to the laws of Quantum Physics is not an idea that only a few less well-known thinkers hold. It is also that of notable and respected figures such as the renowned neurophysiologist Karl Pribram (1971, 2006) who comes to the conclusion that '...spiritual experiences seem to parallel the descriptions of quantum physics' (2006).

The work of David Bohm (1980, 1987), taken together with that of Karl Pribram's, creates a theory – the holographic paradigm – which reveals the holographic structure of reality, where all substance contains information about the whole and no thing is a fixed separate entity, as all things are in a constant state of change and flux.

Overall, quantum mechanics may be a useful lens through which to view transpersonal phenomena, particularly so as some models make 'modal interpretations' (Vermaas, 1999), a view positing that quantum mechanics applies to all things and not just microscopic systems that can only be seen in a laboratory at temperatures near absolute zero. Moreover, they are also 'Observer-independent theories' and thus posit that things exist without a consciousness observing their existence. All postulates that are in accord with Zohar's (1991) view of the universe, which culminates in the contention that reality is a relational field of potential and that consciousness is created and does not originate in matter.

The quantum perspective challenges all that a Cartesian interpretation holds dear, with its view of a world where boundaries are fluid and relativistic. This, if applied to all levels of consciousness, suggests that consciousness itself has a universal character and cannot be bound to individual sentience.

A concept that is in accordance with the Jungian concept of the collective unconscious and the existence of non-local, acausal phenomena such as synchronicity. And today post-Jungians, such as Mansfield and Spiegelman (1989), like Jung himself are looking towards the quantum perspective as providing the foundations from which to explain psychological phenomena. Their research is limited to one area of study, transference and counter-transference as an interactive field condition, whilst others such as Mindell (2000) abandon Cartesian rules in order to offer psychological models. Mindell, the father of process-orientated psychology, includes the insight offered by Jungian theory combined with the thinking of Everett (1930–1982), a viewpoint that presents reality as comprised of many parallel realities (worlds), all of which exist and are equally valid.

Although participative views of reality can be alluring, relaxation of Cartesian rules must be approached with care, as alternatives can present at first glance what can appear as simple and elegant answers that do not offer a well rationalized argument, a carte blanche approach that claim to explain all things including the transpersonal. These words of caution are necessary in order to not be guilty of claiming that quantum theory or transpersonal psychology is a 'Theory Of Everything' (TOE), a one-theory-explains-all-reality model. (This idea is the 'hard sciences' version of grand theories not having a place in Post-modernism as mentioned earlier in this section.) The concept of the possibility of, and search for, TOEs is well known in the Physics community and consequently hotly debated.[4]

One aspect of this debate is philosophical and centres on the idea that if a TOE is 'the' fundamental law of the universe all other theories of the universe can only be a consequence of that TOE. However, another view is that there can exist 'free floating laws' (Weinburg, 1993), the possibility of which would suggest that they are related to the TOE, yet could not be seen as being less primary than the TOE.

---

[4] Albert Einstein, regarded as one of the most influential thinkers within modern physics and the father of quantum mechanics, spent the last 30 years of his life seeking a TOE.

A good reason to include a thinker such as Weinburg in the conclusion to this section is that he is a highly respected and prominent 'hard' scientist, who has no compunction in openly espousing his strong feelings regarding the next field I examined, philosophy. He is vehement in his assertion that philosophy has brought scant contribution to objective truth, and he is hard-pressed to find an important scientist whose work has been developed in the last 40 or 50 years who has been substantially influenced by philosophy.

Yet, philosophy's inclusion in this work is important for it is able to cast off the limitations that scientific realism places upon the work of thinkers such as Weinburg (a Nobel laureate recognized for his contributions in physics), who, being confined by empirical observation, is not free to move beyond materialistic dualism.

Moving beyond traditional scientific epistemic hegemony is central to transpersonal models and is a position considered imperative by thinkers such as Singer (2001), Wallace (2000), Goswami (1995), Searle (1992) and Needlman (1993). They all recommend that the exploration of our inner world is a valid and legitimate means by which to understand reality. This method is not only familiar to transpersonal thinking, for it is proposed by most of the philosophical/religious philosophies that underpin transpersonal thinking. A position that is recognized by Wilber (1997), who proposes that an 'integral theory of consciousness' is needed to make use of the insights offered by the many schools that vie for inclusion.

Within this section I have included the voices of many who claim there is a need to move beyond the present scientific climate. A position that would bring greater recognition of transpersonal psychology being a valid constitute of most schools or an important school in its own right. For the foregoing to be realized, the present scientific community will need to go through a Kuhnian scientific revolution (Kuhn, 1996), which will require a paradigm shift that would negate any suggestion that the transpersonal is little more than a pseudoscience.

With no individual transpersonal theorist or transpersonal school claiming to posses a magic wand or secret formulae for a scientific revolution to overthrow orthodoxy, perhaps science needs to expand its correspondence-rules to include the transpersonal, or to recognize that at present transpersonal thinking presents a challenging underdetermination of theory. And instead of one stance trying to claim theoretical supremacy, there is the opportunity that competing theories may point to the possibility that a one-size-fits-all approach cannot adequately explain the whole breath and depth of the human condition and the universe in general.

Transpersonal psychology itself, as the next chapter demonstrates, is comprised of competing ideas. However, the one central tenet that ties all the theories together is that the transpersonal is a valid constituent of the universe, one that has the possibility of being realized or experienced by all.

And whilst various theorists vie with each other, none claims with dogmatic insistence that they hold the key to the absolute truth; this inclusive stance typifies the field yet is not a statement that can be made for all the fields that underpin the field. So, having explored the fields that go to support and underpin transpersonal psychology, the next chapter presents the rich theories that the major contributors to the field have made.

# 4
# Transpersonal Theories

So far I have not as yet offered an account or an outline of the best-known transpersonal theories, a situation I will remedy forthwith. However, to do so I feel it important to point out that, whilst without exception the thinkers I portray do not arrive at general agreements amongst themselves concerning the nature of transpersonal experience or a cohesive praxis, they all do include the transpersonal in their theories of human nature in order to account for a fuller range of functioning, both pathological and healthy. And without exception they all consider that those thinkers that only account for a psychological life devoid of spiritual elements or influences are less able to offer a picture that portrays the full spectrum of the human condition.

Whilst disparity could be said to rule the day in much of the transpersonal literature, a shared transpersonal-biased lexicon is generally adopted to be able to best describe and include energies or realms of experience that do not meet traditional scientific criteria. However, though a generally homogenized discourse could be claimed to have emerged over the last 40 or so years, care must be taken so as not to jump to conclusions regarding the numerous theories on offer, all heading in a general direction, as there is much debate concerning all things transpersonal within the transpersonal community itself. The risk is that diversity could be construed as inconsistency because there is neither one unified theory nor a general set of principles, as in the hard sciences, other than that the transpersonal exists, which they all aspire to.

If this were not enough to engender potential confusion, many thinkers, in an effort to not have their ideas confused with similar sounding propositions espoused by others, have also created their own terms or borrowed from other fields to describe their theories. Grof and Wilber are two good examples of well-known theorists within the field with large bodies of published work who have both created their own terminology to enable their readers to follow their thinking.

Putting philological debate to one side, my own studies and the understanding that has been born out in my clinical practise has lead me to see the divergent explanations offered as a healthy situation that speaks of a genuine attempt to understand the human condition. The difficulty that differing opinions regarding something that cannot be measured or in some way captured could however lead to the view that transpersonal theory is at best a mishmash of competing worldviews engendered by the biography or interest of their authors, or at the least the outcome of the social milieu of differing historical/philosophical eras that have been built one on the other to end up with a plethora of half-baked ideas that fulfil a 'best fit' criterion. All of this it could be claimed is needed to make sense of the indefinable and replace centuries of making sense of the world through a religious outlook.

At the same time as considering interpretations or possible reasons for claiming a transpersonal view of the world that in themselves are not aided by any hard evidence for validity, I invite you to make up your own mind whilst taking careful consideration of your own bias.

In order to support an inquiring attitude, I have endeavoured to make my portrayal of the various theorists and their models as neutral as possible, as I do not want to suggest or imply that one model is in any way superior to another.

With this aim in mind I have chosen not to compare and contrast the work of the thinkers I portray; however, I have naturally compared in places one view with another because some contrasting the work of some theorists is helpful, as there are some areas of transpersonal thought that at first glance seem to share similar qualities, yet differ from each other in distinct though subtle ways.

Deciding whose work to discuss was not that difficult, as the transpersonal community has a relatively small body of literature (which openly claims the transpersonal as its field of study) when compared to other schools of psychology.

However, it was more difficult to decide in what order to present the various authors. This was made a difficult task as some theorists such as Assagioli, whilst being recognized as influential in the field, wrote very little that is available to those outside the psychosynthesis community. Moreover, it would be easy to claim his writing style is turgid, or archaic as he wrote the majority of his work in the 1920s and from today's perspective it can seem old-fashioned and lacking reference to the now much wider body of psychological literature.

I also chose a loose chronological order starting with R. M. Bucke followed by C. G. Jung, the 'doctor of the soul', and his contemporary Roberto Assagioli before moving onto present day theorists.

This choice was made with the awareness that like many fields the transpersonal community has taken the work of its founders and built upon their thinking in the same way that a house builder would ensure adequate foundations upon which to erect a structure. Moreover, carrying on the analogy, present day transpersonal theories, like most buildings, rest upon foundations that are not normally seen and which are often taken for granted as existing.

Finally, I could have written much more about each of the theorists and their theories; unfortunately, to offer each true justice it would have required a separate book for each of them. Therefore, in order to give a broad enough overview I have either offered the bare bones of their work or not fully explained the theoretical postulates of the thinkers they have built upon. Furthermore, for some thinkers I have mentioned biographical material to highlight how their personal life or the historical/social milieu they were situated within may have influenced their thinking.

## Maurice Bucke

As I stated in the introduction William James was not the only early theorist to claim that the transpersonal needs to be included in psychological discourse. A lesser-known figure (in psychology) is the Canadian Richard Maurice Bucke (1837–1902), known as Maurice Bucke. I include a very brief overview of his thinking here as he was the first psychological theorist to posit a model that offered an explanation for human consciousness and reality as having a transpersonal element that is not exclusively the preserve of religious dogma.

Like many theorist Bucke's research was engendered by his own life experience. In 1872 he encountered a life-changing event when he had a short-lived mystical experience that he looked upon as a few moments of 'Cosmic Consciousness'. Following his profound experience of imminence (an intense experience of connection with the universe) he was to spend the next quarter century researching and writing a book entitled *Cosmic Consciousness* (1902). Though he completed this project in 1898, he was unable to find a publisher until the year before his death in 1901, and over 100 years later it is still in print (1992).

In addition to describing his own experience, he posited the theory that mankind is able to experience three main stages of consciousness – simple-consciousness, self-consciousness, and the not so commonly experienced cosmic-consciousness – which can be seen as belonging to a developmental hierarchical spectrum. As well as the three levels available to mankind he recognized another level that is experienced by rudimentary life forms such as amoeba.

Simple-consciousness is not only solely attributed to mankind, as animals also experience it. It is characterized by a lack of awareness of the inner world. For example, a dog is aware of the things it sees and smells, yet does not know that it is conscious of doing so. Basically it is not conscious of its own consciousness.

Self-consciousness is the next level and is the everyday or 'normal' consciousness of the human condition. At this level mankind differs from animals, for we have the ability to think in concepts. For example, like the dog I previously mentioned, I am conscious of what I see and smell, though I also know that I am conscious of knowing that I am doing so, for I can, as a healthy human adult, metaphorically stand outside of myself and contemplate myself, as I possess the ability to observe the contents of my own mind as well as external objects and events.

Cosmic-consciousness would be best described as a level of experience that is similar if not the same as those generally termed mystical. Here normal consciousness is radically different, as object–subject boundaries dissolve, thus offering an experience of the whole of creation, an immediate perception of the cosmos, which is defined by a sense of unity or oneness.

Bucke gave 13 examples of individuals who he considered to have possessed cosmic-consciousness: Gautama, Jesus, Paul, Platinus, Mohammed, Dante, Las Casas, John Ypes, Francis Bacon, Jacob Behmen, William Blake, Balzac and Walt Whitman. Whitman may seem an odd choice in comparison to the other 12; however, as May (1991) points out Bucke was not only a friend of Whitman, but also idealized him and saw him as a teacher with himself as a devoted disciple with an almost religious veneration for the poet.

As a man of his time and a practising psychiatrist (in his day the term had not yet been coined, instead he was a practitioner of medico-psychology), he was keen to incorporate developments in the understanding of human biology. It may come as no surprise, therefore, to find that he was keen to find correlations of his model within biological sub-systems.

In a similar vein to the possibility that human beings can experience three levels of consciousness, he was also to postulate that man has a tri-partite psychological make up that consists of what he termed the active, intellectual and moral natures.

In a speculative manner he linked the intellectual nature to the cerebro-spinal nervous system, and the moral nature to the autonomic nervous system.

Like the autonomic nervous system that has two branches, sympathetic and parasympathetic, he posited that the moral nature is also bipartite with a positive and negative element, the positive being love and faith, whilst the negative, its counterpart, hate and fear.

Following this supposition he posited that mankind is evolving from the negative of fear and hate, to the positive of love and faith.

Given the three natures in his model, he put forward that the intellectual nature is responsible for philosophy and science, and the moral nature responsible for religion and aesthetic functioning. He understood the world's religions as being expressions of faith, whereas aestheticism and the arts as the expression of love. Although he did not follow a faith, he considered that the intellectual nature is able to make use of tools for the expression of faith such as the understanding of doctrines.

Bucke was certainly a man of his time who was exploring a subject that until then had not been scrutinized from a psychological perspective; therefore, we need to view his work in the light of the era he was situated within. During his life, 'evolutionary theories' were in ascendancy, and 'Darwinism' with its basis in the concept of 'Evolution *sans divine* intervention' was becoming widely accepted by the scientific community.

Even if nowadays Darwin is likely to be the best-known evolutionary theorist, Bucke would certainly have explored the work of other equally influential theorists, who were also positing evolutionary theories that explained mankind's ascendancy, such as Herbert Spencer (1820–1903).[1]

However, his was a lone voice that proclaimed that consciousness needed to be included in any evolutionary model.

Although for brevity's sake I have not given an in-depth account of his model, it may be unwise to discount all of his thinking, particularly so as my brief account fails to offer the evidence and examples he uses to validate his thinking. Moreover from today's perspective, with all the

---

[1] Although Spencer is best known for his work regarding social evolutionism, he posited models that were not confined to sociology and political theory. In 1855 (2004) he wrote the 'Principles of Psychology' which concentrated upon a theory that contended that man's intelligence had slowly developed as a response to the physical environment, and that the mind is biological and therefore not separate to the body.

hypotheses and research carried out over the last century, a viewpoint that would consider his work as anything other than overly simplistic may be unfair, as he was not able to include nor critique others' thinking solely because of his pioneer status.

Regardless of questions about the soundness of his model, what cannot be underestimated is that he was one of the first psychologists to include spiritual experience, which was not bound by any one religious dogma or theology. Thus it is a moot point if he or his contemporary William James could claim to be the father of modern day transpersonal psychology.

## C. G. Jung

So far I have mentioned C. G. Jung on numerous occasions and have given account, often indirectly, of some of his thinking concerning the transpersonal and his influence upon other transpersonal thinkers such as Washburn. Now I feel an overview of his thinking regarding the place of the transpersonal in his theories of human nature will highlight his contribution to the field. However, like my exploration of bodies of knowledge such as 'the psychology of religion' care must be taken not to jump to the conclusion that thinkers who look towards experience that can be described as being beyond ego functioning are proposing a transpersonal orientation or theory.

A case in point could be levelled at an exploration of Jungian thinking. To my mind no study of the transpersonal in psychotherapeutic practise would be complete without mentioning his work, whilst concurrently recognizing that he cannot be considered a transpersonal theorist from the present academic climate. This may seem strange at first glance, particularly so because, as I have already mentioned in a previous chapter, he is credited with introducing the term 'transpersonal' (ueberpersonliche). In itself this may not be so important; however, his thinking, whilst being regarded as seminal in the whole field of psychology, concomitantly provides a major contribution to the development of present day understanding of transpersonal practise.

There is much that could be used to build a case that would posit that it is natural to consider him a transpersonal theorist, foremost because, like many if not all modern transpersonal theorists, he was influenced by fields of knowledge that claim that a spiritual element infuse all areas of creation, or at the least that a spiritual element is a discrete constituent of reality.

In Jung's case we only need to look at his life-long fascination with many of the mystical ideas that were in vogue in his early adulthood: Theosophy (Blavatsky, 1966) and parapsychological phenomena such as mediumship and spiritualism (Charet, 1993) as well as alchemy, which he saw as having a correspondence to psychology (Jung, 2004). Moreover, his academic interests from the current academic climate could be seen to include much that is now relegated to pseudoscience, his first published paper (1902), *Zur Psychologie und Pathologie sogenannter occulter Phänomene* (*On the Psychology and Pathology of So-Called Occult Phenomena*), later formed the basis for his doctoral thesis and was largely based upon his report of séances (communicating with the deceased, often attempted in groups) which he had observed over a 2-year period. This work now can be found in the beginning of his *Collected Works* in Volume 1. Academics in many of the departments where Jungian theory is discussed and taught today would more than likely consider topics such as this at least strange. Moreover his work cannot stand up to rigorous academic scrutiny.

To explore the foregoing we need to look towards his biography to find clues to why, whilst being a 'force major' in psychology, as we know it today, his academic credentials as a scientist are at the least shaky. Doing so will also highlight the confusion that surrounds his interest in the paranormal and the place of a transpersonal viewpoint in his psychological models. The possibility for confusion can be seen when looking towards his childhood. Jung grew up in a household where his father and eight of his uncles were clergymen in the Swiss Reformed Church, and his mother regularly held séances (her father also regularly practised 'spiritualism' and claimed to be in weekly communication with his deceased first wife). An upbringing such as this may well have sown the seeds of his interest in all things spiritual and occult, and although the impact these factors had upon Jung is mere speculation, it is clear that Jung the psychological scholar was caught between what we now regard as reductionism and the need to see himself in a scientific light and a steadfast attraction to the paranormal.

The untangling of the influences upon Jung and his thinking is a very complex (no Jungian pun intended) task.

The split between Jung the 'Mystic' and Jung the 'Scientist' is easiest to find through a careful examination of his account of the séances that he used as the core material of his doctoral thesis (1902), *Zur Psychologie und Pathologie sogenannter occulter Phänomene* (*On the Psychology and Pathology of So-Called Occult Phenomena*).

His conclusion is clear in that he regarded that the ghostly voices of the dead did not originate from a source beyond, yet through the medium, and were instead the product of a mental illness. His speculative diagnosis was that of hysteria being responsible for the induced dreamlike states of dissociation. This is a position that would meet ready acceptance from the medical model and nearly all present day psychological schools, and could be seen as validation for Jung the 'Scientist'.

However, the split between the young man with an interest in the paranormal and the scientific medical student is not that apparent until it emerges upon investigation that he was to conceal and misrepresent much of his research and its findings.

His paper was not to reveal that he had organized the séances himself, and that he had induced the medium's trances by hypnosis. Nor is it revealed that the fifteen-and-a-half-year-old medium Hélène Preiswerk (disguised as Miss S. W.) was in fact his cousin, and that she was only an impressionable thirteen-and-a-half-year-old girl when they began.

Rowland (1991) exploring the women in Jung's life finds evidence that she was in love with Jung and that the emotions were not wholly one-sided.

Any claims of objectivity or validity would further be refuted as he failed to state that he had given her a book about a clairvoyant, much of which held a significant resemblance to some of what she claimed she channelled at a later date, and that at least one of the disembodied spirits 'grand-father' that Preiswerk contacted was in fact a mutual relation of them both.

Whilst the foregoing raises very serious questions regarding his ability to be the 'objective scientist', it does not reveal his passionate interest in spiritualism as something other than the delusional creations of a troubled mind.

His interest in all things mystical was carried on into later life and he was to lend his academic weight to several mystical texts. He wrote forewords or commentary to the texts of Richard Wilhelm's translations of the *1 Ching* and *The Secret of the Golden Flower*, and W. Y. Evans-Wentz's translations of *The Tibetan Book of the Great Liberation* and *The Tibetan Book of the Dead*, as well as *D. T. Suzuki's Introduction to Zen Buddhism*, all of which can be found in the collected works, Jung (1958).

Jung himself recognized that these two sides, the scientist and mystic, were present since early childhood. He experienced a sense of being split early on in life, and was to refer to two distinct aspects of his persona, a

No. 1 self and a No. 2 self. Moreover, as an adult he did not dispute claims that he had been subject to schizophrenic episodes in childhood. His mother, Emilie Preiswerk, also suffered with similar symptoms and was hospitalized when Jung was a small child.

He was not to take offence at this diagnosis, as he felt that it was not a sign that the symptoms should be relegated to being purely as signs of illness and abnormal pathology. His view was that the symptoms could also be regarded as a sign that it is possible to experience facets of the mind that do not surface in 'normal' circumstances, and thus are not so readily available to everyday consciousness.

Thus far I have given an account of his work as scientist in a less than favourable light, and have not I made any claims of validity concerning the more mystical aspects of his thinking.

I would hope that my portrayal of the circumstances surrounding the research method he employed for his doctoral thesis has not lead to conclusions that his thinking and his immeasurable contribution to psychological thinking is flawed, or that all his work should be discounted in any way. His great effort of trying to place his work in the legitimate scientific climate of just over a century ago, to my mind mirrors some of the challenges met by transpersonal psychology in the present era, as transpersonal psychology too could be conceived as straddling the divide between mysticism and science.

Putting epistemological arguments and questions of validity to one side leads to the conclusion that, as in other areas of psychology, Jung has made a considerable contribution to the field of transpersonal psychology.

However, I would not suggest that it is only his abiding interest in phenomena construed as para-psychological that could be taken as evidence of his contribution to the field, for what appears to be his major contribution is centred around his pioneering work regarding the legitimization of the mytho-poetic aspect of the psyche as well as his mastery in making connections between the individual, the collective and the universal which up until then had not been recognized.

In my opinion it is the influence of the legitimization of the mytho-poetic and in particularly Jung's and post-Jungian thinkers' thoughts regarding mid-life as a developmental turning point that offers the potential for greater spiritual awareness that can be misconstrued as being solely the preserve of transpersonal thinkers.

There is one quote, perhaps the best known and most quoted, that speaks of this and can be found with ease when searching for Jungian ideas from within many fields,

Among all my patients in the second half of life…there has not been one whose problem in the last resort was not that of finding a religious outlook on life. It is safe to say that everyone of them fell ill because he had lost that which the living religions of every age have given their followers and none of them has really been healed who did not regain his religious outlook.

(1933, p. 264)

However, when considering the above in a Jungian light it reveals that Jung was not using the term 'religious outlook' to donate solely the encompassing of a spiritual realm; he did regard that post-midlife's developmental norm is the recognition of the transpersonal or spiritual awakening, which he considered a natural occurrence within the maturation process. In his model the maturation or growth process is a developmental means towards encompassing the goal of 'individuation'. Individuation can be best regarded as the achievement of bringing together the collective and universal, the unique and individual, within the psyche. Though Jung regarded this as an ultimate goal, he posited that individuation is never complete and remains an ideal concept. When exploring this concept, care must be taken to not confuse individuation with the attainment of an individual ego-identity or individuality, which he saw only as fundamental developmental stage, and not the goal of the maturation process. He developed this theory through his observations in clinical practise, and was to make a distinction between the struggles and goals of individuals in the first and second half of life.

In his view individuals in the first half of life are engaged within a drama that he conceived of as a struggle of the heroic ego which fights to be free from the mother to gain the establishment of independence. (This concept requires mytho-poetic license, as 'mother' represents, or stands for, all that is entailed within the journey of maturation from helpless newborn to the adult who contributes to their society and the birth of future generations.) This drama he posited leads, however, to an unavoidable one-sidedness that the psyche will seek to remedy.

The negotiation, or transition, between the first and second half of life is sometimes regarded as the mid-life crisis that Jung saw as a transition that is at heart a process of re-valuation which, if negotiated skilfully, leads towards the recognition that life is more than ego-differentiation and the mastery of personal identity. This task, once navigated, leads to the individual changing their life focus, as they have a mature ego that is able to constellate around a locus that encompasses meaning and suprapersonal (more than the concerns of the individual) values.

Though I previously claimed that Jung could not be considered a transpersonal theorist from the present vantage point because of his need to be seen as a scientist, equal care must also be taken not to assume that he was an early proponent of the 'psychology of religion' just because he was to equate the exploration of meaning and the suprapersonal with terms such as 'religious outlook'. Therefore, when reading Jung's works in the present academic climate it needs to be recognized that in his day lexicology was even less able to describe transpersonal experience than it is today. Consequently well-known quotes such as the one I chose are easy to take out of context and can be used without care to support claims that Jung is a proponent of a variety of fields.

Moreover, the same care to not label clinicians as transpersonal practitioners must also be applied to those that claim to be Jungian or at the least hail Jungian thinking as the primary force in their thinking and approach to practise. A good example was highlighted in the previous section when exploring the work of James Hillman as being the best-known figure from the archetypal school, with clear examples of the differences between archetypal psychology and transpersonal thinking.

Having claimed twice that Jung cannot be regarded as a transpersonal theorist because he insisted upon a self-identification, as a scientist he needs a little explanation, particularly so as it could be considered to be central to his view of the transpersonal.

Jung as scientist could only take an empiricist stance and thus could only use reductionistic logic to inform his thinking. Therefore, he was unable to equate the transpersonal, in his terms the spiritual or numinous, as being anything other than a constituent of the collective unconscious, simply because it is universal. Moreover as Jungian thinking places reliance upon the idea of archetypal influences upon the individual, a fair assumption to make is that the collective unconscious contains 'spiritual' material, although not all archetypes can be considered spiritual, as some better fit a description of being archaic or primitive. With the contents of the collective unconscious available to all they may be better understood as being transindividual, although containing material that can be thought of as undifferentiated,a similar though very different concept to the transpersonal. The difference between the transpersonal and the transindividual is at the heart of an ongoing debate within the transpersonal community, one that will be revealed when examining Washburn's and Wilber's theoretical postulates. Essentially transindividuality is a concept that clearly points towards a theory that recognizes that the individual is situated within and is an integral part of the collective. It does not suggest that the contents of the collective unconscious, as potentially available to or influencing all, are transpersonal just because they transcend the individual and cultural or social identifications.

Although Jung did not differentiate between differing levels or types of unconscious material, others do. The next thinker I examine certainly does.

## Alberto Assagioli and psychosynthesis

Within the same era that Jung was developing his theories, one of his colleges Roberto Assagioli, a young Italian psychiatrist who was also interested in the noetic aspects of human nature, was likewise formulating theories that spoke of a psychology that explicitly included the transpersonal, and like Jung was an early associate of Freud. In fact he was charged with the responsibility of championing psychoanalytical thinking and practise in Italy.

Psychosynthesis, 'a psychology with a Soul', is an orientation that looks towards addressing the whole person: the physical, the emotional, the mental and the spiritual. The last, the spiritual, is regarded as having no dogmatic or religious connotation; rather it is regarded as being the divine essence within an individual and an alive vibrant aspect of creation.

Psychosynthesis is composed of two Greek words; 'Psycho' meaning self or soul, and 'synthesis' the root meaning is 'to put together', or 'the combining of various parts to form a coherent whole'.

Although more commonly practised as a therapeutic approach used in one-to-one counselling and psychotherapy, psychosynthesis has a broad field of application. It can also be considered as a philosophy that offers a set of principles as well as a tool that introduces a dynamic, multifaceted approach to personal and transpersonal integration and synthesis. Whilst its aims are applicable to the individual, it concurrently seeks to affect a larger perspective, one that ultimately leads from inner freedom and responsible expression to the unfoldment of order and harmony both within the individual and in society at large.

If sentiments such as the foregoing put you off and conjure up images of charismatic zealots, fanatical cults or food for the narcissistically wounded, I ask you to suspend belief for the present. However, with its overtly transpersonal aims combined with an outlook that seeks universal synthesis it comes as no surprise that psychosynthesis concepts and tools have been borrowed by many adherents of a 'new age outlook', Heelas (1996), Hanegraff (1998), Ferguson (1982).

Looking towards a marriage between the medical and the mystical, Italian psychiatrist Roberto Assagioli (1888–1974), the founding father of psychosynthesis, in 1910 in his MD thesis criticized psychoanalysis and outlined the principles of psychosynthesis, a theory that in the present day would be regarded as a holistic approach to psychology. He was the first practising psychoanalyst in Italy whom Freud hoped would firmly establish psychoanalytical ideas in Italy. In addition to his medical and psychoanalytic studies he also trained in psychiatry with Jung under Bleuler at the Burgholzli in Zurich.

Whilst he recognized the importance of exploring the more primitive elements of the psyche and the working through of Freudian concepts such as the Oedipal drama, he was to emphasize that an exploration of biography and its effect in the present is only part of what is needed. For him psychological growth was much more than this, and he considered it necessary to include the spiritual dimension of human experience, a form of psychology that strove to include the whole person. His intention was not to replace psychoanalysis, but to offer a complimentary approach that could supplement and offer a fuller map of the whole psyche and praxis for its exploration and integration.

Assagioli had developed his theories predominantly by the second decade of the twentieth century, and whilst he could rightly be considered one of the founders of transpersonal psychology whose work can be seen as being influential in the development of the school, it was not until the advent of the human potential movement in the 1960s and 1970s that his work received wider recognition.

Like the whole field of transpersonal psychology, psychosynthesis flowered in this period and Assagioli was to make many links between his ideas and those being put forward by the thinkers establishing humanistic psychology. His call for the need for a 'height psychology' that recognizes a drive for self-realization was being explored by other prominent thinkers such as Maslow, who was investigating 'the farther reaches of human nature' (Maslow, 1993).

In addition to being a theorist Assagioli was a practitioner who pursued an active interest in developing methods for accessing the unexplored aspects of the psyche in order to facilitate a transformational process. Unlike 'the talking cure' that necessitated an expert who relied upon rational language and discourse, he maintained that the patient had equal access to truth and understanding, the individual's implicit wisdom. Therefore, he suggested that the client was able to utilize practical techniques and exercises in order to experience and explore their potential as well as their biography. Thus tools that relied upon a more intellectual focus and included the use of argument analysis and interpretation were incorporated, though techniques that made use of symbolism, metaphor, imagery and myth were also utilized to enhance or bring about therapeutic change.

It is not surprising to see why he developed a model that offers a practical empirical approach when taking into account his interests and the expertise of those he conversed and communicated with early in his career. They included S. Freud, C. G. Jung, V. Frankl and R. Desoille (the originator of the guided day dream) from the world of psychology and the Sufi mystic and teacher Inhayat Khan, Zen authority T. D. Suzuki and esoteric philosopher P. D. Ouspensky from the mystic/religious field. Moreover, he grew up with a mother who, as a theosophist, would have accepted spirituality as being a valid area of interest.

Whilst it is easy to see that much of the focus of his theories looks towards what can be described of as 'the higher aspects of human nature', a realm of spiritual functioning, he did not completely reject psychoanalytic ideas. As part of the original psychoanalytic group in Italy he understood and appreciated the place that psychoanalysis can play in supporting the integration of an individual's biography and the need to address conflicts of the inner world.

His model, however, suggests that whilst a thorough psychoanalysis can be an important means by which to harness and work through the more primitive aspects of the psyche, a successful analysis is not enough and what is called for is an equally comprehensive exploration and actualization of potential and mankind's 'higher' aspects a 'psycho-synthesis'.

He regarded these two equally important and mutually dependant aspects as a *personal psychosynthesis* and a *transpersonal psychosynthesis*. In my terms this perspective offers both a depth and height, psychologies that are likewise at home exploring the shadow side of human life with all the basic drives, needs and pathology as well as meaning and qualities such as beauty, truth and goodness. Whilst the foregoing can be seen as a worthy goal, it is only part of the aims of psychosynthesis. As the purpose is not to create solely personal mastery and gain, it aspires to a self-realization and an understanding that naturally leads to a goal where the individual contributes towards the well-being of all life, a similar concept to Jung's individuation. Whitmore (1991, p. 142) clearly sums this up,

> The successful outcome of psychosynthesis counselling may be described as an expanded sense of identity, in which the Self (number six in the egg diagram) is viewed as the context of life experience. This expanded sense of identity often awakens a motivation which includes self-enhancement but one which interfaces with the larger whole. What is good for the individual is good for the larger whole and ego boundaries enlarge towards more social and global well-being. Increased tolerance for paradox and ambiguity is exhibited, and inner and outer experience becomes more harmonious and confluent.

She goes on to say, 'Paradoxically the experience of the transpersonal dimension is often accompanied by an increased sense of personal freedom and a fresh sense of inner direction and purpose'.

Whilst the concept of increased freedom and personal gain is in accord with many schools of psychology, including basic psychoanalytic theory, it is the focus upon the well-being of the collective as well as the spiritual that distinguishes psychosynthesis as an overtly transpersonal theory.

Psychosynthesis can at first glance seem as if it presents a fairly simple model; however, upon closer examination a more complex picture emerges one that perhaps is testament to the ease with which Assagioli is able to include and make use of the tenets of many fields of knowledge.

This may also offer good reason for how the model is applied not only to individual therapy, but has been adapted and applied by those from diverse fields such as: Education – Vargiu (Undated), Whitmore (1986); Group work – Crampton (1972), Kull (1976) and Yeomans (1994); politics/sociology – Rueffler (1996); ecology and ecopsychology – Brown (1997); business – Cullen and Russell (1990).

A convenient means of portraying the bare bones of the model is the pictorial representation of the psyche 'The Egg Diagram'. It was first published in 1933 in the *Hibbert Journal* and, unlike Freud's early topographical model that portrays the conscious preconscious unconscious elements of the psyche, Assagioli's includes both personal and transpersonal dimensions.

# The egg diagram

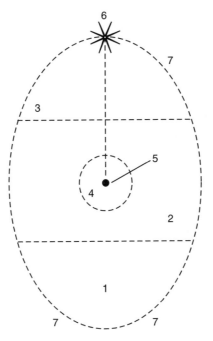

1. The lower unconscious
2. The middle unconscious
3. The higher unconscious or superconscious
4. The field of consciousness
5. The conscious self or 'I'
6. The higher self
7. The collective unconscious

Assagioli's suggested that the unconscious has three levels.

1. The lower unconscious can be equated with both the psychological past and the Freudian concept of the 'id': a realm of instinctual drives and impulses and neuroses.
2. The middle unconscious, which is analogous to the psychological present can be accessible to our waking consciousness, Freud's preconscious.
3. The higher unconscious or superconscious represents the individual's psychological future and is the realm of potential, aspiration and

intuitions, the home of latent spiritual energies. It is also the seat of qualities such as beauty, love and harmony.

4. The field of consciousness contains all that is of immediate awareness: the thoughts, feelings, images and sensations that are consciously observed.

5. The 'I', or personal self, is considered to be a point of pure consciousness and will. An inner 'still point' that is aware of the contents of consciousness yet distinct from the continual ever-changing material that is experienced. However, it is not an individual's ultimate identity, as it is a reflection of the self.

The dotted line between the self and the 'I' portrays the connection between the two, which Hardy (1996, p. 30), quoting Assagioli recounts, describes as symbolizing that though pale the reflection has the same qualities as its source. The simple analogy being that the reflection of the sun upon water or in a mirror shows the same quality of light.

6. The self, sometimes referred to as the higher self, is purposely placed on the edge of the collective unconscious (7) and the higher unconscious, and is linked to the 'I'. It can be seen as being the 'still' centre of the higher unconscious and the context of the personality. It can be easily equated with a mystical concept of a divine essence that has an existence both within and outside time.

It is considered that the creation of the means by which to facilitate a life where self is the unifying centre of our being is the primary goal of psychosynthesis. Whitmore (1991, p. 115) is keen to point out that the self is an ontological reality, the source of superconscious energies and the centre of life, ' ... the self is a *field* of energy containing phenomena of a superconscious nature, providing the conditions for evolution development and growth'.

7. The collective unconscious is seen as the unconscious of the human race, and the home of archetypal form, and is equivalent to the Jungian concept of the same name. The contents of this realm are considered to be transhistoric and transcultural, and are conveyed by the likes of fairytale, myth, religious and sacred symbols.

The outer line of the oval is seen as delimiting, and is analogous to the permeable membrane of a cell, which allows an active interchange with the whole body, thus recognizing that an individual is in constant interaction with a wider interpersonal, transpersonal and psychological environment (Assagioli, 1990, p. 19).

In addition to offering a map of the psyche, Assagioli also created a pictorial representation of what he saw as the functions of the personality: the 'Star Diagram'.

## Functions of the personality

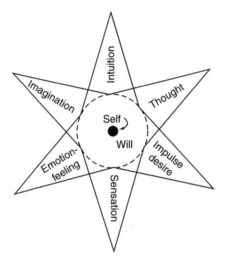

The seven functions of the personality are fairly self-explanatory, and are expressed through three modes, or experiential channels: body, feeling and mind. All human beings have all the basic functions, although a given individual would likely have a natural inclination to emphasize some more than others, as they may have developed one or two modes more than the others – an over-identification. For instance, the academic with a well-honed and trained intellect may have a different experience of the world of body than say an athlete or perhaps not be so able to express and experience their feelings in a manner that may come with ease to an artist. Thus individuals may have differing views of the world because their perceptual function is predominantly directed through one mode. Psychosynthesis with its holistic emphasis aims to broaden choice in the way we act, therefore less-used functions and modes are actively developed.

## The will

At the heart of the star is placed will and the personal self, the 'I'. Assagioli regarded the will as the function closest to the self, and is the energy employed by the self to regulate and direct all the other functions, '*Through* the will, the *I* acts on the other psychological functions, regulating them and directing them' (Assagioli, 1994, p. 12).

Although not any more important than any other human function, the importance of the will in the psychosynthesis model needs to be recognized in order to fully appreciate Assagioli's theories. Therefore a brief outline of his thinking concerning will and willing could help explain his model further.

He considered the will to have three distinct dimensions: aspects, qualities and stages.

> The first category, *aspects*, is the most basic and represents the facets that can be recognized in the fully developed will. The second category, *qualities*, refers to the expression of the will: these are *modes of expression* of the will-in-action. Finally, the *stages* of the will refer specifically to the *process* of willing, the act of will as it unfolds from beginning to end.
>
> (ibid., p. 14)

He classified the major aspects of the fully developed human will as 'strong will', 'skillful will', 'good will' and 'transpersonal will'. The qualities he named are: energy, mastery, concentration, determination, persistence, initiative and organization. He recognized the qualities of will as being within all individuals, though are latent if not developed. Moreover, he also posited that will can be experienced or expressed in pure or distorted ways. For instance, strong will unskilfully directed can be likened to the Victorian conception of a brutal will used as a means to impose, with sheer power, upon others or aspects of the self. Although using will in this way can have benefits there are 'horses for courses', and the use of a sledgehammer to crack an egg may not be the most skilful use of such a tool.

## Assagioli's ten psychological laws

Ever the practical mystic, he conceived that, whilst the other psychological functions can interpenetrate and interact with each other, the will can be utilized to direct their relationship; thus the will itself can be regarded as a regulating influence. Taking this idea further, he posited that the will in turn is subject to the following ten psychological laws (Assagioli, 1994, pp. 51–65).

1. *Images or mental pictures and ideas tend to produce the physical conditions and external events that correspond to them.* Energy follows thought. This suggests that thoughts in some way can be considered to be 'living entities in potentia' that can tend to actualize.

2. *Attitudes, movements, and actions tend to evoke the corresponding mental images and ideas; these in turn (according to the next law) tend to evoke and intensify the corresponding emotions and feelings.* This idea can be seen in approaches such as Gestalt, psychodrama, NLP and encounter groups when clients are asked to 'act as if'.

3. *Ideas and images tend to awaken emotions and feelings that correspond to them.* The elicitation of emotive material is well used in advertising and the media, who understand and make use of both laws three and four.

4. *Emotions and impressions tend to awaken and intensify ideas and images that correspond to them or are associated with them.* This can lead to both 'virtuous and vicious circles' where law one interfaces with law four repeating memories and their psychological effect increases or creates an outcome.

5. *Needs, urges, drives, and desires tend to arouse corresponding images, ideas, and emotions.* The maxim that 'Awareness brings choice' is applicable here in as much as an individual who is aware of the incessant contents of the lower unconscious can choose to not follow or negate an impulse or desire leading to greater freedom from the potential of 'acting out'.

6. *Attention, interest, affirmations, and repetitions reinforce the ideas, images, and psychological formations on which they are centered.* This recognizes that once an unconscious process is acknowledged consciousness can be employed like a magnifying lens that enables material to be seen in clearer detail and greater clarity.

7. *Repetition of actions intensifies the urge to further repetition, and renders their execution easier and better, until they become performed unconsciously.* This is likened to a learning process where behaviour once learned becomes repeated, the norm and no longer requires conscious attention.

8. *All the various functions and their manifold combinations in complexes and subpersonalities adopt means of achieving their aims without our*

*awareness, independently of, and even against, our conscious will.* Here it is suggested that conscious co-operation is not needed by discrete aspects of the psyche, an outcome that leads on to the following law.

9. *Urges, drives, desires, and emotions tend to demand to be expressed. And do not need conscious effort or direction.* That is, they can be considered to behave as if autonomous aspects within the individual.

10. *The psychological energies can find expression (a) directly, discharge of catharsis. (b) Indirectly, through symbolic action. (c) Through the process of Transmutation.* Transmutation is regarded as the process whereby something is changed into something else. It is a process that Assagioli sees as being a natural and occurring all the time.

> The transmutation of energies is a natural process going on at all times, both 'horizontally', *within* each level-physical, biological, and psychological-and 'vertically', *between* levels, where it can be seen as *sublimation* or *degradation*, according to whether energy is carried to a higher or lower level. These transformations often occur spontaneously, but they can be induced by deliberate acts of will.
>
> (ibid., p. 62)

Although the training of the will has a place of importance in Assagioli's model, another idea that is central to his thinking is the postulate that the psyche contains sub-personalities.

## Sub-personalities

These can be likened to Berne's (1988) transactional analysis concept of parts of the personality (parent, adult, child), or the claiming of a sociological role (Rowan, 1990), or Jung's concept of the 'complexes' (Jacoby, 1999), as their definition is very similar.

Put very simply, the personality as a whole, is seen to be composed of what can be likened to discrete and distinct personalities, each of which have their own needs, drives, motivation and worldviews, and are regarded as semi-autonomous small personalities each of which has its own physical, emotional and mental life that is seeking to have its particular need set met.

Within the psychosynthesis model many practical approaches by which to explore the psyche and effect psychological change utilize exploring and meeting the underlying needs of sub-personalities. As with any concept that regards the personality as being comprised of a multiplicity of discrete smaller personalities, danger can befall when there is internal conflict between individual aspects or internal groups. And equally, total identification with one would lead to a position where its needs and perspectives are put in front all else, acting out unconscious motivations to the detriment of the personality as a whole. Sub-personalities, however, often present in pairs as polar opposites with one being more obvious or nearer to everyday consciousness than its contrary twin: stern parent and frightened child, mystic and pragmatist, critic and the judged.

Although this view of the personality can seem overly simplistic, the exploration of the psyche utilizing this model can bring about profound and lasting change.

Psychosynthesis suggests that we are controlled by what we identify with, a situation that can often be our unconscious identifications, so when unconsciously identified with any sub-personality the individual has no choice but to act as it dictates. The therapeutic task is to be able to identify with the 'I', the personal self, which, not being a sub-personality, offers the possibility of acting as an organizing function as well as connection to the transpersonal. This leads to discovering and meeting the underlying needs of the whole individual, and allowing higher qualities to be harnessed. The distorted behaviours can then be transformed and energies released for the benefit of the total person.

Assagioli (1983), like Jung (1958), created a set of personality classifications – a typology. Jung's typology explored factors that contributed towards evolutionary success; although not so well-known in its original form, it has been used extensively in the business community, is the basis of the well-known Myers-Briggs (Briggs Myers, 1995) personality assessment, and places a focus upon personal preference.

Assagioli's typology, however, represents a set of seven different approaches to the expansion of consciousness and the expression of the transpersonal. He termed his personality typology the 'Ways' to transpersonal realization, a transpersonal/psychological typology.

As with much of his written work, many find his style outdated and stilted and thus may find Ferrucci's (1990) more readable description an easier read. He explores the 'Ways' by highlighting how well-known and gifted historical figures have shown themselves to emphasize the transpersonal.

The seven different personality types can be regarded as each offering a discrete approach to expressing and manifesting the transpersonal in the world, or if you prefer a path to self-realization. Assagioli termed

Campion (1998) presents in tabular form a simple summation of each of Assagioli's 'Ways to Self-realisation' with their approach to the world, main qualities, primary motivation and key task.

**Summary of the Ways**

| | Approach | Qualities | Motivation | Key task |
|---|---|---|---|---|
| Hero | To make the world a better place through force of will | Dynamic, powerful and indepedent | A unique vision single mindedly pursued regardless of risk | Develop compassion and intuition |
| Illumination | To bring illumination into the world through unity of consciousness | Compassion intuition and wisdom | A compulsion to reveal inner truth and share in the service of others | Develop will and discrimination |
| Action | To make the world a better place through directing and serving others | Clear intellect and skilful will | A practical vision leadership and determination | Develop a deeper awareness of the transpersonal |
| Creative Artistic | To bring beauty and harmony into the world through creative struggle and its resolution | Imagination Intutition | A passion for beauty | Develop will and trust |
| Science | To make the sublime manifest through observation, questioning, hypothesis, and research | Rigorous intellect and inspiration | A hunger to understand the mystery of the Universe | Develop compassion and intuition |
| Devotion | To make the divine manifest through surrender and union with God | idealist, total surrender | A yearning for union with the beloved | Develop compassion and a deeper understanding |
| Ritual | To make the world a better place through organization and working with others | Discipline, clearminded | A drive to work others to achieve the most effective effecient delivery of the desired objective | Cultivate devotion |

(After Campion 1998)

them: The way of the hero, The way of illumination, The way of action, The way of the creative artistic, The way of science, The way of devotion and The way of ritual. He posited that each path has qualities that are commonly associated with it, with individuals who fit each type sharing common motivations and key tasks. In addition to these personality characteristics each type/way/path also has a commonly held set of distortions or challenges.

Although I have been unable to find in his work a reference to a connection between the 'Ways' and theosophical thought, they bear a remarkable resemblance to the 'Seven Rays' that theosophist Alice Bailey (1991) talked of in her book *Esoteric Psychology* which was published in 1936. Her description of the individuals who are under the influence of one of the 'Seven Rays' is that they share common virtues as well as vices, and all who are governed by the same ray are in need of acquiring the same set of qualities.

## Psychosynthesis today

All the forgoing encapsulates much of Assagioli's thinking, and as one of the pioneers of the transpersonal approach his influence can be found in many others: for example, as the next section reveals, his contribution to S. Grof's and C. Grof's thinking. In addition to those who do not claim psychosynthesis to be their core model, others do use his work as a springboard from which to posit theories that augment and add to the model. Firman and Gila (1997) are a good example. They put forward a theory 'the primal wound' that concentrates upon the development of wounds and the creation of a survival personality through identification with both internal and external 'false' unifying centres, a condition that leads to loosing touch with one's authentic personality.

With a basis firmly situated within the psychosynthesis model, they look, like Assagioli, towards integrating the transpersonal in psychological theories. They utilize a broad range of theoretical constructs from other thinkers, including Maslow, Jung, Winnicott, Kohut and Balint. Their model is not a psychological one with the transpersonal bolted on, nor the reverse, a spiritual model that has been psychologized; in this sense it is like the diamond approach presented by Almass (1996). The integrative element of these models is not the only similarity as both also share many theoretical similarities.

Firman and Gila, like many contemporary analytical thinkers, look towards the insights that object relations bring to bare upon the creation of identity and the potential defence mechanisms created to deal with threat and psychological pain.

Their theory, based on Assagioli's model, responds to the postulate that a relationship, or lack of, to the transpersonal is going to affect the individual as well as the society that they are situated within. To make the most sense of their thinking it is necessary to understand the psychosynthesis model.

Their argument starts with the contention that a good degree of 'I', self-unity, connection, is a prerequisite for psychological health, with a tenuous connection engendering the threat of experiencing non-being.

They suggest that for the forming personality, disruptions of the connection between the 'I' and self can be brought about by abuse or neglect by the caregiver, an 'empathic failure', leading to an experience of non-being. Although it is easy to see this occurring early in life, they also recognize that 'empathic failure' can occur throughout the whole lifespan.

They recognize that this concept has been explored by others, though with differing terminology: Winnicott's annihilation (1987), Kohut's 'unnameable dread' (1971b), Binswanger's 'naked horror' (1958) or Balint's 'basic fault' (1968).

They claim that it is natural to create a defence against the threat of non-being, primal wounding, and posit that splitting is a primary defence which then leads to the formation of a false self or selves. The result of this is succinctly described on the cover of their book,

> ...our intrinsic, authentic sense of self is annihilated. This primal wounding breaks the fundamental relationships that form the fabric of human existence: the relationship to oneself, to other people, to the natural world, and to a sense of transpersonal meaning symbolized in concepts such as the Divine, the Ground of Being, and Ultimate Reality.
>
> (Firman and Gila, 1997)

In sum, psychosynthesis offers a model that is still being developed and refined, one that, due to its expansive view of the person, could easily claim to be a height and depth psychology with practical tools that can be harnessed to facilitate consciousness being both the instrument and the object of change within individuals, groups and social systems.

Assagioli had a very open non-dogmatic attitude to how his work was utilized; Firman and Gila sum this up succinctly,

...keep in mind that psychosynthesis therapy denotes an overall orientation to the therapeutic process and is not a particular technique or methodology. It is rather a context within which any and all appropriate methods may be employed, depending on the training of the therapist. Foreground here is not technique, but the unique person of the client.

(1997, p. 209)

With the foregoing and psychosynthesis having an interest in the whole gamut of human functioning it is not too hard to find critics of the model.

A common criticism of psychosynthesis is expressed by Cortright (1997) who claims that, since Assagioli died in 1974, psychosynthesis has undergone a process of stagnation, and the model has a small literature.

The first is clearly not the case, with thinkers such as Firman and Gila (1997) taking Assagioli's model as a springboard for new innovative thinking.

The second criticism – the model has a small literature – however, is a truer statement when compared to other influential models such as Jung's analytical psychology. Assagioli published only two works, with a third published 13 years after his death (1993), and whilst he also wrote many papers, they are not easily accessible to the general public, although they can be obtained from many psychosynthesis training bodies. In addition to works by Assagioli, there are scores of papers written by others psychosynthesis thinkers as well as journals that are equally available from the same bodies. Hardy (1996, p. 229) as apposed to relying on textbooks, Assagioli's model was disseminated more in an orally transmitted tradition as he taught until the end of his life. My own experience is that he wrote in a rather turgid and old-fashioned manner, and it is more rewarding to read contemporary accounts by other authors.

Another criticism I have met, which has been levelled at psychosynthesis and transpersonal psychology in general, is that there is a shying away from disturbing pathology and the more instinctual elements of the psyche with spirituality being given precedence.

Although in my experience this is far from the truth, I have come across various 'space cadets' who, with little training or understanding of the tools they apply, gladly claim to be professional experts in psychosynthesis or some other form of transpersonal therapy whilst asking for payment for their professional services. These so-called practitioners have often found that if they proffer impactful tools and exercises they can come across to their clients as credible practitioners.

Sadly at present in the United Kingdom it is possible for an individual with little or no psychotherapy or counselling training to call themselves a therapist, and individuals who profess to be therapists of a wide range of models do make unsubstantiated claims regarding their competence and theoretical understanding.

This lack of professional rigour could, to my mind, also be levelled at Assagioli as a writer, as I find he is not as persuasive in his arguments as those that followed him. His work can seem simplistic and it commonly lacks reference to others in the field. This however may not be surprising when considering that he was writing in the late 1930s. Furthermore, he was not a prolific writer, and did not produce a prodigious body of work, unlike some of his contemporaries such as Jung. However, if one is to study his work in depth it is possible to appreciate the extent and scope of his thinking.

Finally, I think it is true to say that the model is still evolving: a very psychosynthetic position and a state of affairs that would not surprise Assagioli himself, as he had a very open non-dogmatic attitude regarding his work. He strove to encourage an inclusive posture that looked towards complementing other psychological approaches rather than offering an alternative to them, with an aim to allow psychosynthesis to be guided by its fate rather than trying to control it or direct it towards a predetermined goal.

## Victor Frankl

Victor Frankl (1967, 1975, 1984), the founder of 'logotherapy', is an influential thinker who is sometimes considered to be a transpersonalist, though he is commonly recognized as an early proponent of existential psychology (1967), a position that could be in some ways justified as his thinking centred very much around meaning. Like all his contemporaries, he was trained in the analytical tradition and his school is sometimes referred to as the 'third Viennese school of psychotherapy'.

He saw being-in-the-world important though was to place much of his exploration upon another area: the Noölogical, a dimension that is closer to how this study conceives of the transpersonal.

Frankl envisioned it as a dimension of noetic (spiritual) processes that are accessible because mankind, unlike other sentient beings, can transcend the level of the psychic and physical environment.

Man is the only being which is able to transcend himself, to emerge above the level of his own psyche and physical conditions. By this very fact man enters, nay creates a new dimension, the dimension of noetic processes – call them spiritual groping or moral decisions – in contrast to psychic processes in general.

(Frankl, 1959, pp. 102–103).

He was also to posit that mankind has an innate motivation to find a meaning and purpose in life, and that working towards life goals fosters an acknowledgement that the individual is responsible for their own life.

This is a position that would not be refuted by the existential movement; however, he went further and was to posit a 'dimensional ontology' (1967) that regards mankind as being comprised of a tri-partite structure with three realms: the noetic (spiritual), psyche (psychological) and somatic (physiological), a view that is in accord with Bucke's thinking.

Although I have only given a brief account of his work, Frankl wrote more than 30 books, many of which have been translated into many languages; and whilst his model cannot be considered to fully meet the definition of a transpersonal approach, it does broaden the analytical tradition's view of mankind's nature to include much more than basic drives and needs.

## Ken Wilber and integral psychology

Any study that examines transpersonal psychology would be incomplete without including the work of Ken Wilber. His thinking has made a significant contribution to transpersonal theory. His name is often taken to be synonymous with transpersonal psychology, and since early on in his academic career he has championed the movement through his writing. However, in 1983 he began to refer to his work as 'integral psychology' (Wilber, 2000a). To him integral psychology, whilst including all the four forces, so also the transpersonal, transcends them all. To me this could be considered as Wilber splitting hairs, as one of the most basic stances of the transpersonal psychology movement is its inclusive nature when looking towards the whole spectrum of human experience. My own experience of the whole field of psychology is that whilst the four-force taxonomy may be a useful means to understand the historical place and knowledge base of various schools, in the present academic climate there may be a general trend towards approaches that seek integration and eclecticism.

Moreover, care must be taken here because, as in other areas of transpersonal psychology, terms need to be clearly defined if confusion is not to ensue. In addition to any potential confusion with eclectic approaches, one of the influences upon Wilber's thinking is a model that shares the same name: Sri Aurobindo Ghose's 'integral psychology' (Aurobindo, 1951). Although Daniels (2005, pp. 175–215) includes Aurobindo's work in his exposition of nine major theoretical approaches in transpersonal psychology, in my opinion it could be better thought of as a metaphysical philosophy that draws upon the Hindu scriptures.

Returning to Wilber's involvement in the field, he brings a prodigious body of work, with over 16 books, many of which have been translated into several languages, in which for the last 30 years he has been honing and elaborating his theories, the foremost of which is without doubt his hierarchical/developmental model 'The spectrum of consciousness' that he first posited in 1977 (1993a).

The 'spectrum of consciousness' is a fairly simple and elegant model; this, however, is not so easy to see, as Wilber tends to include a plethora of background information from diverse fields. His rationale may be to enlighten his reader with information that substantiates his thinking, though my own experience has lead me to need to often reread his work in order not to be overwhelmed by the encyclopaedic nature of his argument. He describes his vast and in-depth model, with its accompanying elaborations and supporting theories, as an 'Integral Psychology' which he suggests is '... merely the briefest outline' (2000a, p. xii). Yet, what he attempts to offer is an integration of ancient and up-to-date theories of human nature that span all levels of reality or, to use his term a 'pluridimensional' conception.

The foregoing statement that he 'draws upon diverse fields' to elaborate his thinking cannot be taken lightly, for it would be no exaggeration to say that all the bodies of knowledge which I recounted in the previous chapter are just some of those he integrates within his model.

To condense 'Integral Psychology' is a difficult task, yet if simply put, he presents a model that is a systematic rationalization suggesting that consciousness, like light or radiation, takes on numerous distinct forms as it steps down into the space–time continuum familiar to Western physics. Thus consciousness can be viewed within a spectrum composed of various levels.

As well as formulating a theory that places the transpersonal in a central position he became the first theorist to give a cognizant view of the overlap and differences between Western psychological theory and Eastern accounts of spiritual growth.

It is not hard to recognize the influence of Wilber's work and the significant contribution in present day thinking within the whole field of transpersonal psychology. Certainly it is hard not to find a mention of his work in the majority of papers and books concerning the transpersonal. Moreover, some writers in the field such as Rowan (1993) base much of their work upon Wilber's model.

Wilber, however, was not the first psychology theorist to create a developmental model nor was he the first to include a transpersonal element; yet he created a truly original vantage point from which to view the psyche. Without losing sight of his originality, it is not too hard to identify some of the less-orthodox as well as better-known bodies of knowledge that have influenced his thinking. An obvious contender is the influence of Eastern wisdom and spiritual traditions such as Hindu's Vedic scriptures, a cosmology that includes the chakra system found in the yogic schools such as Advaita Vedanta (Ramana Maharishi, 1972) as well as other schools and traditions that originated in the East, such as Zen Buddhism (Suzuki, 1972). Though the Eastern spiritual aspect of his work can be easily recognized, Western esoteric influences are also present such as Blavatsky (1966), the founder of the Theosophical Society in 1886.

With influences such as this it is not surprising therefore to find that his work was first published by the Theosophical Publishing House.

Wilber, particularly in his earlier works, sees the perennial philosophy (discussed in the previous chapter (Huxley, 1947)) as having '... formed the core not only of the world's great wisdom traditions, from Christianity to Buddhism to Taoism, but also of the greatest philosophers, scientists, and psychologists' (1993a, p. 214). He sees his 'spectrum of consciousness' model as the latest in a long lineage that seeks to explain and elucidate this transhistorical explanation of mankind's spiritual make up and the potential of its manifestation, a theory of human nature viewed through the lens of a 'perennial psychology'. Wilber states this clearly, 'The Spectrum of Consciousness, in fact is a modern presentation of this perennial psychology (...) drawing equally upon Western as well as Eastern insights' (1977, p. 165). Though the foregoing clearly shows the importance he placed in the perennial philosophy in later works, he does not give it the same prominence as did his earlier works.

Wilber thus brings a contemporary vista from which to view the wisdom traditions. Whilst recognizing and incorporating modern

Western psychological theorists such as Freud (1961a), Jung (1958), Erikson (1980) and Piaget (1954). He weaves within the spectrum of consciousness their models concerning stages of human development and maturation familiar to Western psychological thinking.

An obvious influence upon Wilber's work from the field of Western (transpersonal) psychology is Maslow (1993), who developed the well-known 'hierarchy of needs' model. It is easy to draw parallels between Maslow's scheme, with its three-phases of development, and Wilber's 'spectrum of consciousness' that is also grouped into stages within three bands.

Maslow suggests a deficiency-motivated stage, a humanistically motivated stage and a transcendentally motivated stage. His model portrays needs and motivations, beginning with the most basic physiological drives for the basics – food, water and shelter – which culminates in the development of a drive towards self-actualization and self-transcendence, with the emergence of 'meta-needs' and a move to self-identification beyond the ego. This expresses many similarities with Wilber's model's three major bands or categories that he terms the pre-personal, personal and transpersonal.

Wilber, however, further divides these three bands or stages, giving each three sub-stages, which he terms 'fulcrums'.

- The pre-personal comprises sensoriphysical, phantasmic and rep-mind. Functioning within the pre-personal fulcrums is largely instinctual in nature and forged by basic biological needs. He suggests that functioning within this spectrum is seen in young children as well as some psychotic individuals who are able to live without full rational competence and/or an intact ego.
- The personal comprises rule/role mind, formal-reflexive and vision-logic. Functioning within the personal fulcrums is where behaviour is organized around and directed towards the concerns of the ego. It is within this part of the spectrum that through maintaining identification with attachment (such as 'I want that, and I do not need this') thoughts and feelings are engendered that support an individual in creating their own 'sense' of being, and thus the experience of their own separate identity.
- The transpersonal comprises psychic, subtle and causal. Functioning within the transpersonal fulcrums, where ego boundaries are diminished or absent, gives rise to personal concerns lessening, and the realizing of states of being and modes of knowing allied with connection with levels that are beyond personal identity.

It is important when looking at his model to remember that each of the levels he posits is a distinct level of consciousness. This means that each can be seen as offering an indication of growth or development within a hierarchical spectrum. 'Growth and development occur through a series of stages or levels, from the least developed and least integrated to the most developed and most integrated' (Wilber, 1993d, p. 183). This also means that there is the possibility for dysfunction giving rise to the hazards of pathology or development arrest/failure at any stage.

I will give a brief description of the psychopathology that he posits is brought about by development arrest/failure in each of his three bands/stages.

I think this is important, as Wilber makes a clear argument when presenting a case for integrating a transpersonal perspective when viewing the psyche as well as positing that differing clinical approaches are needed, depending upon the type of presenting psychopathology.

Within the pre-personal would be found psychosis, narcissistic and borderline disorders and neurosis, familiar ground to the 'depth psychology' psychotherapeutic community where considerable study has taken place.

Within the personal band Wilber moves away from the well-known psychoanalytic map that the former band speaks of. Here he posits that there are three further levels of psychopathology that appear similar to psychotic, borderline and neurotic disorders. To discuss them he coins the terms 'cognitive script pathology', 'identity neurosis' and 'existential pathology'.

Cognitive script pathology he sub-divides into two distinct categories: 'Role pathology' – evidenced by the use of multilevel messages and hidden agendas, which he suggests gives rise to duplicitous transactions and role confusion, and 'Rule pathology' – evidenced by distorted beliefs about the self or self-limiting self-conduct rules.

At first glance the next level, 'identity neurosis', seems to be identical to the former. However, here the emphasis is upon problems of identity, *who am I?* as opposed to an individual's role and the previous levels focus upon *how* individuals conduct themselves.

Finally, 'existential pathology' is typified by the concerns familiar to those from the existential psychology school (Spinelli, 1997; Van Deurzen-Smith, 1997; Yalom, 1980). Here disturbance is centred around how an individual deals with concerns typified by existential questions such as the meaning of life, death, loneliness and isolation.

Within the transpersonal band there are other three sub-divisions that he terms: psychic disorders, subtle pathology and causal disorders. These are areas that could be seen as the furthest from mainstream Western psychological thinking and practise, and have hitherto been the preserve of those who have embarked upon following esoteric and spiritual traditions.

We must bear in mind that in this band Wilber argues that there is a lessening of ego boundaries, which leads to subject/object relationships (to other and/or aspects of self) which are altered or completely collapsed, creating the possibility of profound experiences of connectedness.

As in the first two bands these sub-divisions are in turn sub-divided.

In psychic disorders he places nine separate pathologies: spontaneous, psychotic-like, psychic inflation, structural imbalance, dark night of the soul, split life goals, pseudoduhkha, pranic disorders and yogic illness. For the sake of brevity I chose not to describe each of these in depth. However, they all share an aetiology suggesting that individuals who consciously follow a prescribed series of spiritual practise and techniques can find themselves facing similar disturbing symptoms to those who inadvertently find themselves experiencing energies that manifest at a transegoic level. Many of these disturbing symptoms are present in descriptions of spiritual emergency and can be found in the spiritual emergency literature such as Grof and Grof (1998) that are discussed in the next section.

Wilber breaks down subtle pathology, placed in the second fulcrum of this band, into a further three categories: Integration-identification failure, pseudonirvana and pseudorealization.

The last fulcrum offers the potential for disorders that he terms the causal level. Here he identifies two separate areas: 'Failure of Differentiation', seen as an inadequate ability to accept the disintegration of the archetypal self; and 'Failure to Integrate', a failure, as the term suggests, to integrate what is commonly seen as the spiritual realms with everyday consciousness. This in common parlance would be an inability for the Zen master to be self-realized whilst still chopping wood and carrying water.

The idea that there is a spectrum of consciousness that can give rise to divergent and distinct categories of psychopathology draws attention to another aspect of his model that is pertinent to the view that transpersonal psychology can offer a valid theory of human nature which is applicable in the consulting room. His hypothesis is that differing schools of psychology may in fact be viewing differing levels of consciousness, with their own attendant pathologies, or to use his term 'dys-eases'.

He puts this very clearly when stating,

> (...) a primary reason so many different and yet seemingly valid schools of psychology exist is not, as is generally assumed, that they are all viewing the same level of consciousness and arriving at contradictory conclusions, but they are each approaching a *different* level of consciousness and thus arriving at *complimentary* conclusions. (...) For if we agree with the great metaphysical traditions that consciousness is pluri-dimensional (i.e., apparently composed of numerous levels), and if we then *add* the insight that pathology can and does occur on any of these levels (except, of course, the Level of Mind), we will thereupon discover that the *various schools of psychotherapy, East and West, fall naturally into an order that spans the entire Spectrum of Consciousness.*
>
> (1997, pp. 186–187)

My own lived experience and the lessons that my clinical practise has afforded me lead me to agree on a conceptual level with much of Wilber's thinking.

I appreciate his ability to articulately distinguish that consciousness can be viewed in a spectrum that spans basic drives to transpersonal experience, and that pathology can and does occur on all of them. However, I find his model far too complex to apply in the moment in the consulting room. This is particularly so when trying to distinguish the discrete differences between symptoms that he would place in either the subtle and causal. A situation that is highlighted by it being common for clients to present with a multitude of symptoms and mechanisms that span more than one of Wilber's levels.

I also find that due to its hierarchical nature Wilber's model seems to insinuate that psychology is a needed step that leads to spiritual transcendence. My own clinical experience and understanding, however, leads me to think that neither is a prerequisite of the other, and that both have equal importance. Moreover, each can be addressed simultaneously, and can be thought of as a position that does not detract from Wilber's notion that there are divergent and distinct categories of psychopathology.

Rowan (seminar report) suggests that our present day Western vocabulary is not refined enough to discuss with ease the finer points of the transpersonal band. My own experience nevertheless is that it is not my vocabulary that is lacking, even though I am not familiar with the profusion of Sanskrit terms that Wilber amongst others uses. The potential for confusion could lie in the theoretical distinctions he makes, as they are so subtle.

This potential for confusion is not surprising, as often transpersonal functioning is seen to bring or be comprised of transegoic qualities, energies and phenomena. Thus where ego boundaries are diminished or absent, it can be hard to define difference. Moreover, it seems likely that the attendant breakdown, or lack of object–subject relations, which are commonly regarded as one of many manifestations of transpersonal functioning, could further highlight the possibility for confusion.

Although the spectrum of consciousness is Wilber's biggest contribution to transpersonal theory, he has also offered a valuable contribution to recognizing that transpersonal experience is a phenomenon that can present in the consulting room, and that it can be beneficial to consider it when addressing clinical concerns. He offers a theoretical understanding of the inherent potential for confusion when differentiating between mystical experience and psychotic regression, a model that he terms the 'pre/trans fallacy' (1993b).

The concept of the pre/trans fallacy highlights the necessity of healthy ego development as a prerequisite for beneficial transpersonal experience. Without it, Wilber argues, an individual would be unable to integrate their experience and could be at risk of psychological rupture and regression into lower functioning states. Simply put, Wilber recognizes that without care pre-personal and transpersonal experiences can be confused as they can display similar characteristics, and both can be considered as being non-rational states.

The vantage point from which these states are considered is of vital importance, as from a reductionist stance all phenomena are likely to be reduced to basic functioning or regressive impulse, a view that can be found in Freud's view of the transpersonal.

The other stance would be better described as an elevationist view, one that could metaphorically elevate regressive states, such as experiences of feelings of unity with others or objects, as being in fact transpersonal. Jung in Wilber's opinion is a good example of a thinker who takes an elevationist stance (2000a).

For Wilber the importance of recognizing the lens one views symptom through is vital, as he recognizes there two distinct types of experiences, both of which can, without care, be misunderstood as being the other: a situation that leads to diagnostic error. He terms the first type 'The Pre-Trans Fallacy1 (PTF-1)', in which he suggests that some phenomena, which in fact correspond to lower level stages of development, can be mistaken for transpersonal experience. In this case magic or mythical type thinking may appear real, and Wilber recognizes that an unskilled transpersonally biased therapist may not recognize the pre-personal and thus not encourage needed ego integration, whereas a clinician more familiar with the analytical model would better understand the aetiology of what is being presented and look towards attending ego integration needs.

With his second category, which he terms 'The Pre-Trans Fallacy 2 (PFT-2)', the inverse happens. Here genuine transpersonal experience is mistaken for early childhood developmental stages, which to the uninformed appear as a form of developmental regression, such as a form of narcissism, oceanic fusion or unitive state. In this case Wilber recognizes that clinicians who do not acknowledge the transpersonal may view a spiritual orientation in a reductive light, misconstruing it merely as a desire to return to the narcissistic oceanic fusion of early development. What is in fact required is a clinician who is able to recognize transpersonal experience and can support and aid their client in seeking means for its integration.

Though I have given little space to presenting the concept of the pre/trans fallacy, if the transpersonal is a valid part of human functioning, it plays an important part in recognizing that transpersonal psychology does have a role in emotional and mental well-being, as it clearly recognizes that there is a need to include a transpersonal perspective in at least psychotherapy if not all practises that seek to aid individuals making sense of their world and integrating their life experience. Wilber is clear in his assertion that the transpersonal is a valid aspect of our psyche/reality; moreover, he posits that it can be facilitated in order to enhance one's life through experiencing greater depth and meaning. Earlier I questioned the place that the 'Spectrum of consciousness model' may have in the consulting room, the same, however, cannot be said of the concept of the pre/trans fallacy, for its clinical application is much easier to see. The concept of the pre/trans fallacy also suggests that psychology is not the only avenue available to individuals who are experiencing transpersonal phenomena, as it recognizes the importance that spiritual growth practises can play in an individual's developmental journey.

Wilber is not the only theorist to address the perils of confusing mystical experience with psychotic regression, and with the danger of mixing up the two presenting challenges in how individuals are supported and any treatment plans formulated, I examine the need for differential diagnosis in the next section.

As stated earlier Wilber's contribution to (transpersonal) psychology is not inconsiderable, and he is continually refining his models; his latter work, based on and expanding his earlier thinking, offers an even more detailed map that he terms 'AQAL' (2000a) – all quadrants, all levels – a model that incorporates the physical, neurological, social, cultural, philosophical and spiritual dimensions of human consciousness. It can be portrayed diagrammatically with two axes, one that divides individuality/collectivity and another that differentiates between subjectivity/objectivity.

With Wilber's substantial contribution to and commentaries upon the field it will be difficult, as I continue to introduce and examine the work of other transpersonal thinkers, to not include his understanding of their work, since he is prolific in voicing his comments regarding his examination of the thinking of those that agree and disagree with his thinking. However, although it is easier to find him offering robust criticism of others' thinking, I do not intend to criticize Wilber for his vociferous rejoinders, as doing so may be one of the means by which he has developed and refined his own thinking.

Finally, although Wilber's models cannot claim to have had an influential effect upon academia in general, without doubt his has continued to be the most well-known voice when exploring transpersonal psychology.

However, for many clinicians, as well as the general public, his work can be challenging to read, particularly so with its encyclopaedic nature, and thus for many picking up one of his works can be daunting. And like Jung's work, some may find it more useful to read works by others who examine the literature. Visser (2003) provides such a work, which, endorsed by Wilber, gives a fairly full and comprehensible account of Wilber's thinking and its development.

## John Nelson

Although there can be no denying that Wilber has brought a significant contribution to transpersonal thinking, he is not the only theorist who looks towards the Eastern Wisdom in order to explain transpersonal experience and create theories that include transpersonal functioning. Nor is he the only thinker to synthesize psychological theory with spiritual growth practises and thinking to create an expansive psychological model. There are others such as Nelson (1994) who, unlike Wilber, is also a clinician. He presents a unique theoretical framework that is firmly rooted in Eastern thought. His work includes the perspective that quantum theory brings as well as the work of Washburn (1988) and Grof (1985).

Like Wilber he explores the Hindu Vedic system and posits a theory that contains a marriage of the Vedic Chakra system and neuropsychiatry. His study and interpretation of the three-thousand-year-old Vedic scriptures is juxtaposed with mainstream psychiatric thought, and seeks answers that create a synthesis that he recognizes as providing an applicable and vital component of psychiatric diagnosis.

It is therefore no surprise that abnormal psychopathology takes centre stage in his thinking, as he explores the links between mental illness and spiritual experience.

Speaking of his research he states,

> I have found that the system of the seven chakras from ancient Tantric yoga provides a near-ideal way to determine an individual's level of personal and spiritual growth. Using this system, modern transpersonal therapists can respond to their patient's spiritual stumbling blocks with techniques that are specific to that level, techniques that neither demand more of a patient than he can accomplish, nor devalue the higher strivings of spiritually advanced individuals.
>
> (Nelson, 1996, p. 307).

He, however, does not give a clear indication of what it is that constitutes a 'spiritually advanced individual'.

Like other transpersonalists Nelson endeavours to bridge the divide that exists between Eastern philosophy and Western psychology, recognizing that both try to make sense of man's inner world by creating their own theories of human nature. Nelson claims that understanding and reconciliation are called for between the orthodox psychiatric community and transpersonal psychotherapists. He argues that the former need to recognize the validity of mystical and transcendent states of consciousness. This would enable them to expand their diagnostic criteria to include problems that obstruct or hinder spiritual growth without pathologizing and labelling them as aberration or abnormal psychopathology.

With the continuance of the dominance of reductionism in the medical model the recognition that 'reconciliation' is needed may be the only avenue open to rapprochement between the transpersonal and orthodox psychiatric communities. And it may be the only means of ensuring that transpersonal functioning can find a place in mainstream thinking other than being regarded as little more than at best naive philosophical enquiry and at worst symptomatic of atypical psychopathology.

It is clear to see that Wilber's assertion (the heart of his thinking) that consciousness spans a spectrum of '...stages or levels, from the least developed and least integrated to the most developed and most integrated' (Wilber, 1993d, p. 183) will be a difficult concept to accept and incorporate into the prevailing worldview, in spite of his use of theoretical structures that are commonly accepted by the medical model, such as hierarchical and developmental models. However, as transpersonal thinkers such as Wilber and Nelson are addressing 'reality' from a vantage-point that is not situated solely within 'classical mechanics', described by the Cartesian/Newtonian perspective, their work is not likely to be widely accepted until the current epistemological hegemony can subscribe to a view that is not stuck in its present narrow confines. This then may facilitate greater acceptance of the transpersonal, and that reality may be better understood as some form of quantum field, or may operate under differing laws than those that classical physics suggests.

## Michael Washburn

The next thinker I present is Michael Washburn (1988, 1995, 1999), another academic philosopher who like Wilber is able to draw upon a plethora of differing fields and schools, yet relays primarily upon one tradition (Jungian) to create a transpersonal theory that is at odds with some of Wilber's thinking, a position that is highlighted in their view of the pre/trans fallacy. In addition to his own models and thinking, he as the editor for University of New York Press, a prominent publishing house that publishes many works that address transpersonal psychology, will have been immersed in the whole of the transpersonal literature.

Like Wilber's his model too centres upon developmental stages that once negotiated lead to greater coherence and integration. However, although also his model is based around stages, it is a much simpler theory, one that concentrates upon three areas that he terms 'infancy', 'ego' and 'transcendence'.

Whilst it is apparent that he looks towards Jungian thought his work is concerned less with the understanding of man's psychological life from solely a mythological aspect and more within a model that draws upon Jungian developmental theories. These too however are based on conjecture and not hard evidence, and use language that is more often found in texts that explore religious, philosophical and mythical concerns.

Washburn's model is based upon the premise that the self (the essential core of mankind's being) originates from before birth and returns to the same source after death. Thus a developmental schema is created that could be conceived of as being circular. However, Washburn portrays it instead as being better represented by a spiral as the start and end points whilst containing similar characteristics are different. He phrases the human beings developmental journey as ' ... the ego follows a path that returns it to origins so that, taking root in these origins, it can grow to new heights' (1995, p. 239). A position that is clearly in accord with Neumann's (1973) developmental model, which suggests that the self embarks upon a journey that starts within a unitive state and passes through stages of self-consciousness and division that progress to a higher degree of coherence and synthesis.

Washburn terms his concept of the pleromatic and undifferentiated consciousness as 'the Dynamic Ground', which he recognizes as the source of spiritual power (1988).

Before moving on, however, I want to make clear that Washburn is not limiting the dynamic ground to only being the source of spiritual power. For he sees it as the non-static fundamental source and basis of the psyche, that includes active psychic potentials such as instinctual impulses and feelings, and as a source of energy that includes libidinal or psychic energy as well as spiritual energies.

This, however, is a view that is at odds with the greater number of psychoanalytic thinkers who regard these as two opposed forces.

In relation to the aetiology of the dynamic ground he does not give many clues and openly wonders if it has an ultimate source beyond the psyche.

Washburn's model concentrates upon the interplay and relationship between the ego (our individual self) and the dynamic ground: a relationship that he likens in its early stages to that of the relationship between a child and their primary caregiver. This relationship, he posits, is also experienced at the same time internally as a relationship between the ego and the dynamic ground.

His hypothesis is that a very young baby like the young ego is somehow embedded in the dynamic ground, feeling absorbed in its numinous power. This position is mirrored by how the baby finds it hard to distinguish between feelings that arise from within its own body and feelings that come from its interaction with the primary caregiver, whilst the forming ego, likewise, has difficulties in identifying object/subject relationships.

This he suggests leads to the young emerging ego finding itself both attracted to the dynamic ground and fearfully dependent on it; a relationship equivalent to the young toddler's reliance upon their primary caregiver as both the principal source of love and frustration. Therefore, in order to achieve some measure of independence from these immense and overwhelming experiences, the young ego inevitably seeks to buffer or separate itself. It creates a primal (or original) repression as a necessary part of its development, creating an independent space in which the forming ego can grow. This he recognizes as a necessary infrastructure for the development of the ego, the drawback of which however is that the potentialities inherent within the dynamic ground are rendered dormant and reduced to being latent and primarily instinctual.

During this latency he posits that even if there is not the same relationship between the ego and the dynamic ground its potential and power is still available, though in diminished form as psychic energy. For some, the possibility, and rare experience, of moments of numinous awe ('peak experiences').

Washburn's theory proposes that for adults the formation of a strong ego and ego identity is not adequate. Thus the search for higher meaning is a normal developmental need and not a luxury, a regressive self-absorption, an indication of abnormal personality, nor atypical psychopathology.

His model suggests that while the ego is striving for full development there is a bias towards an outward focus such as the creation of wealth, career, relationships and so on (Vaughan's (1985) outward arc). Yet this focus can lead to disappointment and disillusionment, as the assumption that if we are successful then fulfilment will naturally occur is not born out to be true.

He recognizes that intellectually many may realize that this is not so, yet can be so caught up in pursuing the fruits of success that they ignore or defend against the transpersonal elements of the psyche. Thus creating a continuance of the primal repression, which at this stage of development the mature ego can experience as a hindrance, as it now no longer needs to be separated from the dynamic ground to grow.

Simply put, at this stage the ego no longer needs the protection of original repression for its own growth, yet at this point there arises the conditions in which the ego can use repression as a protection from its further growth. Growth here is seen as typified by the ego expanding beyond its own limitations and therefore being able to encompass a wider range of realities, resources and potentialities.

This brings to focus the recognition of transpersonal, or spiritual awakening, which he, like Jung, sees as a natural occurrence, a developmental norm post midlife, '... the spiral path of transcendence and reunion with the Dynamic Ground is the developmental course of the second half of life' (1995, p. 315).

This he regards as being a higher stage of development, rather than a return to a lower stage (pre-birth). Although he claims that this is neither a return to an earlier infantile state nor to formative ways of being, it can appear regressive. In order to seek clarity he terms this step, when successfully negotiated, as 'regression in the service of transcendence' (1995). This concept can, without careful consideration resemble a transpersonalization of the Freudian concept of 'regression in the service of the ego' (Khan, 1960; Kris, 1950). In this model the ego, fulfilling its regulatory function, can aid in the exploration of primary process and then organize and make use of the material explored whilst not being overwhelmed. Primary process (unlike secondary process which is governed by the reality principle) is regarded as being held within the id, and as such operates as an aspect of the pleasure principle, is the realm of sexual, aggressive and instinctual drives, and is totally unconscious and unsocialized. The task of regression in the service of the ego would be regarded from the analytic stance as an ego-controlled regression that is accomplished in order to fulfil an ego-syntonic task. A good example could be the working through, not acting out, of biographical material in the course of an analysand's psychoanalysis.

Although the above may seem a far cry from Washburn's model, both theories suggest that the exploration of repressed material, once it is integrated, will bring increased health and well-being, though without careful consideration the process may appear to be merely regressive.

The Freudian model suggests that regression in the service of the ego will aid the ego to repress material only when necessary. By doing so neurosis will be avoided whilst offering the individual greater choice in mediating between the impulses of the id, the injunctions demanded by the superego and the constraints of a socialized world.

Washburn's model, however, although positing a form of positive regression, differs from the Freudian unconscious primary process, as he suggests that the domain that is visited includes a spiritual element as well as instinctual impulses and libidinal energy.

This clear distinction between the Freudian-biased and Washburn's model is easy to recognize; even so, the possibility that areas of the psyche that are predominantly unconscious, undifferentiated and include material that is spiritual in nature is not an arena that the greater majority of Freudian-influenced thinkers have chosen to explore.

In order to find an argument that tackles this, we need once again to look towards Wilber to find a thinker who explores the subtleties of Washburn's model whilst creating a robust argument that questions his thinking.

Thus far Wilber could be seen as being in agreement with much that Washburn proposes; nonetheless, a disagreement between the two arises concerning their concepts of undifferentiated consciousness, which engenders an argument that suggests that there is a subtle though important difference between various states, which can be conceived of or experienced as undifferentiated consciousness.

Wilber and Washburn base their disagreement upon the claims that phenomenologically two differing states that share many similar attributes are not necessarily the same state.

Washburn (1995) argues that the oceanic, infantile (pre-personal) stage and the mystical transpersonal stage are similar in essence, claiming that similarities between the developmental stages before and after the ego has developed – the pre-personal and transpersonal – indicate they are essentially of the same ontological nature, though differ from each other phenomenologically.

Wilber, however, is forthright in his objection to Washburn's (and the whole Jungian) proposition that the oceanic infantile state may be a type of mystical state, claiming that in fact infantile fusion is a state of undifferentiation, whereas total integration (union) is reached through a higher level of development, a state embodied by mysticism, '...many theorists, following Jung, maintained that since mysticism is a subject/object union, then this early undifferentiated fusion state must be what is somehow *recaptured* in mystical unity' (Wilber, 1993, p. 187).

In relation to this study their argument highlights the importance of diagnostic models that can differentiate between pre-personal and transpersonal states regardless of whether the state is a form of mystical union or some form of undifferentiated fusion. A discussion of the importance for the correct diagnosis of these states forms much of the next chapter, as both could be construed as states that include regressive features though in fact be progressive.

I would like to conclude by saying that I imagine that their debate will carry on for some time. However, though I find it intellectually interesting, I will only cheer from the sidelines whilst they slug it out in the halls of academe. For when I am confronted with an individual who may be suffering with psychotic symptoms and the attendant discord and challenges to themselves and those around them, my first concern will be to aid them finding methods to integrate their experience and find a means to function in the world.

This would be my short-term therapeutic aim, while my working hypothesis would include the awareness that they are struggling with experiences that also fit the description of spiritual emergence. Thus I would have at my disposal a therapeutic framework that can encompass transegoic functioning and moreover not be constrained by a model of the fully functioning human as one that can only regard regressive-like symptoms solely as non-ego syntonic and pathological. An outlook that is in line with both Wilber's and Washburn's models, as both could be used to establish the cause of an individual's symptoms and the material underlying the presenting issues. Wilber's model offers sophisticated and complex diagnostic criteria, whilst Washburn's allows the opportunity to differentiate between regression in the service of transcendence and regression that hints at underlying psychopathology that upsets the psychological equilibrium and needs integrating and/or the successful negotiation of psychological developmental steps.

## Stanislav Grof

Claiming 'that no account of the transpersonal in psychotherapeutic practise would be complete without including the work of Ken Wilber' is a statement that is also true of the next thinker I discuss Stanislav Grof. However, although his contribution could be conceived of as bringing equal significance to the field, he may not be as well-known outside the transpersonal community, regardless of the prodigious body of his published work, a body that equals if not surpasses Wilber's not perhaps in its breadth of influence but in the sheer quantity of published material. Moreover, as a qualified and practising psychiatrist his thinking is founded upon his systematic and comprehensive clinical observations over more than 40 years.

The focus of his past and ongoing research is examining non-ordinary states of consciousness (NOSC), for which he coined the term 'holotropic'. His research career is comprised of over two decades of clinical psychedelic research with psychoactive substances, including LSD, and another 20 plus years of work with holotropic[2] breathwork, a therapeutic method that he developed with his wife Christina Grof.

As well as the above fields of study where altered states of consciousness have been purposely elicited either through psychoactive agents or some form of technique such as spiritual practises or breathing, he also has examined non-consciously induced or spontaneous mystical experiences and episodes of 'psycho-spiritual crises or spiritual emergencies' (Grof & Grof, 1998).

Before continuing with an overview of his work it is interesting to note that, like Washburn, Grof (1985) concurs with much of Wilber's model, yet has strong views that challenge his thinking particularly so when regarding pre-birth experience as well as the dynamics of spiritual development and its interface with psychopathology.

I will, as I portray Grof's thinking, further elaborate upon their respective conceptual disagreement (Grof, 1985; Wilber, 2000a).

Grof, like all transpersonal theorists, takes as given the assumption that humankind is more than a highly complex biological being which has a psychological aspect that can be measured or at least defined by physical laws, in that we have a spiritual nature and a form of consciousness that exists throughout life, a transpersonal domain of the psyche, a realm of being or domain that he posits exists before birth and post-biological death.

Whilst regarding spirituality as a natural and legitimate dimension of the human psyche, he recognizes, like all transpersonal thinkers, that care must be taken to not confuse it as being the preserve of the dogmas and practises of organized religion.

His findings, he claims, show that it is possible to experience this aspect of our nature in our everyday life, and that our awareness of it can be fostered through numerous 'spiritual practises', for example the trances of shamans or initiates in aboriginal rituals and the states encountered in the results of systematic meditative practise; or the experience some have encountered as the result of the use psychedelic substances such as LSD or natural psychotropic substances from natural sources such as some fungi and cacti.

He also acknowledges that the realization and awareness of this realm of experience can be a surprise for some individuals, with spontaneous

---

[2] Holotropic: *moving towards wholeness*, from the Greek *holos* = whole, and *trepein* = to move in the direction of something.

mystical-like episodes that bring symptoms that can be misdiagnosed as they are concomitant with those of psychosis.

He argues that the range of awareness and realms of being recognized by an academic psychiatric community that is limited to biology post-natal biography and the individual (Freudian) unconscious cannot adequately cover the whole spectrum of the human condition, nor explain disorders which do not have an organic basis or a foundation in post-natal biographical trauma.

Moreover, it is not just in the understanding of psychopathology that he recognizes the paucity of the psychiatric community's thinking, for he also acknowledges that they are unable to account for all the phenomena occurring in holotropic states.

Though his theories speak about areas of the psyche that are not commonly discussed in the psychiatric literature, Grof, like most transpersonal thinkers, includes the insights offered by the academic psychiatric community whilst including two additional domains as important: the transpersonal and the inclusion of the influence upon the whole psyche of prenatal and perinatal consciousness, the experience of the foetus and perinatal trauma (the trauma of birth).

Though for convenience's sake I make a differentiation between the two domains, Grof would argue that prenatal and perinatal consciousness are aspect of transpersonal consciousness, as in his view mankind is a psychospiritual being in which the spiritual and psychological nature of mankind and the human condition cannot be divorced nor seen in isolation from the other.

With the foregoing in mind I will elucidate more on his understanding of prenatal and perinatal consciousness, whilst bearing in mind that his understanding of the transpersonal domain is that it includes a collective nature that is comprised of ancestral, racial, collective and phylogenetic memories, all of which can be experienced directly by an individual. Moreover, he makes a case for reincarnation and posits that the transpersonal domain can also act as a catalyst to the working through of material that may have its roots in previous lives, as it is the container of karmic material (the effect of actions in previous lives).

I will conclude my portrayal of his thinking by examining holotropic breathwork, his experimental technique for purposefully creating the opportunity for individuals to experience NOSC's as a therapeutic tool.

The importance Grof places upon the domain of pre-birth consciousness is the area that most distinguishes his thinking from others in the whole transpersonal field, and is also a position that would certainly engender criticism from the psychiatric community, as the possibility that prenatal and perinatal events could have psychological importance and ramifications in other life stages has not been accepted. This is likely to be the case due to a widely held belief that the brain of the newborn is not capable of registering the traumatic impact of birth simply because the neurons in the neonatal cerebral cortex are not fully myelinized, and that somehow consciousness only begins following the birth process.

Grof's premise, however, is that the foetus has a form of consciousness, and that pre- and perinatal events will play a critical role in the individual's psychological history. Therefore, the possibility exists that memories of intrauterine experience are available for conscious recall and reliving, and that equally the memory of birth can be an important reservoir of difficult emotions and sensate experience that can in later life act as a factor in the development of numerous emotional and psychosomatic disorders. He postulates that a difficult birth and poor post-natal circumstances can establish a profound trauma that can colour an individual's entire life. Moreover, it is not just those individuals who recognize they had a difficult birth who suffer from birth trauma. He acknowledges that the birth process is an event of paramount significance within the psychobiological evolution of the individual, and that the birthing experience, including those without complications, is a process of extreme intensity within the context of the radical transition, from an aquatic form of life whose needs are constantly satisfied by placental circulation to a fundamentally new existence as an air-breathing organism.

His suggestion therefore is that by actively seeking to become aware of the prenatal and perinatal domains (and the transpersonal) a means is created that serves to activate intrinsic healing mechanisms that can bring about healing and profound psychospiritual transformation.

His research has lead him to formulate a model that recognizes that the birth process can be broken down into a series of distinct phases or complex experiential patterns, each of which is associated with the consecutive stages of biological birth. His model thus presents a map that charts the psychological aspect of each stage in the birth process that he terms the four 'basic perinatal matrices' (BPMs).

Though Grof's claim that prenatal and perinatal events occurring within the context of the early psychobiological evolution of the individual can be seen as important, as mentioned earlier it raises a controversy regarding the possibility that the stages of the birth process can be consciously experienced by the foetus and thus somehow recorded as memory and worked with in later life stages.

To counter this argument, he maintains, with the data from his years of research, that the perinatal matrices are more than early psychobiological events or simple records of the original foetal experience; thus they cannot be solely defined as stages of the psychobiological evolution of the foetus. He instead regards them as needing to be seen as being principally related to psychospiritual evolution and therefore not just evidence for the importance of the early psychobiological events. For they are, he maintains, much more than simple records of foetal experience, since they also function as an important interface with the archetypal and historical domains of the collective unconscious. He makes this statement after evidencing that the BPM's can be re-encountered as experiential patterns in adults facing NOSC and as such they are a natural experiential interface with the transpersonal domain.

His insistence that intrauterine consciousness is important and needs to be included in psychotherapeutic thinking is rare in all schools of psychology, including the analytical and depth psychology schools, for they take the stance that biological birth is an event that has little if any psychological relevance. This of course is a vantage point that is similar to academic psychiatry, which also does not consider birth to be a psychotraumatic experience. Therefore both stances fail to see that it has any implications for the development of healthy personality (lacking abnormal psychopathology) unless irreversible damage to the brain cells has occurred.

Although the foregoing is the norm, Grof is not alone in positing that intrauterine consciousness is important. There is one notable exception, Otto Rank (1929). Rank was a close collaborator of Freud and his ideas were influential in the great man's thinking; however, Rank began to consider and write about how intrauterine experience and the trauma of birth play an important role in the development of the psyche. Ideas such as this suggest that there can be psychological phases that are 'pre-Oedipal' complex, and with the 'Oedipal' complex, one of his central tenets, under threat Freud distanced himself from Rank's work whilst suggesting that others did likewise.

As I have shown, it is easy to see the disparity between Grof's work and mainstream thinking. And regardless of the fact that he undoubtedly an influential thinker in the transpersonal world, his is a lone voice calling for the importance of intrauterine consciousness and the birth process in recent times. This is also mirrored in some ways in the transpersonal community, where he could be seen as a lone voice championing the importance of the prenatal and perinatal domains as a vital component of the transpersonal nature of the psyche.

Though his insistence on the inclusion of the prenatal and perinatal domains in transpersonal thinking is not clearly apparent in the literature (other than in his own published works), the most obvious place to find his extensive research influencing the field has been in his ongoing debate with Wilber.

Whilst acknowledging Wilber's significant contribution to the field, Grof is forthright in his claims that Wilber's theories have not taken into account the importance of the pre- and perinatal domain in his spectrum psychology.

In response to these criticisms, Wilber (2000a, pp. 585–588, 741–763) included an additional category in his developmental scheme, fulcrum 0 (F-O), which, like all his categories, is further divided into three sub-phases.

However, although Wilber acknowledges Grof's thinking, it appears as if Grof regards Wilber's addition as still not placing enough importance upon intrauterine experience.

Another area that is of more importance to Grof than to Wilber is his thoughts regarding the other end of the lifespan, the psychological importance of 'Biological Death'. Grof understands the psychological importance of death not as the Freudian concept of *Thanatos*, a biological instinct, but as a psychological response to the individual's encounters with life-threatening events. This could be conceived of as the remit of the existential schools; however, Grof is keen to point out that encounters with life-threatening events will inevitably include psychological material from the perinatal period.

Grof also claims that without importance being placed upon pre-birth and post-death experience/consciousness traditional views of psychopathology cannot adequately account for the fullness of the human condition.

This, he asserts, is especially so when psychogenic disorders need to be recognized. For with only post-natal consciousness as the source of validity, the analytic and ego psychology schools can only look towards post-natal biographical events and related psychodynamic processes. Thus they can only look for explanations of normality or abnormality as resulting from the negotiation of specific stages of post-natal libidinal development, the evolution of the ego, the negotiation of the object relationships and conventional biological functioning.

This is once again a similar view to the position held by the medical model that focuses upon searching for correlations between neurobiological functioning and abnormal psychopathology.

The need for understanding the implications of functioning that is influenced or directly caused by consciousness that is other than biological or post natal biographical, and thus often seen as being a NOSC, is taken up in the next section in which I explore spiritual emergence and emergency.

To bring this overview of Grof's thinking to a close, I will briefly portray another of his theoretical postulates, the COEX systems or 'systems of condensed experiences', which again was conceived through careful observation in clinical practise. The model of COEX systems shares many similarities with Jung's theory of the complex (Jacoby, 1999), and Assagioli's (1990) sub-personality model. Basically it recognizes that memory is organized into collections of memories that have similar feeling tones. He observed that if a particular effect is engaged, it can activate a set of specific repressed memories from infancy and early childhood, memories that are somehow linked by the presence of this common effect (1975). Thus at its core each COEX system has a particular affective tone associated with it. These systems, however, are not fixed entities that once created are set in psychological concrete, because, like Jung's notion of the complex and Assagioli's sub-personalities, as an individual grows each COEX system also develops. Yet the development of the COEX, due to its semi-autonomous functioning, includes the honing or creating of its own set of defences.

Despite his work's similarities with other models, Grof sought a very different avenue by which to practise psychotherapy so that working with COEX's is the core task. In his search to find the means for individuals to contact and completely (re)experience the core memories and associated effect constellated within each COEX system, in the earlier part of his career he utilized psychedelic medication. When cultural and political changes meant that research into 'psychedelic therapy' became more difficult, he developed 'Holotropic Breathing' as a way of creating a method to explore COEX systems without the need to administer drugs (1985). Grof's holotropic breathwork is intended to induce powerful NOSC's as well as access repressed memories and perinatal experiences by using hyperventilation techniques, often in large groups with very loud evocative music.

Although the foregoing takes a major focus, the technique also includes processing any material that arises through group process and art therapy. Since this approach is directed towards the working through of suppressed psychological material and the inducing of transpersonal states, it can be hard to ascertain whether he suggests that holotropic breathwork, as a technique, is a form of psychotherapy or a form of spiritual/philosophical quest, as he sees both as often being one and the same.

My own experience of holotropic breathwork, and that of supporting others that have practised it, is that it can be a very powerful tool. However, regardless of how it has been accessed, I have found that, once uncovered, material that has been deeply suppressed or repressed from normal everyday consciousness needs great skill in integrating, if it is to be of lasting benefit. This for me raises an ongoing dilemma, one which concerns all 'depth work', as any technique that seeks to 'work through' historical material that has been experienced as traumatic carries a high possibility of the individual experiencing a re-traumatization, an encounter which brings little overall benefit. This is a circumstance that inadequately trained practitioners may find themselves in, because it is a situation that takes great skill and extreme care to negotiate, if it is not to be some form of encouraged 'acting out' of either the client or the clinician.

With his long career and substantial contribution to transpersonal psychology, Grof can be considered to be one of the elder statesmen of the transpersonal approach, a position that cannot be levelled at Hameed Ali.

## Hameed Ali and the diamond approach

In the first section I quoted Cortright, who claims that the 'diamond approach' (Almass, 1996) is 'perhaps the fastest growing transpersonal approach on the scene today' (Cortright, 1997, pp. 90–91). He, however, does not offer evidence for this claim, and I have not been able to find anything that would substantiate this. I too, though, came across an increasing number of people who have at least heard of this model.

The diamond approach was first posited in its initial form in the early 1970s by A. H. Almass, who uses the pen names Hameed Ali, Karen Johnson and Faisal Muqaddam. They were among the first students of Claudio Naranjo, an anthropologist and psychiatrist whose interdisciplinary work with mind-altering substances lead to a synthesis of spiritual and psychological thinking. Naranjo also taught the ideas and teachings of the esotericist G. I. Gurdjieff, which are commonly referred to as *The Fourth Way* (Ouspensky, 2000).

These influences upon the diamond approach are still very much in evidence today, and it has been Almass who has taken the work forward to offer an in-depth and still evolving model. If it were not for the evolving and deepening nature of his work, I think Almass could be accused of decanting 'old wine into new bottles', an accusation that a brief description of his work may dispel.

Examining the diamond approach will reveal that it encompasses the insights offered by the thinking of Gurdjieff, Sufic thought and Buddhism, particularly the Vajrayana and Zen schools. In addition to this rich esoteric/spiritual strand, ego psychology and contemporary object-relations theory are also present. Thus a model and praxis is presented that views psychological and spiritual growth as inseparable.

It is essentially a simple model of reality that offers a 'psychologically grounded spirituality', and although it could be thought of as a phenomological approach similar to many spiritual practises, it is not dependent upon a religious orientation. Simply put, it can be considered as being a perspective that explains lived experience without the need to separate the psychological and the spiritual.

In the literature the diamond approach is described as offering a twofold move towards spiritual and psychological integration.

It provides spiritual disciplines an understanding of the psychological issues and obstacles that can present throughout the spiritual search, and concomitantly, as a psychological viewpoint, it offers an experiential and intellectual understanding of the human condition, thus making psychological constructs useful to spiritual teaching: in other words, a transpersonal psychology.

Moreover, like psychosynthesis, and unlike most other transpersonal models, as well as offering a theoretical model, it proposes a set of exercises and practises, a practical toolbox of 'hands-on' techniques with which to apply the theory.

The diamond approach posits the premise that greater understanding and the resultant working through of psychological blocks or issues lead to the realization of our true nature, 'Essence' in Almass' terms. It is this psychological material that stimulates our growth and unfolding development in a way similar to the grain of sand that serves as the catalyst and seed in the creation of a pearl.

From a traditional depth psychology perspective this process would be seen as the creation of healthy ego functioning, a position that would bring greater freedom and choice. From Almass' perspective, however, the process is a spiritual exercise, and greater freedom and choice *are* the realization of the universal spiritual element of creation, both within oneself and the world at large.

Like the Sufic and Buddhist schools, from which concepts are drawn, this approach is a taught method, in that teachers are utilized in private sessions as well as small and large groups. Besides taught work, students are encouraged to study independently as well as with peers. The work encourages a method that is designed to heighten perceptual functions, to explore feelings, thoughts and actions in order to integrate emotional, cognitive and intuitive processes.

Although this, for some, may conjure up images that resonate with traditional and orthodox Western teaching modalities, it is more in line with qualitative and not quantitative research methodologies, such as Moustakas (1994), where lived experience and immersion in the field of study is regarded as a valid, if not a necessary, attitude and task.

A student in this context is an individual who is searching for more than intellectual understanding; in fact they are better described as seeking to know themselves and the fullness of reality; in Almass' terms this is the process of inquiry.

> Inquiry is something that arises in the midst of your experience – as part of your experience, not separate from it. In other words there is not a person here inquiring into something over there. The Inquirer has to be within the field of inquiry itself. This is different from inquiry in natural science, where the object of inquiry is outside you and all that is needed is to not interfere with it.
>
> (Almass, 2002, p. 113)

Moving on to examine the theoretical model, what is revealed is a view that considers reality as being both unmanifest and manifest and consisting of multiple dimensions, all of which are infinite, boundless and co-emergent with each other, an ontological hierarchy where potential can become actual and experienceable. 'We use the word "dimension" to refer to a level or plane of being, on which the various qualities of Essence appear in specific ways that differentiate it from other dimensions. Each dimension adds to essential aspects a new characteristic, universal to all aspects in this dimension' (Almass, 2002, p. 271).

The unmanifest is totally non-differentiated and without qualities though somehow, being within a dimension that is empty, it also holds all potential, and through its manifestation what we know as the world or the appearance of reality is revealed, although we may not be aware of its fullness. In other words, we could say that as the unmanifest manifests, it differentiates into dimensions and qualities. Thus what was to all intents and purposes virtual and potential becomes actual and experienceable.

The model can be likened to a spectrum that has an unmanifest that is non-differentiated, without qualities, 'absolute emptiness'. This is not the whole picture, however, as in Almass' view the dimensions become more differentiated and knowable. With spiritual realization regarded as being the recognition and embodiment of these dimensions, the knower becomes the known, a non-dual experience that Almass describes as 'Ontological Presence'. 'It is possible to arrive at a place where we can experience ourselves as the actual phenomenon, the actual ontological presence that we are, rather than as ideas and feelings about ourselves' (Almass, 2002, p. 7). This could also be described as a state of 'pure consciousness' or in a more familiar way 'self-realization'.

> In self-realization we experience ourselves as Presence where Presence is both Being and knowingness. Here, the cognitive act and being are the same experience. (...) The reason we experience knowing and being as a single phenomenon is that Presence is the Presence of consciousness, pure consciousness more fundamental than the content of mind (...) experiencing the direct truth and reality of our consciousness requires no object.
>
> (Almass, 2002, p. 22)

All the foregoing is, broadly speaking, consistent with the phenomenological practises and aims of Sufism, Vajrayana and Zen Buddhism. Almass, however, also draws upon contemporary depth psychology, particularly modern object-relations theory and the work of ego psychologists such as Kernberg (1995), in order to help explain the consequences of and the mechanisms employed to deal with alienation from 'essence' and 'true nature'. He conceived a 'concept of holes', which is employed to bring understanding of this alienation, as is his use of psychopathological constructs, such as Freud's 'drive psychology' with its concepts of integrated ego development, a mature functioning superego and id. Though borrowing some of Freud's model, he rejects the primacy of drives ruling the creation of ego structures. Instead Almass, like Kernberg, regards object relations as existing prior to the full formation of ego structure, and is able to offer explanations of pre-Oedipal function and its effect upon the whole lifespan and all eras of psychological development.

Simplifying the above suggests that psychological experiences, particularly emotions, arise directly from object experiences and are managed primarily by splitting. Thus it is these experiences that create the drives, and since effect and splitting are ego functions, the ego makes use of the repressed material to create the id.

The models posited by ego psychologists such as Kernberg look towards internalized and external objects relations, whilst Almass, although doing likewise, places more importance upon the internal world, with relationship to essence as the primary source of growth and development. This idea shares many similarities with Firman's and Gila's (1997) ideas about internal relationship to spirituality, as well as Washburn's (1988) Jungian-influenced ideas that revolve around internal relationship to the dynamic ground.

With the integration of contemporary psychology he also uses other depth psychology constructs such as psychopathological classifications.

Schizoid defences (Almass, 1998, pp. 75, 398) are one such mechanism he explores, though it is the detailed account of his understanding of narcissistic wounding that takes centre stage.

Like all psychological constructs he relates narcissism as having an aetiology firmly embedded in the experience of essence and the transpersonal. At its heart, he regards the narcissistic constellation as being the natural outcome of the lack of self-realization, and therefore all human beings have some degree of narcissistic wounding. From this perspective narcissism occurs when, '(...) the experience of the self is disconnected from its core, from the depths of what it is. It is estranged from its true nature, exiled from its primordial home' (Almass, 1996, p. 26). Explaining in greater depth he regards it as,

> (...) not simply alienation from being, but more specifically it is the loss of the Essential Identity. Given our discussion of the function of the Essential Identity to allow identification with one's true nature, it is clear that this loss is the central factor in our incapacity to know ourselves as Being, and thus, in our narcissism.
>
> (Almass, 1996, p. 148)

He explains the disconnection or alienation from 'essence' and 'true nature' with the theory of holes (Almass, 1987, 1998).

According to Almass, the pain and anxiety that we feel is the result of the experience of the loss of elements of our essential selves, and it is not caused by the external factors that are often blamed, such as feelings and thoughts concerning social standing, personal wealth, self-image or the actions of others. Therefore, he contends, seeking fulfilment in these areas does not work, as it is an essential aspect that is missing or unavailable to consciousness, leaving in its place a deficiency, a hole. To deal with this, a false facet, that resembles the lost essential aspect, fills or covers the deficiency. What is required, however, is the ability to bear the feelings that arise without defence, a process that will allow essence to emerge once again. Almass describes his theory of holes by stating that,

> A hole refers to any part of you that has been lost, meaning any part of you that you have lost consciousness of. What is left is a hole, a deficiency in a certain sense. What we have lost awareness of is, of course, our Essence. When we are not aware of our Essence, it stops manifesting and is lost. Then we feel a sense of deficiency. So a hole is nothing but the absence of a certain part of our Essence. It could be the loss of love, loss of value, loss of capacity for contact, loss of strength, the loss of will, loss of clarity, loss of pleasure, and any of those qualities of Essence. There are many of them. But when they are lost, they are not gone forever; they are never gone forever. You are simply cut off from them.
>
> (Almass, 1987, p. 17)

All is not lost, however, as Almass suggests what at first glance may seem a simple and undemanding remedy.

> When we stop defending against feeling a hole, the actual experience is not painful. We simply experience empty space, a feeling that there is nothing there – but not a threatening nothingness – a spaciousness, an allowing. This spaciousness allows Essence to emerge and it is Essence and only Essence that can eliminate that hole, that deficiency from the inside.
>
> (Almass, 1987, p. 22)

Although the foregoing can seem to be simplistic, in practise it will reveal myriad defences, and will point towards the idea that the majority of human kind is perhaps caught up in a web of holes and hole filling, as the following final quote sums up.

> Most of us spend our lives within a thin layer of reality, unaware of the deeper realms of our consciousness. What we call emotional reality – the layer where most people believe richness lies – is only onion-skin deep compared to the totality of reality. Beneath this thin layer of emotions and thoughts lie indescribable beauty and freedom. Many people wander in that onion-skin layer forever, but in the inquiry process, it's a layer we need to go through and not get stuck in.
>
> (Almass, 2002, p. 285)

I would imagine that the diamond approach as a taught method would be appealing to many though not all, particularly as it offers a fairly structured context and method that includes personal psychological work as well as a phenomenological exploration of personal and transpersonal themes.

The 'taught' method has been de rigor for centuries for many spiritual and religious traditions, both Eastern and Western, and is a method that certainly can be said to have been tried and tested. However, in master acolyte disciple structures there is the potential for dysfunctional relationships and power struggles, which can occur sometimes hand in hand with the increasing success of the system or body of teachings. For, whilst human nature may well have a transpersonal element, the ego needs of those involved with spiritual teaching are not always met in ways that are commendable to the core teachings or ethos of the body that teaches them. The master–disciple relationship is one that can engender basic and primitive psychological material, and as history reveals the 'road to realization' is littered with those who have been wounded. This can be the result of factors too numerous to mention, and can be from the hand of any figure or group, from the leader to the newest convert within the organization.

I would hope that if the diamond approach does indeed become as popularized as Cortright seems to suggest, it can maintain its integrity and find a means to practise what it preaches.

The final theorist whose work I discuss is also a relative newcomer, though unlike Almass her work is described as being firmly situated with a psychological framework.

## Isabel Clarke and the discontinuity model

Thus far I have included thinkers who claim wholeheartedly to be situated firmly within the transpersonal field, and as such I can with confidence examine their contribution from a transpersonal viewpoint. Clarke (2001), however, is clear that she does not want to be labelled a transpersonalist nor have her contribution to the field, 'the discontinuity model', seen as a transpersonal approach. Primarily she offers a perspective on the relationship between psychosis and spirituality, one of the key areas of debate within the transpersonal psychology community.

She sums up her views succinctly by stating that,

(...) the difference between madness and mysticism is not located within the experience, but the experiencer; that human beings are an incomplete instrument for apprehending reality; but we are capable of getting hold of different bits of it when in two different states of mind, with gradations between. The ability to reach these states of mind, and move smoothly back and forward between, is what distinguishes the saint and the diagnosed individual. However, this distinction is not absolute – the same person can have elements of both, at the same time.

(Clarke, 2002, p. 45)

This view, as she herself makes clear, is at odds with the postulates put forward by Wilber (1993b), particularly his ideas concerning the pre/trans fallacy, a position that will be more evident in a brief exploration of her contribution to theoretical debate within transpersonal psychology.

Her discontinuity model (2001, pp. 129–142) offers a very contemporary and differing approach, though what sets her work apart from all the other thinkers I have discussed is that it is more allied with the CBT School. Therefore she uses differing terms and reference points from which to explore and explain her concepts. The most obvious linguistic difference is that the transpersonal falls in her model within a form of experience that is termed 'transliminal' experience. Her description of transliminal experience embraces material that would fit the descriptions of being both psychotic and spiritual.[3] Though her use of language may be different, it is not the biggest difference between her model and that of others I discuss. It is not surprising that coming from a stance influenced by CBT she does not place great importance upon ego boundaries and ego-identity or regressive states. Instead, she uses two CBT models, Kelly's 'personal construct theory' and some elements of Teasdale's 'interacting cognitive sub-systems theory' as the foundations of her thinking.

In order to give a fair account of her model, I will briefly explain these theories to illuminate her thinking. First however I feel it is important to recognize that, though her thinking springs from within a differing school to the others I discuss, it distinguishes some similar states to those recognized by other thinkers in this section. A good case in point would be her acknowledgement that often it is common for a euphoric stage to precede psychotic breakdown. A phenomenon which may appear similar to those reported by individuals who experience what they

---

[3] Here, her thinking could be likened to that of Jung who in his model (as I discuss later in this section) placed the transpersonal within the collective unconscious.

construe as a spiritual experience. Moreover, she recognizes that this can cause confusion when distinguishing between the two. However she sees the euphoria encountered in psychotic states as being a sign of breakdown as other signs of psychological distress or distortion, such as paranoid delusions, persecutory voices.

Returning to 'personal construct theory' and 'interacting cognitive sub-systems theory', the first is a model that posits that what we experience is regulated by the way we make sense of the world. Clarke, taking this, posits two possible experiential modes in which we are able to encounter our environment. She describes the most common and familiar of the two as 'ordinary consciousness' and 'everyday functioning'. The second mode is a less-focused state, in which both psychotic and spiritual experience can be possible. Moreover, she sees this latter mode as the source of creativity and personal growth.

Her proposition is that these two modes constitute a continuum. The first would include states of everyday focused thinking such as problem solving, and from this end of the continuum moving towards the other, the experience of reverie (unfocused thinking) would be found; the other end, she suggests, would be where discontinuity is encountered.

Her account of Kelly's theory of personal constructs of thought processes sees mankind as being rational cognitive beings that make hypotheses and predictions based on information from their environment and past experience.

These predictions are termed 'constructs', and constitute an individual's unique model of the world. They configure their perceptions and actions, and are constantly adjusted following the feedback that experience brings.

In order to meet all of life's ups and downs with relative ease, an individual needs a sufficient range of constructs, though importantly an individual needs to be flexible enough to be able to assimilate new situations. This flexibility requires the ability to sufficiently loosen construct systems in order to accommodate new material, which in turn expands the system. Flexibility, however, is not enough, as it is important that a 'consolidation phase' follows the loosening of construct systems; simply put, the constructs are tightened again. If this 'consolidation phase' is not met, an inability to make valid predictions will result. This cyclical expansion and tightening followed by a loosening of constructs is seen as a natural rhythm, which is analogous to breathing. She suggests that the state of reverie would be seen as the 'breathing out'.

This model, therefore, sees 'reality' as being filtered through a series of modifiable constructs. A position that Clarke agrees with, though she also suggests that in fact reality is, as well as filtered by constructs, experienced outside the construct system. Her model asserts that both are essential and authentic aspects of being human. She explains that experience beyond the construct system, beyond the state of reverie, is a deconstructive state, and is the home of psychotic and spiritual experience.

It is not only Kelly's thinking that she uses to build her model. She also takes part of Teasdale's and Barnard's (1993) 'interacting cognitive subsystem model' as a means to explain and account for her thinking. This model is an elaborate rationalization that focuses upon the information processing aspect of cognition and, also endeavours to explain differing ways by which memory is stored. She concentrates upon two of nine sub-systems:

- the propositional stands for the logical cognition and thinking processes, and is capable of functioning in a discriminatory manner, with memory stored and coded verbally;
- the implicational sub-system perceives wholes and emotional meaning, and its memory system is coded in more than one sensory modality. In this mode, unlike the propositional, fine discrimination is not possible, for it works with relatively undifferentiated wholes.[4]

Clarke suggests that 'ordinary consciousness' and 'everyday functioning' is evidenced by the propositional and implicational sub-systems working agreeably together in balance. Whereas, in discontinuity that is in spiritual/psychotic states, the two are disjointed, and cognition and functioning are fundamentally driven by the implicational sub-system.

The latter experience, for healthy individuals, is difficult to access. Yet can be brought about by a crisis, or something that engenders a shift in consciousness, such as the effect of certain drugs or spiritual practise.

However, for an individual suffering from psychosis cognition and functioning is primarily processed by the implicational sub-system.

From this vantage point 'reality' has not been mediated (construed) by both the propositional and the implicational sub-systems. It is, instead, an experience of operating only at the implicational level, which can lead to experiences of euphoria, a state that in turn will lead to individuals experiencing a loss of orientation, generated by being unable to rely on or make sense of their environment. This comes about as

---

[4] Observing these two systems it is easy to draw comparisons with Ornstein's bimodal consciousness as discussed in the previous chapter.

a consequence of being unable to access the familiar compass and parameters provided by the construct system, and/or the propositional sub-system.

Clarke gives two examples of how an orderly return to construed reality, everyday reality, can be accomplished,

> In the case of a mystical experience attained through spiritual practice (or, as often happens, occurring spontaneously but within a spiritual context that gives it meaning for the experiencer), managing the transition back to construed reality after the experience generally (but not invariably) occurs naturally and after a short space of time. Where the same state is achieved by taking a drug, the return again normally (but not invariably) occurs when the drug wears off.
>
> (Clarke, 2001, p. 137)

This, however, is not possible for the psychotic or for individuals experiencing unwanted effect of drugs, as they are metaphorically stranded beyond their normal constructs, unable to make use of the propositional sub-system. This is a state of affairs where the dissolution of subject–object differentiation occurs, as well as the differentiation between internal and external experience.

Functioning that is experienced as being beyond the familiar boundaries offered by the space–time continuum may evidence her argument. And it can give rise to experiencing phenomena such as telepathy or the ability of others to read or interfere with their thoughts, which can be construed as 'normal' or 'true'.

From a clinical stance incidents such as these could be recognized as an attempt to make sense of and understand the unfamiliar by grabbing at every connection that presents itself. Within experiences such as these there can be a disintegration of common boundaries where internal concerns can be experienced as external communication, and in extremis as disembodied voices.

Interestingly, although she claims that she approaches her subject solely within the confines of cognitive psychology, it seems to me that she abandons this school moving to psychodynamic/psychoanalytic thinking to explain the variance between psychosis and spiritual experience.

Like the other theorists I explore she claims that individuals with sufficient ego strength can incorporate and make positive use of temporary spiritual experiences; whereas those with scant ego strength become entrapped within a psychotic breakdown,[5] from which escape is not easy. This is not at variance with her assertion that the above can present a clinical dilemma, namely distinguishing between spiritual and psychiatric crisis. However, she states that

> The difference between the position I am adopting, and the more conventional one, will be at the level of conceptualisation. Whereas the standard position, informed for instance by psychodynamic or transpersonal thinking, will be that the course of the condition produces information that enables the practitioner to discriminate between two entirely different phenomena – namely the spiritual crisis and the psychotic breakdown, so that the outcome tells them which it was *all along* – I would argue that this absolute distinction is invalid and essentially meaningless.
>
> (p. 140)

This suggests a form of 'time will tell' attitude that automatically places spiritual experience in a diagnostic category evidenced by an individual returning fairly promptly to 'consensual reality', as opposed to the psychotic who is stuck beyond their familiar cognitive framework.

This is in stark contrast with the other theorists I explore, all of whom propose clear clinical benefits in being able to create taxonomy of transegoic and pre-egoic states that offer the opportunity to optimize treatment.

Clarke presents a well-researched argument for her model; nevertheless, it views psychological experience through the very narrow focus of cognitive functioning. This enables her to achieve clarity, yet it creates a worldview that makes it hard to incorporate the thinking of theorists from differing schools, albeit she does introduce concepts, such as 'ego strength', that are not normally associated with CBT thinking. Moreover, although she is clear in her insistence that her model is situated within the CBT framework, her view explores territory that is far from familiar to the model in general. The following quote amply displays this.

> By giving full weight to our transliminal quality of experience and so giving weight to our implicational selves we become aware of how

---

[5] This is in line with Wilber's 'pre/trans fallacy' model that emphasizes that healthy ego development is a prerequisite for productive transpersonal experience, as well as Washburn's concept of 'regression in the service of transcendence'.

dependant we are on relationship; how our very experience of self is created by relationship, and how that web of relationship extends beyond the immediate significant others, to the wider human race, to the non human inhabitants of our planet, to our earth, to other presences, and to the ultimate relationship in which we are held – whether we call that God or whatever.

(Clarke, 2002, pp. 45–46)

In my experience, passages such as this are not representative of CBT discourse, and could be considered to be more akin to the literature exploring creation spirituality (Fox, 2000) or relational psychoanalysis (Mitchell, 2004).

The focus upon cognition and the thinking function is not the focus for all the other models I discuss, for they can, and indeed do, include the cognitive, albeit not at the exclusion of other spheres of experience. Thus, the CBT framework that her model is situated within is not, I feel, an ideal tool by which to explore and explain transpersonal (transliminal) phenomena other than the changes or the breakdown of 'normal' cognitive process. CBT does however offer a clinical perspective from which to view one of the many aspects of the psychopathology of spiritual emergence, a subject that is explored in the next chapter. Furthermore, any theory that seeks to reveal how the world is experienced, although not addressing what is being experienced, can be a useful addition to transpersonal theory.

## Conclusions

The overview of the most influential models in the field has revealed that, like in psychology in general, no one model or thinker can offer a position that brings no disagreement from some of their peers and wholehearted agreement from others. It also reveals the possibility for non-transpersonal clinicians to create integrative approaches that utilize postulates from their own core model and those offered by transpersonal thinkers. A position that supports a view of human functioning that is greater than that afforded by other models. In addition to differences regarding theory, there is no general agreement concerning the application or inclusion of the transpersonal in practise, a situation that is highlighted in the following section. Although the foregoing may meet agreement from those in the field, underdetermination of theoretical constructs can present challenges regarding the field's theoretical claims, particularly for those that are situated in other allied disciplines. For instance, although many clinicians from the world of psychiatry may be sympathetic to transpersonal theories, perhaps many more would challenge much transpersonal thinking, as it cannot meet their concepts of construct validity. However, no matter the theory that regards human nature and the human condition, some may always say that the proof of the pudding may only be revealed in the application of theory.

With this in mind the next and last section moves from the theoretical constructs that create the field to how theory is utilized in the clinical setting.

# 5
# The Application of Transpersonal Thinking

## Introduction

Having explored some of the 'what is' transpersonal psychology – a look at various fields that underpin its theoretical base and a glimpse at the thinkers who have created or are creating the field as a distinct body of knowledge – I conclude by a discussion of transpersonal psychology in practise.

Those readers who would like an in-depth step-by-step manual containing a how to apply transpersonal theory in the clinical setting will, however, be disappointed when they are looking towards the literature for such a work, as the majority of published material tends to have a theoretical bias. Yet, although the field has not produced a large body of work that addresses the transpersonal in clinical practise, a wide range of approaches can be found.

These cover an eclectic assortment of technique or clinical approach, without one being hailed as the best, most efficient or necessary, because, like in all things transpersonal, there is a general trend towards recognizing that the phenomena under examination can indicate the most advantageous method needed. Moreover, with an openness to approaching psychology as including transegoic functioning, the attitude that the transpersonal is the context in which the work takes place and not always the area of exploration can also be considered.

With an attitude such as this, Wilber's idea that pathology can manifest on a multitude of levels may be a useful concept. And if followed to its logical conclusion this would suggest that different models may be needed, or that clinicians will need to be able to recognize the strength and limitations of their own core models. This, however, is a clinical awareness I would expect from practitioners of all traditions, whether their core model/s accept transpersonal functioning or not. Yet, the obvious difficulty for those that subscribe to schools that do not accept the validity of a transpersonal worldview is that they could misconstrue anything transpersonal, as they will not have the means to differentiate between symptoms of a transpersonal and non-transpersonal nature. In terms of psychopathology this could be seen as differentiating between regressive (pre-egoic) forms of functioning such as psychosis and transpersonal phenomena. With this as a valid concern, much of this section focuses upon the pre/trans fallacy and the idea of spiritual emergence and spiritual emergency.

Although no fixed practises are prescribed, transpersonal psychology can be practised in a systematic manner: for example, both psychosynthesis (Assagioli, 1990; Whitmore, 1991) and Hameed Alis' Diamond Approach (1987, 2002) do offer structured approaches to working with the transpersonal. However, others such as Grof (1985) with 'Holotropic Breathing' suggest specific techniques. Nevertheless, as this work proposes, if the transpersonal is one of many levels of functioning or reality, in practise there is no reason to think that all clinicians with adequate training could include working explicitly or implicitly, if or when the need arises, with the transpersonal. This is a view that is in accord with Hutton (1994), who found that transpersonally orientated therapists tend towards being eclectic in their use of techniques.

This inclusive stance I have found useful in my own clinical practise, so as to be able to make the most propitious use of the tools and methods available, following careful consideration of the needs of the client and their life circumstances.

For instance, individuals who could be considered as being

- refugees from their own disturbance looking towards spirituality as a way to seek the solace they so desperately crave, or
- comparatively well-adjusted individuals, who through spiritual practise or happenstance have found themselves adrift on strange seas,

may present with similar symptoms, yet need very different types of care. The forma may, for example, benefit from a more psychoanalytic stance where transferencial relationships are worked through with basic ego strengthening work, whilst investigating in a contained manner the implications and meaning inherent in their experiences, yet due to their expansive nature, any technique that explores transpersonal energies such as some forms of meditation or guided imagery being a contraindication.

This would be a very different approach to the one adopted for the latter who may be better served by supporting the integration of their experience. A task that could be achieved through various means, many of which, such as meditative practise, visualization and the embodying of qualities, would not be far from the practises of many spiritual or religious schools.

This elasticity of approach for those clinicians who practise within strict confines may not be possible. Yet, as the analytical psychotherapists Wellings and McCormick (2000) and Boorstein (1997), who had a traditional psychiatric and Freudian psychoanalytically orientated training, demonstrate, it is possible to incorporate transpersonal psychology in clinical practise for those who have received trainings in approaches that traditionally do not include the transpersonal. Nevertheless, as Boorstein also recounts, to do so may require a willingness to question basic theoretical assumptions: in his case the orthodox postulate that regards the therapist's anonymity as being sacrosanct and needed for the successful working through of transference, a concept that is one of the corner stones of the traditional psychoanalytic approach.

The recognition that theoretical flexibility may be an advantageous attribute for a clinician who practises within frameworks that allow a transpersonal worldview could not be enough; a clinician will need to have a good working knowledge of the transpersonal realm, although it would be simple-minded to imagine that someone could possibly have a working knowledge of all transpersonal theories, and furthermore naïve to imagine that they may have experienced all of the possible ways that the transpersonal can be encountered.

As well as being a reasonable proposition this line of reasoning could also support the argument that the transpersonal can be the context in which psychological work takes place and not always the area of its exploration.

With this way of undertaking clinical practise, 'doing' transpersonal psychology is in some ways a false or at least redundant statement, as the clinical application of transpersonal psychology may be less about 'doing' and more about 'being', with 'being' meaning an expansive attitude that is open to the fullness of human experience.

This then also goes towards making sense of ideas that need an integrative position such as Clarkson's (2002) 'Transpersonal relationship in psychotherapy', which suggests that the psychotherapeutic relationship, the context, is multifaceted, with five distinct relational spheres, one of which is the transpersonal level.

The idea of the therapeutic relationship having or needing a transpersonal element is not exclusive to Clarkson's model, as Rowan's (2002) 'Transpersonal way of relating to clients' shares some similarities to her views; he brings, though, a more defined postulate, which recognizes that in therapy there are three ways of relating to clients and approaching psychology: the instrumental, the authentic and the trans personal. The instrumental shares similarities to the view of the relationship and practises employed by the first force of psychology; the authentic shares practises and thinking that has similarities to the third force, whilst the transpersonal way of relating to clients is one where object–subject differentiation – therapist–client differentiation – is less defined. This last approach, 'a transpersonal way of relating to clients', he suggests, '(...) requires a form of Being (the state of consciousness necessary), a way of Doing (the actual techniques and methods used), and a form of Knowing (the theory of what is being done)' (Rowan, 2002, p. 101).

To my mind, however, the foregoing could be considered to be important, if not necessary, in all clinical approaches regardless of their view of the transpersonal. Yet, Rowan, focusing upon the transpersonal, regards the consciousness of the therapist to be of utmost importance, as for him what is important is the cultivation of the ability to consciously step into a realm of transpersonal functioning. Because his thinking is very much influenced by Wilber, he regards this as working within the 'Subtle level' (Wilber, 2000a). In addition to Wilber's thinking, Rowan takes a similar position to Cortright's (1997, pp. 56–60) which considers it is the consciousness of the client that takes centre stage in the therapeutic alliance, whilst recognizing that the consciousness of the therapist is of equal importance. Here the general assumption is that the therapist needs to have some lived experience and integration of the transpersonal, as it is the therapist themselves (their consciousness) that is the 'main instrument of therapy'. This is not an uncommon idea: Firman and Gila (1997), for instance, suggest that psychosynthesis psychotherapists need to continually explore and work with all aspects of their own psyches in order to be 'good enough' clinicians (pp. 247–251).

Ideas such as these are as far as one could get from a 'solution-doing things approach', though like in all things spiritual or otherwise, there is the potential for distortion. I would suggest that in the same way that a transpersonal view can be likened to a metaview in which problems can be identified, though not necessarily worked through, a competent clinician will need more than a working experience of transpersonal realities, especially if developmental arrest or failure can and does occur on all levels.

Moreover, suggestions that clinicians need to have reached/explored certain levels of consciousness can lead to various forms of (spiritual) idealization, with the possibility of some sort of guru status bestowed or claimed. I am not proposing that the working through of an idealization transference (Kohut, 1971a) cannot be a useful therapeutic task; however, to do so requires the clinician to be aware of its effect upon the work, as well as have some awareness of this form of defence in the client's life as well as their own. Generally with its non-empirically testable status, and possible grand spectrum of interest, the transpersonal is a field that can draw individuals for whom narcissistic configurations in their psyche have been reactivated, and for clinicians a training in clinical practise and the exploration of transpersonal theories can be the honing or subtly adding to and shoring up narcissistic defences that naturally emerge in the therapeutic encounter.

Although the transpersonal may be conceived as the context of the work, it would be unwise to not also recognize that it can equally offer the content. However, due to the field-like nature of the transpersonal, content must not be confused with outcome, because content is not measurable, other than as subjective and self-reported experience, whilst preferable outcomes and their measurement can be identified. Boorstein (1996) points out that innovative techniques with a diversity of approaches can offer ways of 'doing' transpersonal psychotherapy, yet no one way is presented as 'the' way, '(...) there is no royal road to the transpersonal. Each therapist and each patient must find the road that is right for him or her' (Boorstein, 1996, p. 329).

With no fixed approach or technique recommended, some thinkers do find a means to suggest that a transpersonal orientation can be defined by its praxis. Scotton et al. (1986, pp. 412–415), who regard the inclusion of the transpersonal in psychiatry as vital, do this by positing five clinical principles, which can be summarized as follows:

- Due to the complexity of human functioning a holistic methodology is required.
- Clinical interventions need to be aimed at an individual's developmental level or specific presenting issue, with the caveat that for some individuals a spiritual focus can be a distraction or defence.

- Some issues are transpersonal and thus need an unambiguously spiritual approach.
- Transpersonal interventions can be used therapeutically regardless of an individual's level of development.
- Transpersonal techniques used without prudence can be dangerous or harmful, though with due care and consideration they can be effective and life enhancing.

Although these five principles could be considered to provide a professional and safe clinical framework and praxis, their final conclusion is that

> Because of the many uses of transpersonal experiences, clinical experience and judgment are essential in transpersonal psychiatry for two major issues: (1) defining the therapeutic goals for a particular individual and (2) matching transpersonal interventions to him, choosing from biological, psychological, social and spiritual techniques. This pragmatic judgment is surely the heart of transpersonal psychiatry, just as curiosity and awe for all human experience is its soul.
>
> (ibid., pp. 414–415)

Here importance is placed upon the realistic assessment of the practitioners' competence, a task which includes their ability to make clinical judgments that meet the overall needs of those seeking their service, a position that would be expected from any clinician regardless of the orientation; however, the inclusion of the transpersonal can add additional complexity in the pragmatic assessment process.

This highlights the practical challenges faced when considering Wilber's assertion that psychopathology is brought about by development arrest/failure in any one of his three bands/stages (p. 22). It also highlights the need for particular methods and techniques to be called for, dependant upon the level that corresponds to the presenting pathology.

Although Wilber, as a non-clinician, can only support his arguments at a conceptual level, clinicians such as Boorstein (1997) look towards their practise to substantiate and demonstrate the efficacy of various transpersonal techniques. His particular approach includes transpersonal methodologies in a traditional psychotherapeutic frame that draws particularly from 'self psychology' (Kohut, 1971a) and 'intersubjective psychoanalysis' (Stolorow et al., 1987). He reveals his clinical practise by means of a series of case studies and presents a variety of transpersonal interventions that include practises such as various forms of meditation, the encouragement of clients studying texts and spiritually biased philosophy.

The presenting issues/pathology that he explores and the transpersonal treatment of his clinical vignettes are representative to my mind of the challenges that are presented in general practise: psychotic disorders, the borderline psychotic patient, mood disorders, pre-neurotic character disorders, neurotic illness and existential problems; he also examines the use of transpersonal interventions in Relationship Psychotherapy.

Many of these pathologies would automatically warrant, from the traditional psychiatric view, a suitably qualified clinician to prescribe from a psychopharmacological formulary, choosing drugs that are designed for symptom/behaviour reduction, management or elimination.

This course of action is not only applicable to traditional psychiatric view as it can also be of help to individuals suffering due to the influence of unintegrated material that has a basis in the transpersonal realm. Thus transpersonal psychiatry can also look towards utilizing the same psychopharmacological agents when addressing the needs of individuals who are suffering with conditions that have a transpersonal aetiology or would benefit by the inclusion of transpersonal interventions.

A situation that Kasprow and Scotton (1999) recognize, writing in the APA's, The American Psychiatric Associations' *Journal of Psychotherapy Practice and Research,* as for them it is clear that for some individuals a transpersonal therapy where the prescribing of medication is usefully combined with other therapeutic modalities is the most appropriate course of action.

> Most transpersonal drug therapy involves the use of conventional psychotropic agents (…). Antipsychotic medications, antidepressants, mood stabilizers, and sedatives can be used to modulate but not suppress symptoms in patients undergoing spiritual emergencies. The goal of such modulation is to attenuate the intensity of symptoms just enough to allow affected persons to constructively explore the meaning of their experiences, thereby facilitating the development of cognitive maps linking ordinary consensual reality with transpersonal states. The intention is to help the individual move through and integrate these states, rather than merely suppress symptoms. Such

individuals will probably not require chronic medication, and many may simply require psychological and social support, education, and reassurance.

(p. 20)

The above suggests that the psychiatric profession can be an ideal point of first contact for those who present with symptoms that could indicate one of a group of mental disorders that fall within the general diagnosis of psychoses, particularly so as the profession is perhaps the most knowledgeable when considering mental illness.

Yet, it is not too difficult to find many, in my opinion ill informed, transpersonal therapists, who appear to be wary or hostile towards the prescribing culture of psychiatry. Victor (1986) is unambiguous on this matter and addressing the transpersonal in clinical practise clearly he states that, '(...) it is no longer a viable position for a psychotherapist of any theoretical persuasion to take a stand against medications in the treatment of potentially disabling psychiatric syndromes. Only after integration of neurochemistry and psychopharmacology with transpersonal psychological theory and psychotherapy can a transpersonal psychiatry be achieved' (Victor, 1986, p. 330).

Views such as this are important if transpersonal psychology is to be fully integrated within mainstream psychiatry, and the insights of the psychiatric world to be fully embraced by the transpersonal community, and is perhaps a view that may offer a rapprochement between the thinking of transpersonal clinicians and orthodox psychiatric practitioners.

Returning to Victor (pp. 330–331) he offers four simple principles that a clinician must bear in mind when considering transpersonal psychopharmacology. They can be summarized as:

- The importance of correct diagnosis.
- A good understanding of what medication can and cannot achieve.
- A capacity to integrate spiritual disciplines in treatment plans when appropriate.
- Due to the broad context of transpersonal experience, care must be taken when prescribing medication to ensure the least number of side effects with the awareness that some patients need to work through spiritual crises and not have their symptoms overly suppressed.

These are all in accord with Scotton, Chinen and Battista's five clinical principles mentioned earlier. They also highlight the importance of correct differential diagnosis, separating transpersonal experience and abnormal psychopathology, an argument that can be found repeatedly in the literature.

With the exception of the overtly transpersonal element, the foregoing approach to medication is in line with the prescribing attitude adopted by R. D. Laing (1959) who, in order for the patient to better understand the meaning inherent in their experiences, recommended, combined with existential analysis, the lessening of the dosage of the anti-psychotic drugs that patients received.

This could be conceived as purposely inciting, or at the least not inhibiting, altered states of consciousness, a view and practise that is the opposite approach to the symptom-reduction-leading-to-'normal-functioning' that is the clinical norm; yet, it is in accord with ideas that symptoms, even if experienced as disturbing, are not always signs of deep underlying disturbance. In fact the encouragement of altered states of consciousness, and not always their suppression, is norm for those clinicians within the psychiatry profession who do accept transpersonal functioning.

So far this discussion has only explored the use of drugs administered by a prescriber who has a clinical training that encompasses a good working knowledge of the desired effects and possible side effects of the agents prescribed, and is not under the effect of the drug themselves. This, however, is not the case for individuals who take drugs that have not been prescribed to them; in this category would be included illegal drugs as well as natural substances, 'entheogens', that have a psychoactive effect and can be found in nature such as some mushrooms and fungi.

Self-medication and the seeking of altered states of consciousness is not new phenomena, and there have been countless cultures throughout history where the regular use of mind-altering substances are utilized in religious, shamanic and ceremonial practises as well as in secular contexts, and is/was considered the norm.

Many are claimed to aid the individual in getting in touch with realms that could be considered to meet the criteria of being transpersonal, with an objective that seeks some form of indirect or direct benefit for the individuals who ingest the substance or the benefit of others.

In the present era, in the West, with the advent of modern chemical processes, the procurement of illegally manufactured synthetic drugs that have similar effects is possible. Although this method may give a glimpse or full-blown experience of the transpersonal, their use is not recommended. In addition to legal, moral or social implications, there are three major concerns that govern their use. First and foremost these drugs are powerful agents that change many of the natural chemical balances, and their effect, in the short and long term, upon the whole system is not fully known or understood by those that use them. Secondly these drugs have not undergone rigorous clinical trials and may have been watered down with all sorts of baulking agents, so as to optimize the potential profit for those that sell them. Lastly anything chemical or otherwise that engenders transpersonal experience cannot be considered innocuous, as some individuals may find such an encounter detrimental to their overall well-being.

In my own clinical practise numerous individuals have presented with symptoms that have been exacerbated or caused by ill-advised recreational drug use. These have included a plethora of experiences amongst which experiences of unity with creation, others and inanimate objects, the awareness of a divine presence and the enhancement of the five senses. Generally these experiences have been 'mind blowing', with some finding themselves questioning their self-image and their worldview; this questioning of all the things that they held to be true often has lead to profound and lasting personal changes to their experience of the whole of creation. For some this necessitated supporting the integration of their expanded glimpse of themselves and their world as well as exploring the inner and outer circumstances that lead to their choice to use such substances; overall a focus upon the past, present and potential futures. Others, however, whilst their experience could bring similar questions, needed a completely different course of treatment, as they found themselves lost and unable to function within consensually agreed realities. With a plethora of models by which to explain or discuss their psychopathology they could display symptoms and behaviours that meet the diagnostic criteria of the full spectrum of mental disorders.

In the present political, social and research climate, the use of 'mind altering' psychedelic drugs, such as LSD, in the clinical setting is a contentious and illegal practise; however, until the latter part of the 1960s this was not so, and research into the effects of such drugs was condoned and accepted. Grof (1976) is unquestionably the best-known transpersonal practitioner to have conducted research into their potential benefit in the clinical setting. His findings based on psychotherapy with patients under the influence of psychedelic drugs, he claims, recognized that the careful and clinically administered use of psychedelics such as LSD can be considered to be a means to amplify or act as a catalyst for unconscious material to be brought closer to everyday awareness.

Having recognized the obvious, in that prescribed and non-prescribed drugs can and do affect consciousness, it is also important to bear in mind that for many individuals transpersonal exercises and practises are very effective yet cannot be considered risk-free. A good and obvious example, perhaps due to its abreactive and oft times cathartic nature, is Grof's holotropic breathwork, a very powerful tool that can encourage the loosening of ego boundaries and uncover material that has been deeply suppressed or repressed from normal everyday consciousness as well as allowing access to the transpersonal. Other less colourful techniques that seem more sedate such as vippasena meditation, an intense meditation practise, can equally evoke disturbing material that has not been available to everyday consciousness.

So far this exploration of the application of transpersonal psychology has only looked towards the one-to-one, the dyadic relationship. However, whilst this may be a common way of practising psychology, many transpersonal practises are suitable for group context. The literature covering this area is almost non-existent.

## Spiritual emergence and spiritual emergency

Spiritual emergence and spiritual emergency are two phrases that appear often in the literature, and were first coined by Stan Grof and his partner Christina. They recognized the importance of finding a means to refer to competent and knowledgeable clinician-individuals who are experiencing difficulties associated with spontaneous spiritual experiences and spiritual practises who needed appropriate support.

Though recognizing such a need and the frequency that the terms 'spiritual emergence' and 'spiritual emergency' appear in transpersonal literature may be noteworthy in themselves, what I feel important is that the theories supporting these terms highlight an area of the practical application of much of the theory that has been discussed.

Before exploring these terms and the intrinsic ideas contained in them, it is useful, as in other parts of this work, to define the terms and I turn to Nelson (1996) to furnish with a clear, concise explanation.

> A spiritual emergence is an awakening into a level of awareness and insight beyond the ordinary capabilities of the ego. It heralds passage into higher, transpersonal realms of consciousness. Although the self has not yet learned how to manage the power inherent in these breakthroughs, it recognizes them as important signs that guide it on its upward path.

A spiritual emergence may present itself meekly, perhaps as a sudden intimation of a deeper meaning in nature, a 'runner's high' with a feeling of being at one with the environment, an appreciation of several startling coincidences, or a series of 'hunches' that come true. For a fleeting moment, one feels selfless, boundless, beyond ego. In some cases it presents itself more dramatically as an out-of-body excursion, a near-death experience, or an awesome vision that inspires a new direction in life. Or it may momentarily overwhelm a person with a fully realized mystical experience, an ecstatic ASC [Altered State of Consciousness] that merges self with All. These latter events are unforgettable. Although they cannot be repeated at will, they leave in their wake a lingering sense of the unity of all things that becomes a vital source of energy sustaining the arduous journey back to the Source.

In any case, a person retains his grip on consensual reality during a spiritual emergence even as he opens to a larger sphere of nonordinary reality. This can render him stunned but intact, transformed but able to operate in the world. Although spiritual emergencies are accompanied by a temporary suspension of ego-identity, they do not dissolve the ego as do regressive states.

(pp. 264–265)

The above would be familiar to theological scholars conversant with the revelatory or mystical experiences described in the texts of all the world's great religions as well as, in varying degrees, perhaps to less-informed individuals who follow a spiritual practise. The above would also be familiar to clinicians who understand or/and appreciate that healthy psychological life can include more than the Newtonian/Cartesian paradigm.

However, we must bear in mind that it would not be hard to argue that experiences such as these used to describe spiritual emergence mirror some of the descriptions given to psychotic conditions such as schizophrenia. For example, 'a sudden intimation of a deeper meaning in nature', feelings of 'being at one with the environment', 'appreciation of several startling coincidences' and 'selfless' experiences would sway many clinicians towards making a psychiatric diagnosis that includes abnormal psychology.

This position, though understandable, could speak more of spiritual emergency, and once again I turn to Nelson (1996) for clarification.

A healthy and mature person can tolerate a spiritual emergence without dissolution. But less-prepared people may be overwhelmed by the inrush of spiritual energy, which in extreme cases can temporarily disrupt the ego. (...) In such cases there develops a crisis known as a spiritual emergency.

A spiritual emergency is an ASC [altered state of consciousness] of profound disorientation and ego disruption that sometimes accompanies spiritual emergence. The ASC is often of near-psychotic proportions, lasting minutes, days, or weeks, but it can end with a positive outcome if not interrupted. These upheavals bring to the surface unresolved aspects of the personality that impede spiritual growth. A spiritual emergency differs from both schizophrenia and regression in the service of transcendence in that the self neither regresses nor retreats in any other way, but actively engages the process even though it temporarily forfeits its ego-based ability to function competently in the social world.

A spiritual emergency may take a variety of forms, including ASCs colored by dramatic death and rebirth experiences, out-of-body experiences, extrasensory perception or premonitions, memories of what seem to be past incarnations, revelatory visions, and states of mystical union. Physical manifestations may include feelings of heat or electricity rising up the spine, spontaneous immobile trance states during which an individual is unable to communicate with others and feels he is receiving information from a 'higher source', and feelings of pain or tension that are relieved when the individual assumes certain postures, sometimes resembling the classical positions of Hatha yoga.

(pp. 265–266)

With clear definitions of spiritual emergence and spiritual emergency it is easy to see how without care and consideration both could be confused as being one and the same, highlighting the importance of diagnostic models that can differentiate between the two. Particularly, so as states that include regressive features can in fact be progressive and thus confusing mystical experience with psychotic regression needs to be avoided.

However, with such a complex set of experiences and symptoms, ones that may be unique to an individual, it would be impossible to create a set of diagnostic criteria that places one set of symptoms in the psychotic spectrum and another set in a healthy/normal spectrum.

A state of affairs that could lead to a misdiagnosis, a treatment plan and working hypotheses that may influence clinicians to be caught within Wilber's 'pre/trans fallacy' where pre-personal and transpersonal states are misdiagnosed as being the other.

With the foregoing as a potential issue in the clinical setting, a brief examination of psychotic-like illness and common experiences that are encountered by those experiencing the transpersonal realm may be helpful.

In order to do this it is appropriate to recognize that, though all schools of depth psychology have explored and created maps and models that explain abnormal psychopathology, it is usually the allopathic medical model, the psychiatric profession, that is most often called upon first to support individuals who are suffering with, and display behaviour and traits that do not concur with accepted societorial norms. Yet in the present climate the orthodox psychiatric profession, with its scientific framework that advocates the epistemological principles of empiricism and materialism, may not be the ideal lens through which to recognize disruptive/unintegrated spiritual experiences. However, as it has already been mentioned, an increasing number of clinicians within the psychiatric profession accept that reality may include more than the measurable and quantifiable offered by empiricism and materialism – a view that is not only held by the few published transpersonal theorists who are themselves psychiatrists such as Lukoff (1998), Chinen (1996), Grof (1985), Assagioli (1990), Boorstein (1997), Nelson (1996) and Deikman (1996) as well as Kasprow and Scotton (1999).

Clinicians such as these have undergone conventional psychiatric training, and thus are able to offer transpersonal clinicians and theorists some of the considerable insight and understanding that the medical model has gained in over century of careful, studious research.

And although the traditional psychiatric approach perhaps is not always the best resource to aid those reporting difficulties integrating transpersonal energies, it is eminently suited to, and without doubt, the most desirable choice for the exploration of organic psychoses.

Organic psychoses in psychiatric nosology are recognized as containing underlying influences that stem from anatomical, biological and/or physiological changes or abnormality. With determinants such as these the expertise and understanding of clinicians working within or conversant with the medical model it is clearly required.

Functional psychoses, however, are another matter, and bring a clinician great challenge, as they are typified by psychotic-like states where the determinants of organic psychoses cannot be traced. Unable to find cause or reason for many functional psychotic episodes and states, psychiatry is often successful in the alleviation or control of symptoms using psychopharmacology to suppress symptoms.

It must be recognized, however, that, though psychiatry has expended considerable effort over several decades in the search for the aetiology of functional psychoses, no theoretical consensus has emerged.

It is not just the psychiatric community that has been involved in this exploration. Many within the field accept that psychology offers reasoned debates and suggestions that explain the experience of some that suffer from psychotic conditions and display psychotic behaviour.

For example, Klein (1975) and other theorists, particularly those who see themselves as 'depth psychologists' such as psychoanalytic therapists, have for many years based their thinking in the insights that clinical practise brings. From this viewpoint physiological determinants are not ignored, though emphasis is also placed upon the inclusion of an exploration of life history and conditioning. This often focuses upon childhood events, and can include an examination of possible preverbal and infantile experience, a method that is sometimes referred to as a biographical approach.

It would make this study simple if I could claim that the use of psychopharmacology, or that uncovering and working through biographical history and the insights of depth psychology, fully explain all non-organic psychoses and the accompanying behaviour and personality structures.

It is the above that opens up the possibility that transpersonal psychology may be able to add additional insight concerning the determinants of some functional psychoses, or at the least shed light upon the cause of individuals displaying symptoms that would place them in a diagnostic category seen as a mental illness.

However, like those from the psychiatric profession, transpersonal psychology professionals cannot claim to have all the answers.

Yet, because of the ascendancy that orthodox traditional psychiatric thinking holds in the West many psychiatric professionals are unaware of ideas that do not originate in their own epistemological tradition, thus finding it hard to explain or identify transpersonal experience from within their theoretical confines.

It could be argued that this is due to the transpersonal realm being ineffable; however, a more likely explanation could be that transpersonal experience is located beyond the rational epistemology that psychiatry is situated within.

A good example of the confines that orthodox traditional psychiatric reasoning is bounded by can be seen in how it views Jungian thinking as not having a quantitative and empirically testable and measurable credence. However, Jung (1973) can be accredited as being among the best-known early thinkers to suggest that psychopathology can be influenced by factors that are neither biographical nor organic. One reason for this suggestion could lie in his postulate of the collective unconscious. He postulated that we all have access to a shared universal realm that is distinct from, yet allied to, the personal unconscious.

From the Jungian perspective many experiences that are considered evidence of psychotic states could be seen as the emergence of, or an individual somehow working with, elements of the collective unconscious, which could include experiences such as visions of a demonic or angelic nature, familiar territory to those involved with the diagnosis of psychosis. Here we must also recognize that individuals are situated within their own milieu, and therefore may interpret experience according to prevailing symbols.

This could explain how those that could be diagnosed as suffering from a psychotic illness in 'third world' communities have been known to report experiences of being taken over by 'Djombies' (malign spirits), whereas in the developed and technologically driven first world it is more common to find reports that 'space beings' from UFO's or malicious governmental operatives are interfering with or influencing an individual.

In my own practise, clients have presented with fears or experiences that are couched in the terms, concepts and images that are popular at the time: for example, whilst in the 1980s these fears were often centred around being abducted by aliens or battling with the 'Dark Side', in the present era a larger number of disturbed individuals fear they have been taken over by or are a component of a malign intelligent structure that underlies perceived reality. In these cases blockbuster Hollywood movies could have presented these themes: in the 1980s it was 'Close Encounters of the First Kind' and 'Star Wars', whilst in the present era 'The Matrix' appears to be a better vehicle for trying to create meaning from frightening or strange overwhelming experiences.

It is not just the Jungian perspective that can be seen to be at odds with a psychiatric profession that places individuals that exhibit behaviour that is not seen as 'normal' in a 'model of illness' with a whole taxonomy of abnormal psychopathology.

Romme and Escher (1993) present an interesting alternative approach to the care and support of those who experience hearing voices. (Auditory hallucination is commonly regarded as an indication of severe mental illness, customarily an indication of schizophrenia.)

Although they include the psychiatric and biographical perspective, they identify that it presents a limited outlook and recognize the valuable contribution that transpersonal thinkers such as Assagioli and Grof provide as well as the view afforded by quantum mechanics and parapsychology.

Even if broadening diagnostic criteria is important and relevant, what is significant is that their findings are endorsed and published by MIND, a non-governmental organization (NGO) and charity, which in addition to providing an influential voice in debates regarding governmental policy in all areas of mental health is the largest independent provider of community mental health care in Britain.

As has been shown, transpersonal psychology could claim to have been pivotal in raising the need for the understanding, recognition and care of individuals who are encountering challenges integrating transpersonal experiences, and this need is often discussed in the literature with the terms spiritual emergence and spiritual emergency. Although Grof is often accredited with originating the term, the theoretical underpinnings of much of his work in this area is influenced by Roberto Assagioli (1990), the founder of psychosynthesis.

Assagioli in *Self realization and Psychological disturbances* (1990), the revision of a paper originally published in 1937, explored the subject of what he termed 'spiritual awakening', the awareness by an individual of an inner reality that had been previously unknown. He offers a clear and concise statement about the importance of spiritual development and a discussion of the problems and complications associated with the processes involved with spiritual development.

Assagioli's paper could be considered an important yet recondite work, and Grof states that it '(...) is truly a classic in the field. There are very few other passages in the psychiatric literature that emphasise so clearly the need to distinguish between common psychopathology and the crises preceding, accompanying, and following spiritual opening' (Grof & Grof (eds), 1998, pp. 29–30).

Within this theoretical framework the goal of self-development, psychological in its widest form, is 'Self-realization'. To this end he posited that individuals could, spontaneously or through spiritual practises, experience some form of spiritual awakening.

Assagioli regarded spiritual awakening (spiritual emergence) as involving 'a drastic transmutation of the 'normal' elements of the personality, an awakening of potentialities hitherto dormant, a raising of consciousness to new realms and a functioning along a new inner dimension' (1965, p. 39). He envisaged four distinct critical stages or phases within which there can be the potential for new levels of integration of transpersonal energies, as well as the possibility that emotional and psychological 'disturbance' is experienced. Disturbance here is seen as a potential factor engendering defensive mechanisms, such as denial and projection, that are employed when psychological material is experienced as troubling.

The four phases or distinct critical stages are:

- Crises preceding spiritual awakening.
- Crises produced by spiritual awakening.
- Reactions to spiritual awakening.
- The process of transmutation.

Individuals whose perception of their reality changes from what they have seen as 'normal' may experience crises preceding spiritual awakening. This may be a change in their relationship to their inner world as well as the world they perceive around them. The initiation of such crises, Assagioli suggests, can be experiences such as feelings of bereavement, loss or deep disappointment, which may be sudden or gradual. This area is described often as existential crisis.

There can be pathological symptoms such as the 'loss of contact with reality', an experience that can take many forms. From the psychiatric viewpoint, this would be seen as an indication that the individual is suffering with a psychiatric disorder that would be described as falling within one of the four main categories of dissociative disorders: dissociative amnesia (psychogenic amnesia), dissociative fugue (psychogenic fugue), multiple personality disorder and depersonalization disorder, all of which can be responses to heightened stress and shock.

Crises produced by spiritual awakening are commonly described as the experience of being flooded with feelings such as intense joy, coupled with a sense of release and disappearance of inner conflicts, suffering and disturbances (psychological and/or physical). For those with scant ego strength this can engender distortions such as inflation/grandiosity, leading to religious fanaticism and phenomena associated with delusions of grandeur, all of which are familiar criteria for those seen as suffering from conditions such as narcissistic personality disorder.

Reactions to spiritual awakening concern the potentially painful or severe reactions that can be experienced when the 'state of grace' is lost with the re-assertion of the 'ordinary/normal' personality.

States of heightened consciousness commonly do not last for sustained periods. Following a spiritual awakening normal consciousness can return bringing what is often termed a 'crisis of duality'. This 'return' can bring anguish and distress, as the gap between what could be (potential) and everyday reality is experienced. In extremis enduring this tension can lead to suicidal urges and profound despair as well as feelings of hopelessness, lack of personal worth and incompetence. For some finding themselves back in a world, both internal and external, that includes the negative can be too much to bear. And the longing for 'paradise lost' is sometimes described as 'divine homesickness'.

The last phase, the process of transmutation, is not, unlike the first three, a reaction to transpersonal energies; instead it speaks of the journey or process of self-realization.

> This stage follows the recognition that the necessary conditions to be fulfilled for the high achievement of Self-realization are a thorough regeneration and transmutation of the personality. It is a long and many-sided process which includes several phases: the active removal of the obstacles to the inflow and operation of superconscious energies; the development of the higher functions which have lain dormant or undeveloped; and periods in which one can let the Higher Self work, being receptive to its guidance.

> It is a most eventful and rewarding period, full of changes, or alternations between light and darkness, between joy and suffering. It is a period of transition, a passing out of the old condition without having yet firmly reached the new; an intermediate stage in which, as it has been aptly said, one is like a caterpillar undergoing the process of transformation into the winged butterfly.

> (Assagioli, 1988, p. 41)

As well as a detailed description of the above phases Assagioli also discusses what is needed from therapists who work with clients who are experiencing spiritual emergence. However, he is not formulaic, and does not give clear instructions concerning how individuals can be supported. He does though make clear the need for correct diagnosis,

> (...) it is important to remain aware of the central fact that while the problems which may accompany the various phases of Self-realization can be outwardly very similar to, and sometimes appear

identical with, those of normal life, their causes and significance are very different, and the way to deal with them must be correspondingly different. In other words, the existential situation in the two instances not only is not the same, but it is, in a sense, opposite.

The psychological difficulties of the average person have generally a regressive character. These individuals have not been able to accomplish some of the necessary inner and outer adjustments that constitute the normal development of the personality. In response to difficult situations, they have reverted to modes of behavior acquired in childhood or they have never really grown beyond certain childhood patterns whether they are recognized as such or are rationalized.

On the other hand, the difficulties produced by the stress and strife in the various stages toward Self-realization have, as I said earlier, a specifically progressive character. They are due to the stimulation produced by the superconscious energies, by the 'pull from above', by the call of the Self, and are specifically determined by the ensuing conflict between these energies and the 'middle' and 'lower' aspects of the personality.

(Assagioli, 1988, p. 45)

Towards the end of his article Assagioli points out that

The physical, emotional, and mental problems arising on the way of Self-realization, however serious they may appear, are *temporary* reactions, by-products, so to speak, of an organic process of inner growth and regeneration. Therefore they either disappear spontaneously when the crisis which has produced them is over, or they yield easily to proper treatment.

(Assagioli, 1988, p. 48)

It is also worth noting that he considers the 'process' of self-realization as not being a linear one that follows a fixed sequential pattern.

Returning to spiritual emergency, Grof, as I already said, carried on the theme that Assagioli had been exploring decades earlier. However, he elaborated upon Assagioli's four phases. Although working without a pre-existing taxonomy from which to place or classify disturbing spiritual experiences, Grof and Grof clearly state that no two spiritual emergencies will be alike, though there can be similarities and common factors, '... it is possible and useful to define certain major forms of spiritual emergency, which have specific features differentiating them from others. Naturally their boundaries are somewhat fuzzy, and combinations and overlaps of various kinds are the rule rather than the exception' (1989, p. 13).

They identify ten 'major forms of spiritual emergency', which they name:

- The shamanic crisis
- The awakening of Kundalini
- Episodes of unitive consciousness (peak experiences)
- Psychological renewal through return to the centre
- The crisis of psychic opening
- Past life experiences
- Communication with spirit guides and channelling
- Near-death experiences
- Experiences with close encounters and UFOs
- Possession states.

Taking heed of the different perspectives that this chapter offers supports the hypothesis that clinicians need to recognize the transpersonal in the therapeutic relationship, for it clearly shows that by looking beyond the traditional view of psychosis that psychiatry holds as sacrosanct a perspective can be found that offers the possibility of differentiating between regressive (pre-egoic) psychosis and transpersonal phenomena. Moreover, this view can contribute to a discernment of the differences between various kinds of psychotic states, thus additional diagnostic discrimination is available when considering an appropriate intervention. Consequently, a wider range of therapeutic options can be considered as opposed to merely viewing reports of unusual or extraordinary experiences as pathological.

Therefore, initial and ongoing assessment and evaluation would include the standard elements of a psychiatric assessment and history of pre-morbid functioning, with the inclusion of an evaluation of any spiritual experiences, in order to assist in determining whether the psychotic symptoms are best accounted for by pre-egoic or transegoic mechanisms. Thus two separate treatment plans can be considered.

If the psychosis is regressive, treatment will endeavour to strengthen ego function, a goal and practise familiar to the aims of traditional psychiatric/psychotherapeutic models and the solely pharmacological approach.

However, in the case of a spiritual emergency with psychotic features, appropriate treatment may see pharmacological intervention offered principally to modulate, rather than suppress, symptoms such as loss of boundary. Psychotherapeutic intervention could then address any biographical issues that may arise. Moreover, additional supportive measures such as meditation techniques can be offered in order to aid the individual in working with and eventually integrating the psychotic-like state with a focus on safely supporting and guiding this process rather than suppressing it.

## Conclusion

In conclusion there is no one method or approach that has been found to be the most effective means by which to view or practise transpersonal psychology. Many researchers and theorists claim that a mixed-method approach can be employed. This may include the use of prescribed medicines, some form of 'talking cure' and, for some, practises that may have originated in spiritual traditions, for instance meditation. When considering the latter, it is recognized that although transpersonal or spiritual practises can seem innocuous, they can bring about powerful changes in the psyche that, for some, may not be ego syntonic, or at least require careful and skilful negotiating if lasting benefit is to be found.

Moreover, taking meditation as a good example of what has been regarded for thousands of years as a spiritual practise, one needs to recognize that there are many forms to choose from, and care must also be taken when considering what type may be advantageous or contra-indicated. For instance, methods that encourage concentration on a specific object of meditation, either internal or external, may be better suited to individuals with scant ego strength, whereas other methods such as those that foster undirected free floating receptive awareness may precipitate further loosening and dissolution of internal boundaries leading in extremis to psychotic illness. This awareness of needing to utilize the correct intervention can be likened to the correct prescription of a medication, and like a prescriber of drugs a clinician, regardless of their core model, needs to have adequate training in the tools they use, as, in addition to the broad range of method that can be employed, a transpersonal approach can be advantageous and effective in the treatment of the whole spectrum of psychological illnesses, as well as being an ideal vehicle for self-growth.

Yet care must be taken, as the breadth and death that the inclusion of a transpersonal view and the practical application of such knowledge, when incorporated in psychology, can paint a picture of some wonderful panacea – a view that needs to be avoided. This may be especially true of a transpersonal approach, because the naive and those whose psychological development has been arrested, as well as some individuals who suffer from various mental disorders can mistakenly accept an outlook where the whole realm of transpersonal functioning appears to meet every need.

With all the foregoing in mind it comes as no surprise that throughout the literature the need for correct ongoing diagnosis is repeatedly called for; this is particularly relevant for those who present with symptoms that lead to the psychopathological diagnosis of some form of psychotic disease, as for some individuals any transpersonal approach may be ill-advised and all forms of transpersonal work contra-indicated. However, with such a wide scope of interest and a more comprehensive view of maturation and development, a transpersonal approach to psychosis offers a great deal more than routinely viewing reports of unusual or extraordinary experiences as pathological. Thus a productive means can be sought to help many individuals make sense of and integrate experiences that could just be pathologized and suppressed through medication.

Finally, and very simply put, I found Diana Whitmore's summation of the experiences of those that encounter the transpersonal as being helpful when the transpersonal realm appears in the therapeutic context: 'A mystic swims in the same waters in which the psychotic drowns' (in conversation). And in keeping with the swimming metaphor, a clinician with a good working knowledge of transpersonal functioning can be both a lifeguard and/or a swimming instructor when and if the need arises.

In some ways my search for an answer to the question posed at the beginning of this work has lead me full circle.

Even though the topic is so huge, and I have attempted to portray succinctly my findings, whilst endeavouring to put aside my own prior understanding; a feat that has been an uphill struggle. Yet this pursuit has lead to many fruitful branches of the proverbial tree of knowledge, even if many of the works and viewpoints examined either said the same thing utilizing differing bodies of knowledge and attendant lexicons, or revealed thinkers and traditions that disagreed over the most basic of tenets.

Nonetheless, even with all of this, my off-the-cuff answer to the question 'What is transpersonal psychology, counselling or psychotherapy?' still remains the same:

It's a broad trans-cultural, pan-historical theory of human nature that posits that human beings are more than physical and psychological beings, with some form of spirituality being a reasonable bet. Oh, and by the way, it is also a discrete field of study that could be conceived of as having had about forty years of academic recognition.

Now, however, although the sentiment is the same, I have a wider and deeper admiration for the whole of the human condition. And I have a greater appreciation of why the transpersonal, whether called spiritual, religious or by any other term, has played a significant role in the affairs of human kind since as far back as can be counted. This deeper appreciation also recognizes that although no single method or set of theories can claim to be the truth, in the present day countless individuals, like their predecessors, are consciously or unconsciously asking the same question and coming up with their own unique answers. Whilst some pose this question in an abstract or intellectual manner, others are grappling with the question in a more experiential way, as they find the means to integrate or actively seek out what can only be described as the transpersonal.

With the interest that the transpersonal as realm, phenomena, context, experience or bodies of knowledge has held since ancient times, I find it not surprising in the least that psychology too considers it as an area that proffers rewards for those that venture into supporting their fellows upon the quest for answers.

I look with interest and anticipation to where the field will be taken or will lead the next batch of pioneers in search of themselves and the universe they inhabit; for I, like the imaginary poser of the question at the start of this work, would like to posit even more complex questions and extend possible answers from yet more diverse fields, or over a beer, or preferably two, try to better understand and integrate what can only be described as a transpersonal experience that I had when...

# Bibliography

Assagioli, R. (1983) *Psychosynthesis Typology*. London: Institute of Psychosynthesis.

Assagioli, R. (1988) in Grof, S. & Grof, C. (eds) *Spiritual Emergency When Personal Transformation Becomes a Crisis*. New York: Tarcher/Putnam.

Assagioli, R. (1990) *Psychosynthesis*. Wellingborough: Crucible.

Assagioli, R. (1993) *Transpersonal Development*. The Aquarian Press.

Assagioli, R. (1994) *The Act of Will*. London: The Aquarian Press.

Almass, A. H. (1987) *Elements of the Real in Man*. Berkeley: Diamond Books.

Almass, A. H. (1996) *The Point of Existence*. Berkeley: Diamond Books.

Almass, A. H. (1998) *The Pearl Beyond Price*. Berkeley: Diamond Books.

Almass, A. H. (2002) *Spacecruiser Inquiry: True Guidance for the Inner Journey*. Berkeley: Shambhala.

Allport, G. W. & Ross, J. W. (1967) in Allport, G. W. (1968) *The Person in Psychology*. Boston: Beacon Press.

American Psychiatric Association (1994) *Diagnostic and Statistical Manual*. Fourth edition. Washington, D.C.: American Psychiatric Association.

Atwood, G. E. & Stolorow, R. D. (1984) *Structures of Subjectivity: Explorations in Psychoanalytic Phenomenology*. Hillsdale: The Analytic Press.

Aurobindo, Sri (1951) *The Life Divine*. New York: Sri Aurobindo Library.

Austin, J. (1999) *Zen and the Brain*. Boston: MIT Press.

Avery, S. (1995) *The Dimensional Structure of Consciousness: A Physical Basis for Immaterialism*. Lexington: Compari.

Baars, Bernard J. (1988) *A Cognitive Theory of Consciousness*. New York: Cambridge University Press.

Bailey, A. (1970) *A Treatise on White Magic*. London: Lucis Press.

Bailey, A. (1991) *Esoteric Psychology: A Treatise on the Seven Rays*. London: Lucis Press.

Balint, M. (1968) *The Basic Fault: Therapeutic Aspects of Regression*. London: Tavistock.

Barber, P. (2004) *Researching Personally & Transpersonally*. Guilford: Gestalt in Action.

Barber, P. (2006) *Becoming a Practitioner-Researcher: A Gestalt Approach to Holistic Inquiry*. London: Middlesex University Press.

Bateson, G. (1972) *Steps to an Ecology of Mind*. New York: Ballantine.

Bateson, P. & Martin, P. (1999) *Design for a Life How Behaviour Develops*. London: Jonathan Cape.

Black, D. (1998) Differentiating Psychoanalysis and the Religions. *British Psycho Analytical Society Bulletin* Vol. 34(6).

Black, T. R. (1999) *Doing Quantitative Research in the Social Sciences*. London: Sage.

Blavatsky, H. P. (1966) *The Secret Doctrine*. London: The Theosophical Publishing house.

Beck, A. T. (1979) *Cognitive Therapy and the Emotional Disorders*. London: Whurr Publishing.

Berne, E. (1988) *Games People Play*. New York: Ballantine Books.

Berger, P. L. & Luckmann, T. (1966) *The Social Construction of Reality: A treatise in the Sociology of Knowledge*. New York: Doubleday.

Bidwell, D. R. (1999) Ken Wilber's Transpersonal Psychology: An Introduction and Preliminary Critique. *Pastoral Psychology* Vol. 48(2), pp. 81–90.

Binswanger, L. (1958) The Existential Analysis School of Thought, in May, R. Angel, E. & Ellenburg, H. (eds) *Existence: A New Dimension in Psychiatry and Psychology*, New York: Basic Books.

Binswanger, L. (1963) *Being-in-the-World: Selected Papers of Ludwig Binswanger*. London: Basic Books.

Binswanger, L. & Freud, S. (2000) (Pomeras, A. J. & Roberts, T. Trans) *The Freud-Binswanger Letters*. London: Open Gate Press.

Bion, W. R. (1970) *Attention and Interpretation*. London: Tavistock.

Bion, W. R. (1998) *Experiences in Groups*. London: Routledge.

Bohm, D. (1980) *Wholeness and the Implicate Order*. London: Routledge and Kegan Paul.

Bohm, D. (1987) *Unfolding Meaning*. London: Ark Paperbacks.

Bohm, D. & Peat, D. (1987) *Unfolding Meaning: A Weekend of Dialogue with David Bohm*. London: Ark.

Boorstein, S. (ed.) (1980) *Transpersonal Psychotherapy*. Palo Alto, CA: JTP Books.

Boorstein, S. (ed.) (1996) *Transpersonal Psychotherapy*. Second edition. Albany: State University of New York Press.

Boorstein, S. (1997) *Clinical Studies in Transpersonal Psychotherapy*. Albany: State University of New York Press.

Boorstein, S. (2000) Transpersonal psychotherapy. *American-Journal-of-Psychotherapy* Vol. 54(3), pp. 408–423, Assn. for the Advancement of Psychotherapy.

Boss, M. (1963) *Psychoanalysis and Daseinsanalysis*. London: Basic Books.

Boss, M. (1995) *Existential Foundations of Medicine and Psychology*. Lanham: Jason Aronson.

Boyer, P. (2001) *Religion Explained: The Evolutionary Origins of Religious Thought*. London: Basic Books.

Bragdon, E. (1990) *The Call of Spiritual Emergency*. San Francisco: Harper and Row.

Braud, W. (1998) Can Research Be Transpersonal? *Transpersonal Psychology Review* Vol. 2(3), pp. 9–17.

Braud, W. & Anderson, R. (1998) *Transpersonal Research Methods for the Social Sciences*. London: Sage.

Briggs Myers, I. (1995) *Gifts Differing: Understanding Personality Type*. Mountain View, CA: Davies-Black Publishing.

Brown, M. Y. (1997) *Growing Whole: Self-Realization on an Endangered Planet*. Mt. Shasta, CA: Psychosynthesis Press.

Buber, M. (2002) *Between Man and Man*. London: Routledge.

Bucke, R. M. (1902) *Cosmic Consciousness: A Study in the Evolution of the Human Mind*. Philadelphia: Innes & Sons.

Bugental, J. F. T. (1980) *The Search for Authenticity: An Existential-Anyltic Approach to Psychotherapy*. New York: Irvington.

Byrne, L. (ed.) (1990) *Traditions of Spiritual Direction*. London: Geoffery Chapman.

Calvin, W. H. (1997) *How Brains Think. Evolving Intelligence, Now and Then*. London: Basic Books.

Campbell, J. (1993) *Myths to Live By*. London: Penguin Books.

Campion, H. (1998) *The 'Ways' to Transpersonal Realisation*. Unpublished paper, London: Psychosynthesis and Education Trust.

Caplan, M. Hartelius, G. & Rardin, M. A. (2003) Contemporary Viewpoints on Transpersonal Psychology. *The Journal of Transpersonal Psychology* Vol. 35(2), pp. 143–162.

Capra, F. (1975) *The Tao of Physics: An Exploration of the Parallels Between Modern Physics and Eastern Mysticism*. Berkeley: Shambhala.

Chalmers, D. (1995) Facing Up to the Problem of Consciousness *Journal of Consciousness Studies* Vol. 2(3), pp. 200–219.

Chalmers, D. (1996) *The Conscious Mind*. Oxford: Oxford University Press.

Charet, F. X. (1993) *Spiritualism and the Foundations of C. G. Jung's Psychology*. Albany: State University of New York Press.

Chinen, A. B. (1996) The Emergence of Transpersonal Psychiatry, in Scotton, B. W., Chinen, A. B. & Battista, J. R. (eds) *Textbook of Transpersonal Psychiatry and Psychology*. New York: Basic Books, pp. 9–18.

Clarke, I. (ed.) (2001) *Psychosis and Spirituality: Exploring the New Frontier*. London: Whurr Publishers, Ltd.

Clarke, I. (2002) Mysticism and Madness: Exploring the New Frontier. *Transpersonal Psychology Review* Vol. 6(2), pp. 43–46.

Clarkson, P. (1996) The Eclectic and Integrative Paradigm: Between the Scylla of Confluence and the Charybdis of Confusion, in Woolfe, R. & Dryden, W. (eds) *Handbook of Counselling Psychology*. London: Sage.

Clarkson, P. (2002) *The Transpersonal Relationship in Psychotherapy: The Hidden Curriculum of Spirituality*. London: Whurr Publishers.

Claxton, G. (ed.) (1996) *Beyond Therapy: The Impact of Eastern Religions on Psychological Theory and Practice*. Dorset: Prism Press.

Condrau, G. (1998) *Psychoanalysis to Daseinsanalysis: A Discussion of Martin Heidegger's Impact on Psychotherapy*. Dublin: Edition Mosaic.

Cooper, M. (2003) *Existential Therapies*. London: Sage.

Cortright, B. (1997) *Psychotherapy and Spirit: Theory and Practice in Transpersonal Psychotherapy*. Albany: State University of New York Press.

Cosmides, L. & Tooby, J. (1992) in Barkow, J., Cosmides, L. & Tooby, J. (eds) (1992) *The Adapted Mind*. New York: Oxford University Press.

Cosmides, L. & Tooby, J. (1997) *Evolutionary Psychology Primer*. http://www.psych.ucsb.edu/research/cep/primer.htm.

Crampton, M. (1972) *Toward a Psychosynthetic Approach to the Group*. P.R.F. Issue No. 28, pp. 1–18.

Crane, T. (1995) *The Mechanical Mind*. London: Penguin.

Crick, F. H. C. & Koch, C. (1990) Towards a Neurobiological Theory of Consciousness. *Seminars in the Neurosciences* Vol. 4, pp. 263–276.

Cronin, H. (1992) *The Ant and the Peacock*. Cambridge: Cambridge University Press.

Crowley, A. (1998) *The Revival of Magick and Other Essays*. Tempe, AZ: New Falcon Publications.

Cullen, J. & Russell, D. (1990) IAMOP Monograph 4-6, *The Self-Actualizing Manager: An Introduction to Managerial Psychosynthesis*. Thousand Oaks: IAMOP.

Daniels, M. (2005) *Shadow, Self, Spirit Essays in Transpersonal Psychology*. Exeter: Imprint Academic.

Darwin, C. (1999) *The Origin of Species by means of Natural Selection or, The Preservation of Favoured Races in the Struggle for Life.* http://www.literature.org/authors/darwin-charles/the-origin-of-species-6th-edition/.

Deikman, A. J. (1996) in Boorstein, S. (ed.) (1996) *Transpersonal Psychotherapy.* Second edition. Albany: State University of New York Press.

Dennett, D. C. (1991) *Consciousness Explained.* Boston: Little, Brown.

Dennett, D. C. (1996) *Darwin's Dangerous Idea: Evolution and the Meanings of Life.* London: Penguin Books.

Dennett, D. C. (1999) *Content & Consciousness.* Second edition. London: Routledge.

Denzin, N. K. & Lincoln, Y. S. (1998) *Collecting and Interpreting Qualitative Materials.* London: Sage.

Dilts, R. B. & McDonald, R. (1997) *Tools of the Spirit: Pathways to the Realisation of Universal Innocence.* Capitola: Meta Publications.

Donnington, L. (1989) What is Core Process Psychotherapy? *Self & Society* Vol. 17(8).

Duane, D. (2004) The Socratic Shrink. *New York Times Magazine* 21 March 2004. http://www.nytimes.com/2004/03/21/magazine/21SHRINK.html.

Eigan, M. (1998) *The Psychoanalytic Mystic.* London: Free Association Books.

Ellis, A. (1975) *A Guide to Rational Living.* Hollywood: Wilshire Book Company.

Ellis, A. & Yeager, R. J. (1989) *Why some Therapies Don't Work: The Dangers of Transpersonal Psychology.* Amherst, NY: Prometheus Books.

Epstein, M. (1995) *Thoughts Without a Thinker: Psychotherapy from a Buddhist Perspective.* New York: Basic Books.

Epstein, M. (1996) *Thoughts without a Thinker.* London: Duckworth.

Epstein, M. (1999) *Going to Pieces without Falling Apart.* London: Thorsons.

Erikson, E. H. (1980) *Identity and the Life Cycle.* New York: Norton.

Everett, H. (1973) *Many-Worlds Interpretation of Quantum Mechanics.* Princeton N.J: Princeton University Press.

Fenwick, P., Parnia, S., Waller, D. & Yeates, R. (2001) A Qualitative and Quantitative Study of the Incidence, Features and Aetiology of Near Death Experiences in Cardiac Arrest Survivors. *Resuscitation Vol. 48,* pp. 149–156.

Ferguson, M. (1982) *The Aquarian Conspiracy.* London: Paladin.

Ferrer, J. N. (2002) *Revisioning Transpersonal Theory: A Participatory Vision of Spirituality.* Albany: State University of New York Press.

Ferrucci, P. (1990) *Inevitable Grace.* Los Angeles: Tarcher.

Ferrucci, P. (2000) *What We May Be: Techniques for Psychological and Spiritual Growth.* Los Angeles: Tarcher.

Field, N. (1996) *Breakdown & Breakthrough Psychotherapy in a New Dimension.* London: Routledge.

Firman, J. & Gila, A. (1997) *The Primal Wound.* Albany: State University of New York Press.

Fischer, R. (1978) in Sugerman, A. A. & Tarter, R. E. (eds) *Expanding Dimensions of Consciousness.* New York: Springer.

Fischer, R. (1986) in Wolman, B. B. & Ullman, M. (eds) (1986) *Handbook of States of Consciousness.* New York: Van Nostrand Reinhold.

Fontana, D. (2003) *Psychology, Religion, and Spirituality.* Oxford: BPS Blackwell.

Fontana, D. & Slack, I. (1996) The Need for Transpersonal Psychology. *The Psychologist* Vol. 9(6), pp. 267–269.

Forman, R. K. C. (1998) What does Mysticism have to Teach us About Consciousness? *Journal of Consciousness Studies* No. 2, pp. 185–201.

Foucault, M. (2002) *Madness and Civilization.* Abingdon: Routledge.

Fox, M. (2000) *Original Blessing: A Primer in Creation Spirituality.* New York: Tarcher/Putnam.

Frankl, V. (1959) *Man's Search for Meaning: An Introduction to Logotherapy.* Boston: Beacon Press.

Frankl, V. (1967) *Psychotherapy and Existentialism.* New York: Washington Square Press.

Frankl. V. (1975) *The Unconscious God.* New York: Simon and Schuster.

Frankl, V. (1984) *Mans Search for Meaning. Revised edition.* New York: Washington Square Press.

Freud, S. (1961a) The Future of an Illusion. Standard edition, Vol. 21. London: Hogarth Press.

Freud, S. (1961b) *Civilization and its Discontents.* Standard edition, Vol. 21. London: Hogarth Press.

Freud, S. (1967) *Moses and Monotheism.* New York: Random House.

Freud, S. (2001) *Totem and Taboo.* London: Routledge.

Friedman, H. (2002) Transpersonal Psychology as a Scientific Field, *The International Journal of Transpersonal Studies* Vol. 21, pp. 175–187.

Furman, B. & Ahola, T. (1994) in Hoyt, M. F. (ed.) (1994) *Constructive Therapies.* London: The Guilford Press.

Gazzaniga, M. (1970) *The Bisected Brain.* New York: Appleton Century Crofts.

Gellner, E. (1985) *The Psychoanalytic Movement.* London: Paladin.

Giorgi, A. (ed.) (1985) *Phenomenological and Psychological Research.* Pittsburgh: Duquesne University Press.

Giorgi, A. (1997) The Theory, Practice, and Evaluation of the Phenomenological Method as a Qualitative Research Procedure. *Journal of Phenomenological Psychology* Vol. 28, pp. 235–261.

Gordon, N. S. (2000) Researching Psychotherapy, the Importance of the Client's View: A Methodological Challenge. *The Qualitative Report* [On-line serial], Vol. 4(3/4). http://www.nova.edu/ssss/QR/QR4-1/gordon.html.

Gorusuch, R. L. (1984) Measurement: The Boon and Bane of Investigating Religion. *American Psychologist.* Vol. 39, pp. 228–236.

Goswami, A. (1995) *The Self-Aware Universe.* Los Angeles: Tarcher.

Graham, H. (1986) *The Human Face of Psychology.* Milton Keynes: Open University Press.

Grof, S. (1976) *Realms of the Human Unconscious: Observations from LSD Research.* New York: Dutton.

Grof, S. (1985) Beyond the Brain: Birth, Death and Transcendence in Psychotherapy. Albany: State University of New York Press.

Grof, S. (1988) *Adventure of Self-Discovery.* Albany: State University of New York Press.

Grof, S. & Grof, C. (eds) (1998) *Spiritual Emergency When Personal Transformation becomes a Crisis.* New York: Tarcher/Putnam.

Grunbaum, A. (1984) *The Foundations of Psychoanalysis.* New York: University of California Press.

Guntrip, H. (1969) *Schiziod Phenomena, Object-Relations and the Self.* New York: International Universities Press.

Hanegraff, W. J. (1998) *New Age Religion and Western Culture: Esotericism in the Mirror of Secularism*. New York: State University of New York Press.

Hardy, J. (1996) *A Psychology with a Soul*. London: Woodgrange Press.

Harman, W. W. (1993) Towards an Adequate Epistemology for the Scientific Exploration of Consciousness. *Journal of Scientific Exploration* Vol. 7(2), pp. 133–143.

Haronian, F. (Fall, 1976) Psychosynthesis: A Psychotherapist's Personal Overview, *Pastoral Psychology* Vol. 25(1), pp. 16–33.

Harris, F. (2002) Transpersonal Psychology as a Scientific Field. *The International Journal of Transpersonal Studies* Vol. 21, pp.175–187.

Heath, G. (2002) Philosophy and Psychotherapy: Conflict or Co-operation? *International Journal of Psychotherapy* Vol. 7(1), pp. 11–51.

Heelas, P. (1996) *The New Age Movement, The Celebration of the Self and the Sacralization of Modernity*. Oxford: Blackwell.

Heidegger, M. (1996) (Trans Stambaugh) *Being and Time: A Translation of Sein and Zeit*. Albany: State University of New York Press.

Heron, J. (1996) *Co-Operative Inquiry* . London: Sage.

Heron, J. (2000) Transpersonal Co-operative Inquiry, in Reason, P. & Bradbury, H. (eds) *Handbook of Action Research*. London: Sage.

Hiles, D. (2001) *Heuristic Inquiry and Transpersonal Research*, Paper presented to CCPE, London, October 2001. http://www.psy.dmu.ac.uk/drhiles/HIpaper.htm.

Hillman, J. (1978) *The Myth of Analysis*. New York: Harper & Row.

Hillman, J. (1991) *A Blue Fire*. New York: Harper Perennial.

Hillman, J. (1997a) *The Thought of the Heart & the Soul of the World*. Woodstock, CT: Spring Publications.

Hillman, J. (1997b) *The Souls Code*. New York: Warner Books.

Hillman, J. (2002) *Re-Visioning Psychology*. New York: Harper Collins Publishers.

Hillman, J. (2004) *Archetypal Psychology*, third edition. Woodstock, CT: Spring Publications.

Hodge, D. R. (2001) Spiritual Assessment: A Review of Major Qualitative Methods and a New Framework for Assessing Spirituality, *Social Work* Vol. 46(3), pp. 203–214.

Hodgson, D. (1993) *The Mind Matters: Consciousness and Choice in a Quantum World*. Oxford: Clarendon Press.

Hoffman, E. (1981) *The Way of Splendor*. Boston: Shambhala.

Hollaway, W. & Jefferson, T. (2000) *Doing Qualitative Research Differently*. London: Sage.

Hoppe, K. D. (1978) Split Brain – Psychoanalytic findings and Hypotheses. *Journal of the American Academy of Psychoanalysis* Vol. 6(2), pp. 193–213.

House, R. (2002) 'Psychopathology', 'Psychosis' and the Kundalini: 'Postmodern' Perspectives on Unusual Subjective Experience, in Clarke, I. (ed.) *Psychosis and Spirituality: Exploring the New Frontier*. London: Whurr Publishers, pp. 107–125.

Hoyt, M. F. (ed.) (1994) *Constructive Therapies*. London: The Guilford Press.

Husserl, E. (1977) (trans Cairns. D) *Cartesian Meditations: An Introduction to Phenomenology*. New York: Springer.

Hutton, M. (1994). How Transpersonal Psychotherapists Differ from Other Practitioners: An Empirical Study. *Journal of Transpersonal Psychology* Vol. 26(2), pp. 139–174.

Huxley, A. (1947) *The Perennial Philosophy*. London: Chatto and Windus.

Hycner, R. H. (1993) *Between Person and Person*. New York: The Gestalt Press.

Jacoby, J. (1999) *Complex/Archetype Symbol in the Psychology of C. G. Jung*. London: Routledge.

Jacoby, M. (1984) *The Analytic Encounter*. Toronto: Inner City Books.

James, W. (1958) *The Varieties of Religious Experience*. New York: New American Library of World Literature.

James, W. (1981) The Collected Works *The Principles of Psychology*. *Volume one*. Cambridge, MA: Harvard University Press.

Jaynes, J. (1976) *The Origins of Consciousness in the Breakdown of the Bicameral Mind*. Boston: Houghton Mifflin.

Jibu, M. & Yasue, K. (1995) *Quantum Brain Dynamics and Consciousness, An Introduction*. Amsterdam: John Benjamins Publishing Company.

Johnson, R. A. (1986) *Inner work*. San Francisco: Harper & Row.

Jones, D. (ed.) (1997) *Innovative Therapy*. Milton Keynes: Open University Press.

Jung, C. G. (1933) *Modern Man in Search of a Soul*. New York: Harcourt, Brace.

Jung, C. G. (1958) *Psychology of Religion: West and East*, Volume 11 of *Collective Works*. London: Routledge and Kegan Paul.

Jung, C. G. (1959) *The Archetypes and the Collective Unconscious*. London: Routledge and Kegan Paul.

Jung, C. G. (1973) *The Structure of the Unconscious*, Volume 7 of *Collective Works*. London: Routledge and Kegan Paul.

Jung, C. J. (1974) Hull, R. F. C. (trans) *Structure and Dynamics of the Psyche* Volume 8 *Collected Works*. Princeton: Princeton University Press.

Jung, C. G. (1999) *Modern Man in Search of a Soul*. London: Routledge.

Jung, C. G. (2004) *Psychology and Alchemy*. London: Routledge.

Karl Popper, K. (1968) *The Logic of Scientific Discovery*. London: Routledge.

Kasprow, M. C. & Scotton, B. W. (1999) A Review of Transpersonal Theory and its Application to the Practice of Psychotherapy. *Journal of Psychotherapy Practice and Research* Vol. 8(1), pp. 12–23.

Kelly, G. A. (1969) *Clinical Psychology and Personality: The Selected Papers of George Kelly*. Chichester: Wiley.

Kelly, S. M. (1991) *The Prodigal Soul: Religious Studies and the Advent of Transpersonal Psychology*, in Klaus, K. Klostermaier & Larry, W. Hurtado (eds) *Religious Studies: Issues, Prospects and Proposals*. Atlanta: Scholars Press, pp. 429–441.

Kernberg, O. F. (1995) Psychoanalytic Object Relations Theories. in Moore, B. E. & Fine, B. D. *Psychoanalysis: The Major Concepts*. New Haven: Yale University Press.

Keutzer, C. S. (1984) Transpersonal Psychotherapy: Reflections on the Genre. *Professional-Psychology: Research-and-Practice* Vol. 15(6), pp. 868–883. American Psychological Association.

Khan, M. R. (1960) The Schizoid Personality: Affects and Techniques. *International Journal of Psychoanalysis* Vol. 31, pp. 430–437.

Kirkpatrick, L. A. (1999) Toward an Evolutionary Psychology of Religion and Personality. *Journal of Personality* Vol. 67, pp. 921–952.

Klein, M. (1975) *The Writings of Melanie Klein, Four Volumes*. London: Hogarth Press.

Kramer, S. Z. (1995) *Transforming the Inner and Outer Family*. New York: The Haword Press.

Krippendorff (1991) in Steier, F. (ed.) *Research and Reflexivity*. London: Sage.

Kris, E. (1950) On Preconscious Mental Processes. *Psychoanalytic Quarterly* Vol. 19, pp. 540–560.

Kohut, H. (1971a) *The Analysis of the Self*, New York: International Universities Press.

Kohut, H. (1971b) *The Restoration of the Self*, New York: International Universities Press.

Kuhn, T. S. (1996) *The Structure of Scientific Revolutions*. Chicago: University of Chicago Press.

Kull, S. (1976) *Tape Transcription Group Work Seminar*. London: Psychosynthesis and Education Trust.

Laing, R. D. (1959) *The Divided Self: An Existential Study of Sanity and Madness*. London: Tavistock.

Laing, R. D. (1969) *Self and Others*. Harmondsworth, Middlesex: Penguin Books.

Lajoie, D. H. & Shapiro, S. I. (1992) Definition of Transpersonal Psychology: The First Twenty-five Years. *Journal of Transpersonal Psychology* Vol. 24, pp. 79–98.

Loewenthal, K. M. (1995) *Mental Health and Religion*. London: Chapman and Hall.

Lukoff, D., Lu, F. & Turner, R. (1998) From Spiritual Emergency to Spiritual Problem: The Transpersonal Roots of the New DSM-IV Category. *Journal of Humanistic Psychology* Vol. 38(2), pp. 21–50. www.spiritualcompetency.com/jhpseart.html

Lyons, K. (1999) *Vocation or Call of the Soul*, unpublished M.A. Dissertation London: Psychosynthesis and Education Trust.

Mace, C. (ed.) (1999) *Heart & Soul: The Therapeutic Face of Philosophy*. London: Routledge.

Mansfield, V. & Spiegelman, J. M. (1989) Quantum Mechanics and Jungian Psychology, *Journal of Analytical Psychology* No. 1, pp. 34

Mansfield, V. & Spiegelman, J. M. (1996) On the Physics and Psychology of the Transference as an Interactive Field. *Journal of Analytical Psychology*. http://www.lightlink.com/vic/field.html.

Marinoff, L. (1999) *Plato, Not Prozac!: Applying Eternal Wisdom to Everyday Problems*. New York: Harper Collins.

Marinoff, L. (2002) *Philosophical Practice*. San Diego: Academic Press.

Marinoff, L. (2003) *The Big Questions: How Philosophy Can Change Your Life*. New York: Bloomsbury.

Marseille, J. (1997) The Spiritual Dimension in Logotherapy. *Journal of Transpersonal Psychology* Vol. 29(1), pp. 1–12.

Maslow, A. H. (1968) *Toward a Psychology of Being*. New York: D. Van Nostrand.

Maslow, A. H. (1971) *The Further Reaches of Human Nature*. New York: The Viking Press.

Maslow, A. H. (1993) *The Farther Reaches of Human Nature*. London: Penguin Arkana.

May, R. (1969) *Love and Will*. New York: W W Norton & Co.

May, R. (1988) *Paulus: Tillich as Spiritual Teacher*. New York: W W Norton & Co.

May, R. M. (1991) *Cosmic Consciousness Revisited*. Shaftsbury: Element.

McDermott, I. & Jago, W. (2001) *The NLP Coach*. London: Piatkus.

McNamee, S. & Gergen, K. J. (eds) (1992) *Therapy as Social Construction*. London: Sage.

Meier, C. A. (ed.) Pauli, W. & Jung, C. J. (2001) *Atom and Archetype: The Pauli/Jung Letters, 1932–1958*. London: Routledge.

Miller, S. D., Duncan, M. & Hubble, B, L. (1997) *Handbook of Solution-Focused Brief Therapy*. San Francisco: Jossey-Bass.

Mindell, A. (2000) *Quantum Mind: The Edge Between Physics and Psychology*. Portland, OR: Lao Tse Press.

Mitchell, S. A. (2004) *Relationality: From Attachment to Intersubjectivity (Relational Perspectives)*. Hillsdale: The Analytic Press.

Mitchell, A. M. & Aron, L. (eds) (1999) *Relational Psychoanalysis The Emergence of a Tradition*. Hillsdale: The Analytic Press.

More, T. (1992) *Care of the Soul: A Guide for Cultivating Depth and Sacredness in Everyday Life*. London: Harper Collins.

Moustakas, C. (1990) Heuristic Research, *Design, Methodology and Applications*. London: Sage.

Moustakas, C. (1994) *Phenomenological Research Methods*. London: Sage.

Needlman, J. (1993). Questions of the heart: Inner empiricism as a way to a science of consciousness. In *Noetic Sciences Review*, Summer, 26, 4–9.

Nelson, J. E. (1994) *Healing the Split*. Albany: University of New York Press.

Nelson, J. E. (1996) in Boorstein, S. (ed.) (1996) *Transpersonal Psychotherapy*. Second edition. Albany: University of New York Press.

Neumann, E. (1973) *The Origins and History of Consciousness*. Princeton, NJ: Princeton University Press.

Newberg, A., D'Aquili, E. D. & Rause, V. (2001) *Why God Won't Go Away: Brain Science and the Biology of Belief*. New York: Ballantine.

Noll, R. (1996) *The Jung Cult*. London: Fontana Press and Pacific Grove: Brooks/Cole Publishing Company.

O'Connor, J. & McDermott, I. (2001) *Ways of NLP*. London: Thorson.

Ollinheimo, A. & Vuorinen, R. (2001) *Metapsychology and the Suggestion Argument: A Reply to Grunbaum's Critique of Psychoanalysis*. Helsinki: Finnish Academy of Science & Letters.

Ornstein, R. (1992) *The Evolution of Consciousness: The Origins of the Way We Think*. New York: Simon & Schuster.

Ouspensky, P. D. (2000) *The Fourth Way: Teachings of G.I. Gurdjieff*. New York: Random House.

Padesky, C. A. & Greenberger, D. (1995) *Mind Over Mood*, New York: Guilford Press.

Parfit, W. (2006) *Kabbalah for Life*. London: Rider & Co.

Parlett, M. (1991) Reflections on Field Theory. *British Gestalt Journal* Vol. 1(2), pp. 69–81.

Patton, M. Q. (2002) *Qualitative Research & Evaluation Methods*. Third edition. London: Sage.

Pauli, W. (1981) *Theory of Relativity*. New York: Dover.

Penrose, R. (1994) *Shadows of the Mind*. New York: Oxford University Press.

Perls, F. Hefferline, R. F. & Goodman, P. (1994) *Gestalt Therapy: Excitement and Growth in the Human Personality*. London: Souvenir Press.

Piaget, J. (1954) *The Construction of Reality in Children*. New York: Basic Books.

Piedmont, R. L. (1999) Does Spirituality Represent the Sixth Factor? Spiritual Transcendence and the Five-Factor Model, *Journal of Personality* Vol. 67(6), pp. 986–1013.

Pinker, S. (1998) *How the Mind Works*. London: Penguin Books.

Popper, K. R. (2000) *The Logic of Scientific Discovery*. London: Routledge.

Pribram, K. H. (1971) *Languages of the Brain: Experimental Paradoxes and Principles in Neuropsychology*. Pacific Grove, CA: Brooks/Cole.

Pribram, K. H. & Mishlove, J. (2006) *Thinking Allowed Conversations On The Leading Edge Of Knowledge and Discovery*. Online serial: http://twm.co.nz/pribram.htm.

Ramana Maharishi (1972) *The Spiritual Teachings of Ramana Maharishi*. Berkeley: Shambhala.

Rank, O. (1929) *The Trauma of Birth*. New York: Harcourt Brace.

Reason, P. & Rowan, J. (1981) *Human Inquiry*. Chichester: Wiley.

Reber, A. S. (ed.) (1995) *Dictionary of Psychology*. London: Penguin.

Rizzuto, A. M. (1998) *Why did Freud Reject God?* New Haven: Yale University Press.

Robson, C. (2002) *Real World Research, Second Edition*. Oxford: Blackwell.

Rogers, C. R. (1942) *Counselling and Psychotherapy*. Boston: Houghton Mifflin.

Rogers, C. R. (1959) A Theory of Therapy, Personality, and Interpersonal Relationships, as Developed in the Client-Centered Framework, in S. Koch (ed.) *Psychology: A Study of a Science: Vol. 3 Formulations of the Person and the Social Context*. New York: McGraw Hill, pp. 184–256.

Rogers, C. R. (ed.) (1961) *Becoming a Person*. Boston: Houghton Mifflin.

Rogers, C. R. (1980) *A Way of Being*. Boston: Houghton Mifflin.

Rogers, C. R. (1986) *Rogers, Kohut, and Erickson. Person-Centered Review* Vol. 1(2), pp. 125–140.

Romme, M. & Escher, S. (eds) (1993) *Accepting Voices*. London: MIND Publications.

Rowan, J. (1990) *Subpersonalities*. London: Routledge.

Rowan, J. (1993) *The Transpersonal: Psychotherapy and Counselling*. London: Routledge.

Rowan, J. (2002) A Transpersonal Way of Relating to Clients. *Journal of Contemporary Psychotherapy Vol. 32(1)*, pp. 101–110.

Rowland, S. (1991) *Jung: A Feminist Revision*. Oxford: Blackwell.

Rueffler, M. (1996) *Psychology of Nations: An Exploration of a National Collective Unconscious*, in Schafer, A. K. (ed.) *Psychosynthesis for the Next Century*. Sacramento, CA: Basic Education Strategies and Techniques.

Safran, J. D. (2003) *Psychoanalysis & Buddhism: An Unfolding Dialogue*. Somerville, MA: Wisdom Publications.

Samuels, A. (1990) *Jung and the Post Jungians*. London: Routledge.

Sarfatti, J. (1998) Beyond Bohm-Vigier Quantum Mechanics, Causality & Locality in Modern Physics, *Fundamental Theories in Physics*. Vol. 97, pp. 403–410.

Satir, V. (1990) *People Making*. London: Souvenir Press.

Schacter-Shalomi, Z. M. (1996) *Spiritual Intimacy: A Study of Counseling in Hasidism*. London: Jason Aronson.

Schmitt, C. B. (1966) Perennial Philosophy: From Agostino Steuco to Leibniz. *Journal of the History of Ideas* Vol. 27, pp. 505–532.

Schutz, W. C. (1973) *Elements of Encounter*. Big Sur: Joy Press.

Schwartz-Salent, N. & Stein, M. (eds) (1987) *Archetypal Processes in Psychotherapy*. Wilmette: Chiron.

Scotton, B. W., Chinen, A. B. & Battista, J. R (eds) (1986) *Textbook of Transpersonal Psychiatry and Psychology*. New York: Basic Books.

Searle, J. R. (1992) *The Rediscovery of the Mind*. Cambridge, MA: The MIT Press.

Segall, S. R. (ed.) (2003) *Encountering Buddhism: Western Psychology and Buddhist Teachings*. Albany: State University of New York Press.

Seligman, M. E. P. (2006) *Learned Optimism: How to Change Your Mind and Your Life*. New York: Vintage Books Random House.

Sellars, W. (1963) *Science, Perception and Reality*. London: Routledge.

Shah, I. (1996) *Learning How to Learn: Psychology and Spirituality in the Sufi Way*. New York: Arkana.

Shapiro, S. I., Lee, G. W. & Gross, P. L. (2002) The Essence of Transpersonal Psychology: Contemporary Views. *The International Journal of Transpersonal Studies* Vol. 21, pp. 19–32.

Sheldrake, R. (1981) *A New Science of Life: The Hypothesis of Formative Causation*. Los Angeles: Tarcher.

Singer, J. (1983) From Jungian Analysis to Transpersonal Psychotherapy. *Psychiatric-Hospital* Vol. 14(4), pp. 207–212. US: National Assn. of Private Psychiatric Hospitals.

Singer, M. (2001) *Unbound Consciousness: Qalila, Mind and Self*. London: Free Association Books.

Skinner, B. F. (1953) *Science and Human Behaviour*. New York: Macmillian.

Skinner, B. F. (1974) *About Behaviourism*. New York: Knopf.

Slater, W., Hall, T. W. & Edwards, K. J. (2001) Measuring Religion and Spirituality: Where are We and Where are We Going? *Journal of Psychology and Theology* Vol. 29(1), pp. 4–21.

Sloan Wilson, D. (2002) *Darwin's Cathedral: Evolution, Religion, and the Nature of Society*. Chicago: University of Chicago Press.

Smith, H. (1982) Perennial Philosophy, Primordial Tradition. *International Philosophical Quarterly* Vol. 22, pp. 115–132.

Sokal, A. D. (Spring–Summer, 1996a) Transgressing the Boundaries: Toward a Transformative Hermeneutics of Quantum Gravity. *Social Text*, No. 46/47, Science Wars, pp. 217–252.

Sokal, A. D. (1996b) A Physicist Experiments with Cultural Studies, *Lingua Franca*. Available at http://www.physics.nyu.edu/faculty/sokal/lingua_franca_v4/lingua_franca_v4.html.

Solms, M. & Turnbull, O. (2002) *The Brain and the Inner World. An Introduction to the Neuroscience of Subjective Experience*. New York: Other Press.

Sorenson, R. L. (2004) *Minding Spirituality*. Hillsdale: The Analytic Press.

Spencer, H. (2004) *The Principles of Psychology*. Kila, MT: Kessinger Publishing.

Spinelli, E. (1997) *Tales of Un-Knowing*. London: Duckworth.

Stace, W. T. (1960) *Mysticism and Philosophy*. London: Macmillan Press.

Stapp (1996) paper presented at: Towards a Science of Consciousness, University of Arizona Tucson, 8–13 April 1996. http://www-physics.lbl.gov/~stapp/38621.txt.

Steinar, K. (1991) *Psychology and Postmodernism*. London: Sage.

Stevens, A. (1982) *Archetype a Natural History of the Self*. London: Routledge.

Stolorow, R. D., Brandchaft & Atwood, G. E. (1987) *Psychoanalytic Treatment: An Intersubjective Approach*. Florence, KY: The Analytic Press.

Stuhlmiller, C. M. (1996) Narrative Methods in Qualitative Research: Potential for Therapeutic Transformation, in Carter, K. & Delamont, S. (eds) *Qualitative Research: The Emotional Dimension*. Aldershot: Avebury.

Sutich, A. (1996) in Boorstein, S. (ed.) *Transpersonal Psychotherapy*, Second edition. Albany: State University of New York Press.

Suzuki, D. T. (1972) *Living by Zen*. London: Rider & Co.

Symington, N. (1998) *Emotion and Spirit*. London: Karnac Books.

Talbot, M. (1992) *The Quantum Universe*. New York: Harper Perennial.

Tart, C. (ed.) (1975) *Transpersonal Psychologies*. London: Routledge and Kegan Paul.

Tart, C. (1987) *Waking Up: Overcoming the Obstacles to Human Potential.* Boston: Shambhala.

Teasdale. J. D & Barnard, P. J. (1993) Affect, Cognition and Change. Hove: Lawrence Erlbaum Associates.

Thorne, B. (2002) *The Mystical Path of Person-Centred Therapy.* London: Whurr Publishers.

Tillich, P. (2000) *The Courage to Be.* New Haven: Yale University Press.

Underhill, E. (2001) *Mysticism.* Oxford: One World.

Vale, R. S. & Von Eckartsberg, R. (eds) (1981) *The Metaphors of Consciousness.* New York: Plenum.

Valle, R. (ed) (2006) *Phenomenological Inquiry in Psychology: Existential and Transpersonal Dimensions.* New York: Springer.

Van Deurzen-Smith, E. (1997) *Everyday Mysteries: Existential Dimensions of Psychotherapy.* London: Routledge.

Van Deurzen-Smith. E. (2002) *Existential Counselling & Psychotherapy in Practice.* London: Sage.

Vargiu, J. (Undated) *Global Education and Psychosynthesis. The Application of Psychosynthesis to the Development of Global Consciousness.* San Francisco: Psychosynthesis Institute.

Vaughan, F. (1985) *The Inward Arc.* Boston: New Science Library.

Vermaas, P. (1999) *A Philosophers Understanding of Quantum Mechanics: Possibilities and Impossibilities of a Modal Interpretation.* Cambridge: Cambridge University Press.

Victor, B. S. (1986) Psychopharmacology and Transpersonal Psychology, in Scotton. B. W., Chinen, A. B. & Battista. J. R. (eds) *Textbook of Transpersonal Psychiatry and Psychology.* New York: Basic Books.

Visser, F. (2003) *Ken Wilber: Thought as Passion.* Albany: University of New York Press.

Waldman, M. R. (2006) Understanding Transpersonal Psychology: An Examination of Definitions Descriptions and Concepts. *Alternative Journal of Nursing.* Issue No. 11, pp. 1–23.

Walker, E. H. (1998) Quantum Theory of Consciousness: *Noetic Journal* Vol. 1, pp. 100–107.

Wallace, B. A. (2000) *The Taboo of Subjectivity.* New York: Oxford University Press.

Walley, C. (1996) in Claxton, G. (ed.) *Beyond Therapy: The Impact of Eastern Religions on Psychological Theory and Practice.* Dorset: Prism Press.

Walsh, R. & Vaughan, F. (eds) (1993a) *Paths Beyond Ego; The Transpersonal Vision.* Los Angeles: Tarcher.

Walsh, R. & Vaughan, F. (1993b) On Transpersonal Definitions. *Journal of Transpersonal Psychology* Vol. 25(2), pp. 199–207.

Walsh, R. & Vaughan, F. (1996) in Boorstein, S. (ed.) *Transpersonal Psychotherapy,* Second edition. Albany: State University of New York Press.

Washburn, M. (1988) *The Ego and the Dynamic Ground.* Albany: University of New York Press.

Washburn, M. (1995) *The Ego and the Dynamic Ground.* Albany: University of New York Press.

Washburn, M. (1999) *Transpersonal Psychology in Psychoanalytic Perspective.* Albany: University of New York Press.

Waterhouse, E. S. (1931) *Psychology and Religion.* London: Elkin.

Weinburg, S. (1993) *Dreams of a Final Theory: The Scientist's Search for the Ultimate Laws of Nature*. New York: Vintage Books.

Weir Perry, J. (1987) *The Self in Psychotic Process*, revised edition. Dallas: Spring Publications.

Wellings, N. & Wilde McCormick, E. (eds) (2000) *Transpersonal Psychotherapy Theory and Practice*. London: Continuum.

Welwood, J. (2002) *Toward a Psychology of Awakening: Psychotherapy, and the Path of Personal and Spiritual Transformation*. Boston: Shambhala.

West, W. (2000) *Psychotherapy and Spirituality*. London: Sage.

Whitmore, D. (1986) *Psychosynthesis in Education: The Joy of Learning*. London: Turnstone.

Whitmore, D. (1991) *Psychosynthesis Counselling in Action*. London: Sage.

Whitmore, J. (1997) *Need, Greed or Freedom: Business Changes and Personal Choices*. Shaftbury: Element Books.

Whitmore, J. (2002) *Coaching for Performance: Growing People, Performance and Purpose*. London: Nicholas Brealey Publishing.

Wigner, E. P. (1979) *Symmetries and Reflections*. Woodbridge, CT: Ox Bow Press.

Wilber, K. (1977) *The Spectrum of Consciousness*. Wheaton: The Theosophical Publishing House.

Wilber, K. (1990) *Eye to Eye: The Quest for the New Paradigm*. Revised edition. Boston: Shamballa.

Wilber, K. (1993a) *Transformations of Consciousness*. Wheaton: Quest Books.

Wilber, K. (1993b) in Walsh, R. & Vaughan, F. (eds) *Paths Beyond Ego: The Transpersonal Vision*. Los Angeles: Tarcher.

Wilber, K. (1993c) *The Spectrum of Consciousness*. 20th anniversary edition. Wheaton: Quest books.

Wilber, K. (1993d) *Grace and Grit*. Boston: Shambhala Publications.

Wilber, K. (1994) in Nelson, J. E. (ed.) *Healing the Split*. Albany: University of New York Press.

Wilber, K. (1997) An Integral Theory of Consciousness. *Journal of Consciousness Studies* Vol. 4(1), pp. 71–92.

Wilber, K. (1998) *The Marriage of Sense and Soul*. Dublin: Newleaf.

Wilber, K. (2000a) *Integral Psychology: Consciousness, Spirit, Psychology, Therapy*. London: Shambhala.

Wilber, K. (2000b) *Sex, Ecology, Spirituality*. Boston: Shambhala.

Wilber, K. (2002) *Up from Eden A Transpersonal View Of Human Evolution*. Second edition. Wheaton: Quest Books.

Williams, G. C. (1996) *Plan and Purpose in Nature*. London: Basic Books.

Wilshire, B. (1968) *Williams James and Phenomenology: A Study of "The Principles of Psychology"*. Bloomington: Indiana University Press.

Wilson, E. O. (1975) *Sociobiology: The New Synthesis*. Cambridge, MA: Harvard University Press.

Wilson, E. O. (1978) *On Human Nature*. Cambridge, MA: Harvard University Press.

Winnicott, D. (1953) Transitional Objects and Transitional Phenomena *International Review of Psychoanalysis* Vol. 34, pp. 89–97.

Winnicott, D. (1971) *Playing and Reality*. London: Routledge.

Winnicott, D. (1974) Fear of Breakdown. *International Journal of Psychoanalysis* Vol. 1, pp. 103–107.

Winnicott, D. (1975) *Through Paediatrics to Psychoanalysis*. London: Hogarth Press.

Winnicott, D. (1987) *The Maturational Processes and the Facilitating Environment.* London: Hogarth Press.

Winter, G. (2000) A Comparative Discussion of the Notion of 'Validity' in Qualitative and Quantitative Research. *The Qualitative Report [On-line serial]* Vol. 4(3/4). Available: http://www.nova.edu/ssss/QR/QR4-3/winter.html.

Wright, R. (1994) *The Moral Animal: Evolutionary Psychology and Everyday Life.* New York: Random House.

Wright, R. (1995) *The Moral Animal: Why We Are, the Way We Are: The New Science of Evolutionary Psychology.* New York: Vintage Books Random House.

Wulff, D. M (1997) *Psychology of Religion: Classic and Contemporary.* New York: Wiley.

Yalom, I. D. (1980) *Existential Psychotherapy.* New York: Basic Books.

Yeomans, T. (1994) *The Corona Process: Group Work in a Spiritual Context.* Concord, MA: The Concord Institute.

Young-Eisendrath and Miller (2000) *The Psychology of Mature Spirituality: Integrity, Wisdom, Transcendence.* Hove: Psychology Press.

Zales, M. R. (1978) in Sugerman, A. A. & Tarter, R. E. (eds) *Expanding Dimensions of Consciousness.* New York: Springer.

Zdenek, M. (1986) *The Right Brain Experience.* London: Corgi Books.

Zinnbauer, B. J., Pargament, K. I., & Scott, A. B. (1999) The emerging meanings of religiousness and spirituality: Problems and prospects. *Journal of Personality,* 67(6), 889–919.

Zohar, D. (1991) *The Quantum Self.* London: Flamingo.

Zohar, D. & Marshall, I. (2000) *Spiritual Intelligence, the Ultimate Intelligence.* London: Bloomsbury.

# Author Index

# Subject Index